DATE DUE	
FEB 0 1 2010	
FEB 1 5 2010	
APR 1 9 2010	
OCT 1 0 2011	
FEB 2 8 2012	
MAR 1 4 2013	
AUG 1 1 2015	
GAYLORD	PRINTED IN U.S.A.

THE INDISPENSABLE BOOK OF PRACTICAL LIFE SKILLS

THE INDISPENSABLE BOOK OF PRACTICAL LIFE SKILLS

Essential lessons in everything you need to be a fully functioning adult

Nic Compton • Kim Davies
David Martin • Sara Rose

HAMMOND World Atlas
Part of the Langenscheidt Publishing Group

**This book was created by
Ivy Press**
210 High Street
Lewes, East Sussex BN7 2NS, UK

CREATIVE DIRECTOR Peter Bridgewater
PUBLISHER Jason Hook
EDITORIAL DIRECTOR Caroline Earle
ART DIRECTOR Michael Whitehead
PROJECT EDITOR Sanaz Nazemi
DESIGN J.C. Lanaway
CONCEPT DESIGN Joerg Hartmannsgruber
ILLUSTRATION Ivan Hissey, Coral Mula
PICTURE MANAGER Katie Greenwood
PICTURE RESEARCH Lyana Lanaway, Lynda Marshall
CONSULTANTS Christine Evans, paramedic;
Marie-Eve Foisy, Parks Canada; Vivienne Macey, midwife;
Dr. Christopher Van Tilburg, wilderness physician;
Tony Wafer, RNLI; Professor Greg Whyte, Professor
of Applied Sport and Exercise Science, John Moores
University, Liverpool.

CONTENTS

HOME & YARD

HOME & YARD

HEALTH & BEAUTY

TRAVEL & SPORTS

ACCIDENT & EMERGENCY

HEALTH & BEAUTY

TRAVEL & SPORTS

IN THE WILD

ACCIDENT & EMERGENCY

HOME & YARD

HEALTH & BEAUTY

TRAVEL & SPORTS

ACCIDENT & EMERGENCY

HOW TO USE THIS INDISPENSABLE BOOK

The INDISPENSABLE BOOK OF PRACTICAL LIFE SKILLS is packed with essential techniques and must-have methods, organized into an easy-to-navigate format and clearly explained with illustrated step-by-step instructions. You can quickly find the essential skill that fits your situation, read it, absorb it and get ready to ride to the rescue. It's indispensable. It's practical. And soon you will be, too...

ENTRIES
Whether it's mending a puncture or chopping an onion, it's easy once you know how. Each entry talks and walks you through a skill that every fully functioning adult should have in their repertoire.

INTRODUCTION
Every topic and subject is introduced and explained, so that you're fully prepared to use all the information provided.

PRACTICAL TIPS & INDISPENSABLE WARNINGS
Skills can be made easier with a little inside information, helpful hints and important safety information.

INSTRUCTIONS
Each procedure is divided into clear steps so that even the most impractical will find it easy to grasp the basics.

CHAPTERS

Each section is subdivided into chapters, to narrow down the area of interest. You can navigate your way into the Home & Yard section (In the Home, In the Kitchen, In the Yard); Health & Beauty (Looking After Clothes, Looking After You, Looking After a Baby); Travel & Sports (On the Road, Fun & Games, In the Wild); and Accident & Emergency (Going to the Rescue, Dealing with Emergencies, Surviving in Extremes).

SECTION DIVIDERS

The book is divided into four color-coded sections by theme: Home & Yard (green), Health & Beauty (yellow), Travel & Sports (blue), Accident & Emergency (purple). The colored tabs on the right-hand side of the pages make each section instantly accessible.

ILLUSTRATIONS

Step-by-step illustrations demonstrate and instruct so that you can follow the whole process visually from start to finish making it easy to learn and impossible to forget.

BRAIN TRAINING

Informational panels contain historical facts and trivia for those who like their practical learning accompanied by a quick exercise in brain training.

HOME & YARD

IN THE HOME

Save money on paying professionals and
rise to the challenge of home maintenance
with this indispensable chapter on easy
repairs around the house. From keeping
your home clean to unblocking a sink, all
the essential tasks are covered, with
easy-to-follow instructions, equipment
checklists and terrific tips.

HOW TO CLEAN THE OVEN

Cleaning the oven is an arduous, dirty job that few people relish, so practice prevention to save yourself some elbow grease. Line the bottom of the oven with aluminum foil to catch crumbs and splatters, and wipe away any spills as soon as you can. However, even the most vigilant will still need to deep-clean the oven regularly—once a month is best, before there's too much buildup and food becomes baked on and difficult to clean off.

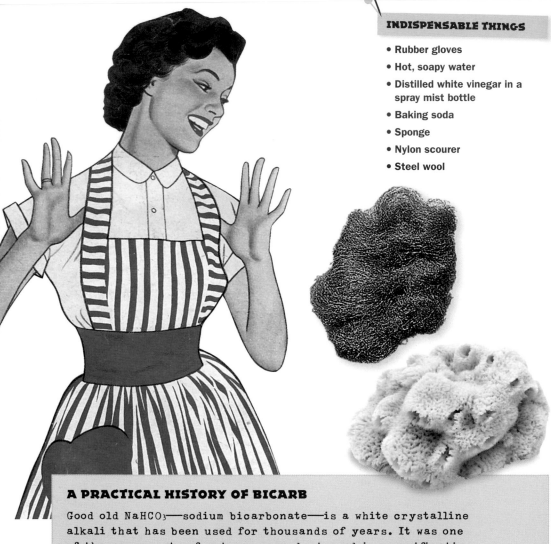

INDISPENSABLE THINGS

- Rubber gloves
- Hot, soapy water
- Distilled white vinegar in a spray mist bottle
- Baking soda
- Sponge
- Nylon scourer
- Steel wool

A PRACTICAL HISTORY OF BICARB

Good old $NaHCO_3$—sodium bicarbonate—is a white crystalline alkali that has been used for thousands of years. It was one of the components of natron, a product used in mummification, and was taken medicinally to treat a variety of minor ailments. Best known today as a leavening agent in baking, the fizzy, scouring action of baking soda also makes it the perfect ingredient in an amazing array of commercial household products, from toothpaste to toilet cleaners. Its continued popularity comes from a combination of its proven effectiveness and the fact that it's a natural, environmentally safe substance.

SURFACES
Prevent grease buildup by wiping all outside surfaces with hot, soapy water.

HOOD
Put metal filters from the hood in the dishwasher or scrub clean with hot, soapy water.

COOKTOP
Wipe up spills when they occur (being careful not to burn yourself) and always wipe down the cooktop after cooking. Depending on the type of burners you have, dismantle gas rings and use a nylon scourer and hot, soapy water; ceramic burners can simply be wiped clean with a cloth dipped in hot, soapy water.

OVEN
Before you begin, make sure the oven is completely cool. Put on your rubber gloves. If you don't want to use harsh chemicals, a mixture of baking soda and distilled white vinegar will work. Lightly moisten the oven interior with water, then sprinkle with a thick layer of baking soda. Let stand for about 3 hours, then spray with the vinegar. Let stand for a couple more hours, then simply wipe out with a damp sponge and warm water. You will still need to rinse out the oven, but at least the next time you cook there won't be a residual smell or taste of oven cleaner!

OVEN DOOR
Make a paste of baking soda and water and apply to stains. Let stand for 10 minutes, then scrub clean with steel wool and rinse off with a clean sponge and hot water.

HOW TO KEEP THE HOUSE CLEAN AND TIDY

A clean and tidy home will help you feel more relaxed, calm and organized, but it's essential to find the cleaning system that suits your personal schedule so that you can keep to it. Some people like to do a major blitz once a week, others prefer less effort, but more frequently. Kitchens and bathrooms are the rooms that make your house look dirty, so try to keep these sparkling, then follow a room-by-room to-do list so you can put your feet up sooner rather than later.

INDISPENSABLE THINGS

- Dustpan and brush
- Broom
- Bucket and mop
- Vacuum cleaner
- Paper towels
- Spray cleaner
- Disinfectant
- Nonabrasive liquid cleaner
- Dusters and microfiber cloths
- Polish
- Sponges
- Scourers
- Rubber gloves

A PRACTICAL HISTORY OF THE VACUUM CLEANER

The 19th century brought with it an increased understanding of the connection between cleanliness and germs, and various machines were invented to clean carpets, including huge horse-drawn contraptions that had to be parked outside the house. In 1907, James Murray Spengler invented a portable electric vacuum cleaner, which was little more than a pillowcase attached to a fan and a box, but crucially it incorporated a rotating brush. He sold the patent to his cousin's husband, William Hoover, the following year, and today the word "hoover" is synonymous with vacuuming.

BATHROOM

Make cleaning the sink part of your daily routine, just like brushing your teeth. Rinse out the bath or shower, wipe the mirror and pour some cleaner around the toilet bowl. Change and replace wet or dirty towels.

KITCHEN

Always start with the sink. Keep it empty and clean, and you'll be inspired to load plates into the dishwasher, wipe down surfaces and remove kitchen clutter from counters. Sweep and mop the floor.

BEDROOM

Always make the bed. Fold and put away clothes and clear clutter from your bedside table. Invest in good-quality cleaning products such as microfiber cloths, which are much more effective than old dish towels.

HALLWAY

Institute a house rule whereby everyone leaves their shoes by the door—this will keep unwanted bacteria, chemicals and dust and dirt from being trodden all over the house. Make spot cleaning a habit: wipe away smudges on walls, baseboards and floors as soon as you notice them.

LIVING ROOM

Plump up cushions, recycle newspapers and remove objects from the floor. Put felt pads under pieces of furniture so you can easily move them for cleaning. When dusting, always put a dab of polish on the cloth, otherwise you'll just shift the dirt around.

HOW TO PUT UP SHELVES

If you lack storage space, putting up a few shelves can make all the difference, but an improperly erected shelf won't last and can be a safety hazard. To reduce the chance of sagging, shelves need to be at least $3/4$in. (18mm) thick and have brackets every 2 ft. (600mm) for adequate support. Plywood and wooden shelves are less likely to sag than particleboard or medium-density fiberboard.

INDISPENSABLE THINGS

- Drill
- Masonry drill bits
- Level
- Pencil
- Goggles
- Screwdriver
- Shelf and fixings
- 2in. (50mm) screws
- Wall anchors

1 The most important step is to determine what type of walls you have. For masonry walls, use wall anchors to secure the shelves. If you have wallboard walls, you must secure shelving to the studs in the wall—use a studfinder or knock along the wall with your knuckles until you hear a solid thud.

2 Paint the shelves before attaching them to the wall. Decide the position of each shelf. Use a level and a pencil to mark a pencil line on the wall where the shelf is to go. Mark the bracket positions on the line. Make sure there are no cables or pipes behind the wall where you'll need to drill.

3 Put on your goggles, choose a drill bit suitable for the wall material that is the same diameter as the anchor, or slightly smaller if you're using screws. Drill into the wall to the depth of the anchor, or slightly less than the length of the screw.

4 If using anchors, insert them and screw the brackets to the wall. Make sure the screws grip firmly. If not, try using a larger wall anchor. Attach the shelves with screws or finishing nails so that they do not tip forward when loaded.

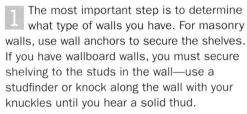

A PRACTICAL HISTORY OF SHELVES

The simple and utilitarian nature of the humble shelf means they can be found in nearly every home. The existence of open wooden shelving can be traced back thousands of years to ancient Mesopotamia, where they were used to store official documents inscribed on clay tablets. However, it wasn't until the development of the printing press in the Middle Ages that books, and shelves to house them securely, became more commonplace. The oldest bookshelves in existence, dating from the end of the 16th century, are in the Bodleian Library, Oxford, England.

HOW TO DRAFTPROOF THE FRONT DOOR

For lower energy bills and fewer chills, draftproofing your front door is a job that can make a big difference in cold weather. There is often a gap between the door and the frame, and even more air is let in by cracks in door panels and around light panels. So take a little time to draftproof your front door, and keep in the heat, save energy and reduce your impact on the environment.

INDISPENSABLE THINGS

- Door sweep
- Hacksaw
- Phillips screwdriver
- Self-adhesive weather strip
- Wood filler or caulk
- Hammer

DOOR FRAME

Wash down with warm, soapy water and let dry. Then cut the weather strip to fit and press it along the exterior edge of the doorstop. It will compress to eliminate drafts when the door is shut. It's a cheap option, but will need replacing every couple of years.

DOOR

Hold the door sweep along the inside of the bottom of the door and mark the length required from edge to edge, less about ¼in. (5mm). Cut the door sweep with a hacksaw to fit. Secure to the bottom of the door with the screws provided with the door sweep.

PANELS

Use wood filler to fill in any cracks in wood panels. If the cracks appear around window or light panels, use caulk to seal.

HOW TO FIX A WOBBLY CHAIR

There are usually two reasons why a chair is wobbly. One of the legs may have worn down more than the others, and in this case, all you need to do is sand away the longer ones until all the legs are of equal length. In other cases, the joints have become loose through wear and tear, which takes a little longer to fix.

INDISPENSABLE THINGS

- Newspaper or protective cover
- Different grades of sandpaper
- Tape measure and pencil
- Hammer
- Wood glue
- Damp cloth
- Clamp

1 Protect a table with newspaper or the protective cover and place the chair on it, turned upside down. Carefully measure the length of each leg to find out which is the short one. Mark the other three legs to the same length, then sand down with coarse sandpaper until all are equal.

2 For loose joints, remove whatever has lost its grip (the wobbly leg or arm) and sand the top of it with fine sandpaper until all the old glue is removed. Use fine sandpaper to lightly sand the inside of the joint, then wipe away the wood dust.

3 Squeeze some wood glue into the hole and insert the arm or leg, turning it a couple of times to make sure the glue is evenly distributed. Wipe away any excess glue with a damp cloth and clamp the joint to keep it in place until it dries. Don't sit on the chair for a day or two.

HOW TO HANG CURTAINS

How you hang your drapes can make a huge difference to the way a room looks. Not only will they reflect your style and personality, but there are also tricks that can make your room look bigger and let in the maximum amount of light, if that is the effect you want. You will need at least one drape hook or ring per 4in. (10cm) of fabric, so although these are usually supplied with the track or pole, buy extra. Make sure you have a sturdy stepladder to stand on and someone standing at ground level to take the weight of the drapes as you hang them.

INDISPENSABLE THINGS

- Stepladder
- An extra pair of hands
- Drill, wall anchors and screws
- Pole or track
- Drapes
- Extra hooks and rings

1 Hanging the rod above the molding makes the window and ceiling appear taller, and prevents the messy heading of the drape being visible to the outside world. Mark the position of the pole on the wall at least 3$\frac{1}{2}$in. (8cm) above the window and drill, anchor and screw the pole brackets Into place. Slide the pole into the brackets, then hang your drapes.

2 For a look that maximizes light, hang the drapes wide of the actual window frame by extending the rod anywhere from 10–18in. (25–40cm) on each side. This way, when you push back the drapes, you will be able to see the whole window.

3 Calculating how wide a drape should be involves not only the size of the window, but how much fullness you want when the drapes are closed. Drapes look their best when there is a generous amount of fabric. Standard drapes use 1$\frac{1}{2}$ times the window width for each panel. If your drapes hang wide of the window, each drape should be twice the window width.

4 Small variations in drape length can make a big difference to how your room looks. For a streamlined, tailored look, your drapes should just hit the floor. If you prefer a more homey look, add 1$\frac{1}{2}$in. (4cm) so that the fabric bunches up a little at the bottom. If your drapes have heading tape at the top, draw the threads to make gathers. Put up one drape and adjust the threads until the drape is halfway across the pole or track. Tie the threads loosely together. Repeat with the other drape. This ensures that the drapes will meet in the middle when closed.

 PRACTICAL TIP

Always take the time to iron your drapes before hanging them up—they'll look much neater. For heavy drapes, choose sturdy poles that won't sag.

HOW TO HANG A PICTURE

Putting up your pictures properly is more important than you might think—one that is crooked or misplaced will always attract the eye, and not in a good way. First, decide where to hang the picture. If in doubt, make a template the same size as your picture and place it where you think you might like to hang the real thing. Avoid hanging one small picture on a huge expanse of wall—small pictures will look better when grouped together.

INDISPENSABLE THINGS

- Tape measure
- Pencil
- Picture hooks or hangers
- Hammer and nails
- Level

A PRACTICAL HISTORY OF HANGING ART

Museums have often hung pictures upside down by mistake, particularly if the art is abstract. The most famous case is that of Matisse's *Le Bateau*, which hung upside down at the Museum of Modern Art in New York for 47 days in 1961. *Long Grass with Butterflies* by Van Gogh briefly hung upside down in the National Gallery in London, England, in 1965. But in the 2008 Rothko exhibition at the Tate Modern in London, two of the artist's best-known works were deliberately displayed on their side, contrary to the artist's original intentions.

1 Measure the distance between the wire at full tension—or from the hanging tab if that's what the picture has to the frame's top edge (A). Large pictures will need two hangers instead of one for stability, so when you measure this distance, spread the wire out to two different points where the wire will rest on hangers. Measure from the top of the frame to both points of tension to get your height. Measure the height of your frame (B) and halve the result.

2 From the floor, measure up the wall to 66in. (170cm), the average adult eye-level, and make a pencil mark. From this mark, measure upward half the height of the frame and make a second pencil mark (C). From the second mark, measure downward the distance recorded in step 1 (from the wire at full tension to the frame's top edge) and make a third mark (D). Place the nail and hanger here.

3 Make sure that the bottom of your hanger, rather than the nail point, is resting on the third pencil mark (D) when you hammer your nail in because this is where your wire will rest. If you are hanging a heavy picture, make sure you use the right hangers: standard sizes generally support 5–10lb (2.2–4.5kg) of weight. Use a level to make absolutely sure your picture is hanging straight.

HOW TO BUILD A FIRE

The key to building a successful fire is to use materials that are perfectly dry and to arrange them so that they leave plenty of air space—if the supply of oxygen is cut off, the fire will not burn. But be careful: fires get very hot! Use a mesh guard on an open fireplace, and never leave children unsupervised by a fire.

INDISPENSABLE THINGS

- Fireplace
- Newspaper, firelighters or cinders
- Kindling
- Logs (and coal)
- Matches

LIGHTING THE FIRE

Make sure the flue is open, or you will fill the house with smoke. Light a match and hold it to the newspaper or firelighters. Blow slightly at the bottom of the kindling to spread the fire. When the crackling has died down and the flames are large and well established, add some larger logs or coal.

BOTTOM LAYER

Place two or three firelighters or a few sheets of crumpled-up newspaper on the bottom of the grate. Some cinders (small pieces of partly burned coal or wood from the previous fire) will help the fire start quickly and easily.

KINDLING

Place small kindling (thin twigs or wood shavings) on top of the bottom layer and criss-cross it so there is plenty of air space between each piece. The more kindling you have, the better.

LOGS

Create a tent shape on top of the kindling with two of your smaller logs. Hardwoods, such as oak, cherry or apple, burn much hotter and longer than softwoods (pine, cedar).

HOW TO CHANGE A LIGHTBULB

To carry out this simple task, make sure you have the right bulb for the job. Keep a supply of spare bulbs of appropriate wattage in the house, then you'll never be left in the dark. Turn off the light or lamp at the wall switch or outlet and let the bulb cool. Hold the bulb in a cloth when changing it in case it shatters in your hand.

INDISPENSABLE THINGS

• Replacement lightbulb
• Clean, dry cloth

INSERTING
Insert a new bulb and turn it clockwise until secure. Turn the lamp back on to make sure the bulb works. Wrap the old bulb in newspaper before putting it in the garbage, so you can dispose of it safely.

REMOVING
Cover the bulb with a dry cloth, firmly grasp the bulb and twist it gently in a counterclockwise direction until it is released from the socket.

A PRACTICAL HISTORY OF THE LIGHTBULB

Until the 19th century, artificial lighting came in the form of candles, oil lanterns and gas lamps. The American inventor Thomas Edison didn't invent the lightbulb, but he did develop the first lightbulb for home use that was practical, safe and economical. In 1879, using a small, carbonized filament, an improved vacuum inside the globe and a lower current of electricity, he introduced a reliable, long-lasting source of light.

HOW TO HANG WALLPAPER

Nothing changes a room's appearance quite as dramatically as a well-chosen wallpaper. For a professional look, a little preparation goes a long way. Always remove any old wallpaper and clean the surfaces to be covered, repairing any holes or cracks. Then size the walls by applying a coat of diluted wallpaper paste. Do any painting (such as ceiling and woodwork) first, because it's easier to remove paste than paint, and calculate how many rolls of paper you need before you begin.

INDISPENSABLE THINGS

- Wallpaper
- Tape measure
- Pasting table
- Pasting brush
- Wallpaper paste
- Paper-hanging brush
- Scissors
- Plumb line
- Seam roller
- Sponge

A PRACTICAL HISTORY OF WALLPAPER

During the Middle Ages, wealthy people used fabric to cover walls and windows to keep out drafts. Wallpaper came into being as a cheap substitute for tapestry and wood paneling, and its use in Europe is thought to date back to the 1400s. The first wallpapers were small squares with images on them printed by wood blocks, which were then colored in by hand. The paper was not attached directly to the wall—it was pasted onto sheets of linen that were then attached to the walls with tacks.

1 Cut your first length of wallpaper so it overlaps the ceiling and baseboard by at least 2in. (5cm) at each end. When you cut each subsequent length, take into account any patterns. Using a pasting table and pasting brush, apply wallpaper paste to the paper, making sure you paste right up to the edges.

2 Begin with your least noticeable wall. Use a plumb line to guide you so that you know where the strips of wallpaper should meet. Slide the paper onto the wall, but be careful not to stretch the paper while you are positioning it.

3 Use a paper-hanging brush to smooth out any air bubbles, working from the center out. If air bubbles remain, or the paper doesn't appear to be straight, gently pull back the paper and smooth it down again.

4 Using your scissors, carefully trim off any excess at the top and bottom. Follow the same procedure to put up subsequent strips of wallpaper, making sure you match the pattern exactly.

5 Wipe off any excess paste with a damp sponge as you go along, and seal the matching edges with a seam roller after hanging each piece of wallpaper. Make sure that you wipe off any excess paste from the woodwork as well.

HOW TO ARRANGE FLOWERS

You can put fresh flowers in almost any container to make an attractive and stylish arrangement. Choose flowers in different stages of development, from bud to full bloom, and use different shapes, colors and textures for a more interesting look. For maximum freshness, lightly spray your arrangement with water occasionally to create a humid atmosphere around the flowers. Add flower food when you first arrange them and then every time after changing the water. Keep flowers out of direct sunlight and away from heat because these will speed up the wilting process. Remove and discard dying blooms when necessary.

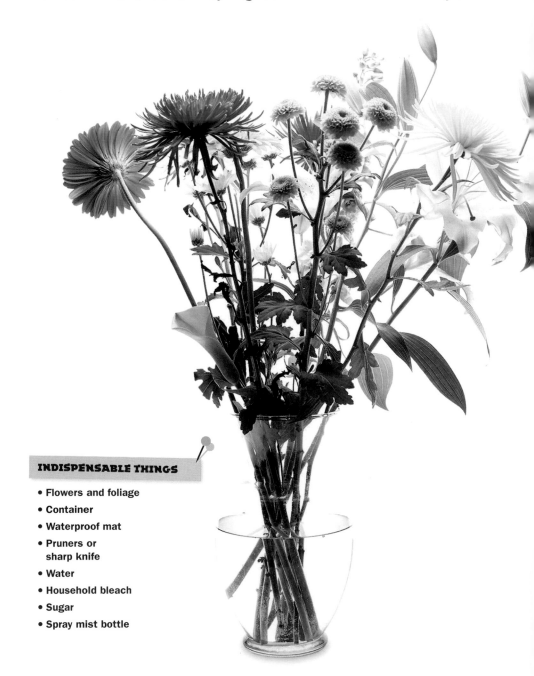

INDISPENSABLE THINGS

- Flowers and foliage
- Container
- Waterproof mat
- Pruners or sharp knife
- Water
- Household bleach
- Sugar
- Spray mist bottle

PREPARING THE FLOWERS

Cut at least 1in. (2.5cm) from the bottom of each stem at an angle; this will create a larger surface area so the flowers can take up water with ease. With woody stems, such as hydrangeas, cut a slit at the end of the stem to facilitate water intake. Remove any leaves that will lie below the level of the water to help keep the flowers fresh.

LINES, GLOBES & FILLER

Put the larger, more dominant flowers (lines) in first to create the focus of the arrangement. Then add the smaller flowers (globes). Turn the flowers to different angles to add interest to the display. Keep the colors balanced and use foliage (filler) to fill any gaps, but don't overdo it.

WATER

Partially fill the container with water at room temperature and add flower food. Don't overfill the vessel; you can always add to it later. Change the water every three days and recut the stems.

FLOWER FOOD

Make your own with a few drops of household bleach and a tablespoon of sugar. The bleach will kill the bacteria and the sugar will help feed the flowers, making them open and bloom faster. Dissolve in a mug of hot water and add to the container.

CONTAINER

Choose a container that's appropriate for your flowers— anything from a jam jar to a teapot or a bottle if you don't have a vase, but remember that smaller flowers look best in shorter, wider vessels, whereas longer flowers look elegant in taller ones. Make sure the container has been thoroughly cleaned, and put down a waterproof mat if you intend to place it on a polished surface (never put on top of electrical appliances).

HOW TO FIX A DRIPPING FAUCET

A faucet that drips is annoying, can cause stains and is highly wasteful—gallons of water a day will go down the pipes—so fixing a drip is a job that needs to be done. If a faucet drips from the spout, even after being tightly turned off, then it's likely that the washer needs replacing. Sorting out the problem yourself is easier than you think, and you'll save on an expensive plumber's fee.

INDISPENSABLE THINGS

- Adjustable wrench
- Cloth
- Screwdriver
- Washer
- Valve-seat dresser

A PRACTICAL HISTORY OF PLUMBING

Ancient civilizations in Egypt, Babylon, Greece, India and China had systems of providing potable water and waste drainage. The word "plumber" comes from the Latin *plumbus* (lead)—the Romans developed lead piping, and public baths helped to spread a culture of cleanliness throughout their empire. As Western civilization stagnated during the Dark Ages, so did plumbing, and very little progress was made until the 19th century, when the importance of clean water and sanitation was once again recognized. The first screw-down faucet was patented by Guest and Chrimes, a Rotherham brass foundry in England, in 1845.

👉 PRACTICAL TIP

Turn off the water supply or you will get drenched later on. Look under the sink or at the main water valve and turn the valve counterclockwise. Turn on the faucet to let out any water left in the pipes. Once it stops flowing, replace the plug to catch any small parts you may accidentally drop.

1 Take off the top of the faucet. You may need to use an adjustable wrench to unscrew the large packing nut, in which case, pad the jaws of the wrench with a cloth to avoid scratching the tap's metallic surface. You may have to first remove a cap and unscrew the handle to remove the stem of the faucet.

2 Using a screwdriver, pry off the old washer from underneath the packing nut. Push a new washer of exactly the same size into place and screw the packing nut back on to the faucet, but do not over tighten. Replace the faucet parts in reverse order and turn the water supply back on.

3 If the faucet still drips, grit or general wear and tear has probably worn the seating. Buy a valve-seat dresser, available from home repair stores. Push the end of the tool into the faucet, adjust the cutter so it touches the seat and rotate it to grind down the metalwork. Reassemble the faucet.

HOW TO CLEAN WINDOWS

Windows look best if cleaned on a regular basis, and sparkling clean windows can really make a difference to your home. Part of what makes window washing such a chore is that people insist on doing it with loads of suds, wads of newspaper and a ton of elbow grease. All that rubbing is a bad idea, because you're just moving dirt around from one spot to another and putting a static charge on the glass, which attracts dust and dirt.

INDISPENSABLE THINGS

- Water
- Toothbrush or cotton swabs
- Dish-washing liquid
- 2 plastic buckets
- Sponge
- Rubber gloves
- Squeegee
- Lint-free cloth or paper towels

A PRACTICAL HISTORY OF THE SQUEEGEE

The squeegee dates back to the Middle Ages, when fishermen scraped fish guts and water off boat decks with long-handle wooden-blade tools called "squilgees." It wasn't until the turn of the 20th century that window cleaners in the United States adopted a rubber-blade version of the tool, which was needed to clean the windows of the newly developed skyscraper buildings. In 1936, Italian immigrant Ettore Steccone invented a light, brass-handle tool with a very flexible and sharp single rubber blade. The "Ettore" squeegee remains a favorite among professional window cleaners.

HOME & YARD

SILLS AND FRAMES

Make sure that the windowsills and frames are cleaned first. Dust and vacuum before wiping with a damp cloth to get rid of dirt and grime. Use a damp, soft toothbrush or cotton swab to clean corners.

SPONGE CLEAN

Prepare a cleaning solution of just a squirt of dish-washing liquid in a bucket of warm water. Dip a sponge into the bucket and wash the surface of the window, starting at the top and working down to the bottom. Never clean windows in direct sunlight, because the sun will dry the cleaner before it can be wiped away and there will be streaks.

SQUEEGEE

After sponging, dip a squeegee into a bucket of clean water. Press the squeegee lightly onto the surface of the window, starting at the top and pulling down vertically. Wipe the squeegee with a lint-free cloth or paper towel. Continue this process until the entire surface of the window has been cleaned, then pull the squeegee horizontally across the bottom section of the window. Wipe off the water at the bottom of the window frame.

AVOIDING STREAKS

Clean windows with up-and-down strokes on one side and side-to-side strokes on the other. This way you will see which side has the streaks, instead of having to redo the whole window.

HOW TO UNBLOCK A SINK

You know you've got a blocked drain when the water drains away sluggishly or not at all. A blocked drain can be smelly and unhygienic, but the good news is that most of the time you don't need a plumber, and it only takes a few minutes to get the water washing away freely again. You won't have to use expensive, toxic drain cleaners either, and these methods can also be used to clear blocked toilets. Begin by pouring boiling water into the sink. This will often clear the blockage—if this fails, follow these steps.

INDISPENSABLE THINGS

- Boiling water
- Plunger, drain auger or vacuum pump
- Bucket
- Brush
- Disinfectant
- Wrench (possibly)

☞ PRACTICAL TIP

Prevention is better than cure, so to keep drains clear, pour a cup of washing soda down the drain once a week, followed by a pot of boiling water to dissolve grease and prevent blockages from forming.

1 The plunger method involves, as you'd expect, an old-fashioned plunger, which is simply a rubber cup on the end of a stick that creates pressure in the waste pipe. Cover the plug hole with the sink plunger. Push until suction holds the cup in place. Plunge up and down quickly several times to create pulses of air and water that should suck or push the blockage out of the way. Remove the plunger and run the hot water to clear out any remaining debris.

2 An auger is a coil of flexible wire that you insert into the drain hole. Push it down as far as it will go. Twirl the wire around, and this should dislodge any matter stuck in the trap and push it out into the waste pipe.

3 Alternatively, cover the drain hole with the end of a vacuum pump. Pull the pump handle up and push down to free the blockage. Remove the pump and run the hot water to rinse away any debris.

4 If the plunger, auger and pump methods fail to clear the blockage, you'll need to remove the trap. Remove as much water from the sink as possible and put in the plug. Place the bucket under the trap. If you have a U-bend trap, loosen the fittings at either end (you may need to use a wrench) and gently pull the U-bend pipe away from the other pipes. Empty any water from the U-bend pipe into the bucket. Clean out the pipe with a brush and some disinfectant, then replace. If you have a bottle trap, untwist the fittings to remove the trap, empty the contents into the bucket and clean out the trap with a brush and disinfectant. Replace the trap.

HOW TO REMOVE STAINS FROM CARPET

Most carpet stains can be removed with water and ordinary household items, although you may occasionally need to buy a special stain remover or have the carpet professionally cleaned. Many carpets have been treated with stain-resistant materials, so spills can be removed if you get to them right away. However, the longer you delay, the more difficult removing carpet stains becomes. When treating stains, simply dab the offending spot—do not rub or scrub, or you will spread the stain and may damage the carpet. If you're not sure how to remove a carpet stain, always try plain water first.

INDISPENSABLE THINGS

- Water
- Distilled white vinegar
- Dish-washing liquid
- Paper towels
- Ice cube
- Spoon or knife
- Hair dryer
- Plastic wrap or plastic bag
- Brown paper bags
- White wine
- Milk

CHEWING GUM

Scrape as much of the residue off as you can with a knife or spoon. Leave an ice cube on the gum for a minute to freeze it. The gum should harden sufficiently so that it can be broken up and removed from the carpet. An alternative treatment is to heat the gum with a hair dryer, being careful not to melt the carpet fibers. Place a piece of plastic wrap or a plastic bag on top of the gum, then pull up and discard.

AFTERCARE

After all treatments, rinse the area well with clean water and dry with paper towels. Place a weight on top of the paper to speed up water absorption, or blow a fan or hair dryer over the top of the carpet. Brush clean and vacuum the carpet when the stain is dry to pick up any lingering particles.

RED WINE & INK STAINS

For red wine, blot the remaining liquid with paper towels. Apply white wine to the spot. This re-creates the initial conditions, especially on old stains, making it easier to remove. Mop up with paper towels and repeat. To treat ink stains, dab the area with a small amount of milk.

CANDLE WAX

Using a spoon or knife, scrape off as much wax as you can. Put a clean brown paper bag over the spot, and place a clothes iron on it, set on low. The wax will liquefy and transfer to the paper. Apply a new paper bag as often as necessary until all of the wax has been removed.

COFFEE STAINS

Soak up the excess with paper towels. Mix a few drops of dish-washing liquid with 1 cup lukewarm water. Sponge the area with the detergent solution. Another method is to mix $1/3$ cup distilled white vinegar with $2/3$ cup lukewarm water. Sponge the stained area with the vinegar solution.

HOW TO REMOVE HEAT STAINS FROM WOOD

If something hot, such as a coffee cup, sits directly on wood furniture, a heat mark is almost inevitable. The wood will gradually change color as it warms, until you're left with a white mark that mars the look of the furniture and will have you reaching for the tablecloth. But fear not, just follow these simple, indispensable tips.

INDISPENSABLE THINGS

- **Toothpaste**
- **2 damp cloths**
- **Clean white cloth**
- **Iron**
- **Dry cloth and furniture polish**

1 Apply some toothpaste (not gel) to the stain and rub with a clean, damp cloth, using a circular motion. Remove the toothpaste from the surface with a second damp cloth. You may have to repeat the process several times to lift the mark. Polish as usual.

2 Double-fold a clean white cloth and place over the scorch mark. Turn your iron to a low or medium setting and let it heat up. Press the iron back and forth over the cloth. Tap the steam release on the iron so that a burst of steam hits the cloth over the stain. Remove the cloth and wipe up any moisture.

📣 INDISPENSABLE WARNING

If your furniture is antique, be extremely careful, because depending on the type of finish used to seal the wood, the above treatments may do more harm than good. Ask an expert first.

IN THE KITCHEN

Impress your friends and family with this indispensable guide to kitchen competence. From the basics of boiling an egg to sharpening a knife and setting a formal table, you'll find practical advice and labor-saving tips to help you achieve culinary success and entertain in style.

HOW TO OPEN A JAR

Jars are vacuum sealed to keep food fresh, but this also makes the lids stick like wasps to flypaper. Some people try to break the vacuum by stabbing the top with a knife, but if you'd rather avoid a trip to the hospital and want to use the lid again, follow these indispensable steps instead.

1 First of all, simply tap the top of the jar with a wooden spoon to break the vacuum. If this fails, wrap the lid in a dishcloth to give your hands traction. Make sure that you have a firm grip on the jar lid and press down on the lid as you twist.

INDISPENSABLE THINGS

- Wooden spoon
- Dishcloth
- Rubber bands
- Rubber gloves

2 Alternatively, try placing rubber bands around the jar or hold it while wearing rubber gloves. Use one hand to grip the jar and the other to grip the lid. Twist the hand holding the jar clockwise and the one holding the lid counterclockwise.

3 If mechanical force fails, run the lid under warm (not boiling) water for a minute to make the metal expand. This increases the radius of the lid, making it a little bigger and looser, and therefore easier for you to open the jar.

HOW TO SHARPEN A KNIFE

It's essential to keep your knives sharp: a blunt knife is dangerous because it requires more pressure and is more likely to slip and cut you. A sharp knife also means a better, faster and easier job. Test for sharpness on a firm, ripe tomato—it should slice through easily rather than crush it. Be very careful when sharpening knives.

INDISPENSABLE THINGS

- **Sharpening steel**
- **Knife**
- **Sharpening stone**

1 A sharpening steel is a metal rod designed for sharpening knives. Hold it in one hand and hold the knife in the other. Place the knife just above the handle of the steel. With the knife at a 10–25-degree angle to the steel, draw the knife blade away from you down the steel.

2 Do the same on the other side and repeat several times until the entire blade of the knife has been drawn across the steel on both sides.

3 If using a sharpening stone, place it in front of you. Lay the edge of the blade nearest to the knife handle on the stone at a 45-degree angle. Slowly scrape the knife blade along the stone in an even motion, keeping the blade at the same angle. Repeat several times on each side. Turn the stone over and repeat on the smoother side.

HOW TO FRY AN EGG

For the perfect fried egg, make sure your egg is as fresh
as possible. You can use a teaspoon of oil instead of
butter, but it should have a mild flavor so it doesn't
affect the taste of the egg. For eggs "over easy," turn
over with a spatula when the whites are just about done
and cook for another 15 seconds.

INDISPENSABLE THINGS

- Egg
- Skillet
- Spatula
- Butter or mild-tasting oil
  (such as peanut)

SKILLET
Use a small nonstick
skillet. This means that
you will need to use less
oil (which is better for you)
and that the egg will slide
easily out of the skillet
once it is cooked.

BUTTER
Only add a little butter to the
pan—2 teaspoons per egg.
Heat the butter for several
minutes until sizzling—if it is
not hot enough, the egg will
spread out and take longer
to cook, becoming rubbery.

EGG
Crack the egg against the side of
the skillet and slide it in. Tilt the
skillet and baste the top of the egg
with the butter. Fry for a couple of
minutes, or until the white is firm
and the yolk has started to thicken,
but is not rock solid.

HOW TO BOIL AN EGG

The perfect boiled egg is mostly due to timing, but there are a few tricks that can help you achieve great results every time. Serve with buttered bread or toast cut into strips for a simple treat.

INDISPENSABLE THINGS

- **Eggs**
- **Pan**
- **Water**
- **Slotted spoon**

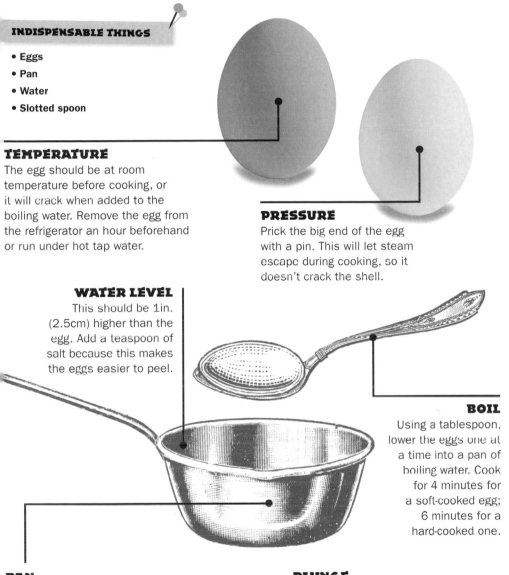

TEMPERATURE
The egg should be at room temperature before cooking, or it will crack when added to the boiling water. Remove the egg from the refrigerator an hour beforehand or run under hot tap water.

PRESSURE
Prick the big end of the egg with a pin. This will let steam escape during cooking, so it doesn't crack the shell.

WATER LEVEL
This should be 1in. (2.5cm) higher than the egg. Add a teaspoon of salt because this makes the eggs easier to peel.

BOIL
Using a tablespoon, lower the eggs one at a time into a pan of boiling water. Cook for 4 minutes for a soft-cooked egg; 6 minutes for a hard-cooked one.

PAN
The pan should just be large enough for the amount of eggs you are cooking. This is to prevent them from breaking as they bump into each other or the side of the pan while cooking.

PLUNGE
As soon as the cooking time is up, plunge the eggs briefly into a bowl of cold water to stop cooking and prevent discoloration of the egg yolk.

HOW TO MAKE AN OMELET

The perfect omelet is one that is just tinged with gold on the outside and very soft and squishy on the inside. The number one rule is not to overmix the eggs. The size of the pan is also vital: too large and the eggs will spread like a pancake and become dry and tough; too small and the omelet will be spongy and difficult to fold. You can vary the basic recipe by using different fillings.

INDISPENSABLE THINGS

- 2 large eggs
- Salt & pepper
- ½ teaspoon butter
- ½ teaspoon olive oil
- Bowl
- Fork
- Nonstick skillet measuring 6in. (15cm) in diameter
- Spatula
- Plate

PRACTICAL TIP

Popular fillings include grated cheese, chopped tomatoes, ham, mushrooms and cooked onion— use any combination or all, adding at the end of step 3 (mix in any herbs in step I). Eggs cook quickly, so have all the ingredients ready before you start.

A PRACTICAL HISTORY OF THE OMELET

The practice of cooking beaten eggs in butter in a pan is an ancient one. According to the *Larousse Gastronomique* (1938), some scholars claim that the omelet derives from *ova mellita*, a classic Roman dish consisting of beaten eggs cooked on a flat clay dish with honey. However, the word "omelet" did not enter the English language until the early 17th century, when it was thus defined by Randle Cotgrave in *A Dictionarie of the French and English Tongues* (1611) as: "Haumelette, an Omelet, or Pancake of Egges."

1 Carefully break the eggs into a bowl and season with salt and pepper. Blend the egg yolks and whites with a large fork. Place the pan on the heat and let it get quite hot.

2 Add the butter with the oil and, when melted, swirl around the pan to coat the bottom and the sides. Turn the heat up as high as possible, then, when the butter is foaming, pour the eggs into the pan, tilting it to spread them evenly over the bottom. Keep the pan on the heat without moving it for a count of five.

3 Tilt the pan to 45 degrees and, using the fork, draw the edge of the omelet into the center. The runny egg will flow into the space. Tip the pan the other way and repeat. Keep tilting the pan backward and forward, lifting the edges with a spatula so the runny egg flows underneath and cooks.

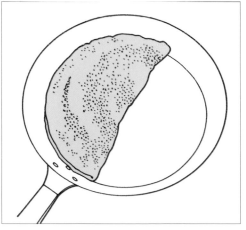

4 When there is just a small amount of liquid left on the surface, tilt the pan again, loosen the edges of the omelet and fold it in half. Slip the omelet on to the plate and serve immediately.

HOW TO MAKE BREAD

A home-baked loaf of white bread is hard to beat. Just follow these steps, or simply place all the ingredients in a food processor with a dough hook and knead for 3 minutes. The longer you leave the dough to rise, the better the bread will be. Dough will also rise at a cold temperature, so if more convenient, pop in the lowest part of the refrigerator and leave overnight. All bread recipes are approximate guides only—the amount of liquid the flour absorbs depends on the type of flour you use and even the weather!

INDISPENSABLE THINGS

- 5 cups strong white bread flour, sifted
- 1 teaspoon active dry yeast
- 1 tablespoon salt
- 1 teaspoon superfine sugar
- 1¾ cups lukewarm water
- Large bowl
- Plastic wrap
- Two 9 x 5 x 3-in. (23 x 13 x 8cm) loaf pans or one 8 x 4 x 2-in. (20 x 10 x 5cm) pan, greased
- Wire rack

1 Put the flour, yeast, salt and sugar in a bowl. Make a well in the center and add enough water to make a soft dough. Place the dough on a flat work surface, then stretch it away from you, using the heel of one hand to push from the middle and your other hand to pull the other half toward you. Then lift the edges over and back to the middle.

2 Repeat the process, turning the dough slightly with each movement. When the dough becomes very smooth and springy, and appears blistery on the surface (anywhere between 5 and 15 minutes), it's ready to rise.

3 Form the dough into a ball and place in a large, warm, oiled bowl, turning to coat evenly with grease. Cover with lightly oiled plastic wrap or a damp cloth and let stand to expand. When risen, the dough should have doubled in size and should spring back, feeling slightly sticky when touched.

4 Punch down the dough by punching all the air out of it with your fists until it's back to its original size. Put the dough into the loaf pan, cover as before and let stand for 20 minutes for a second rising.

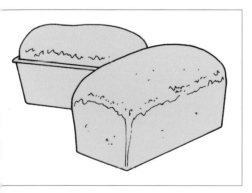

5 Uncover the pan and place on the center shelf of a preheated oven 450°F/230°C). Bake for 30–40 minutes. Remove the loaf from the pan and give the bottom a quick tap with your knuckles. If cooked, it will sound hollow; if not, put back in the oven for a few minutes. Let stand on a wire rack to cool.

HOW TO ROAST BEEF

A succulent slice of roast beef is one of life's simple pleasures. Take the meat out of the refrigerator to bring it to room temperature before cooking. Season with salt and pepper or rub with garlic, herbs or mustard powder, according to taste. Place the meat in a shallow roasting pan with the fattiest side on top.

INDISPENSABLE THINGS

- Cut of beef
- Roasting pan
- Seasoning
- Foil
- Spoon
- Skewer

TEMPERATURE & TIME
Put the beef in a very hot pre-heated oven (475°F/240°C) for 15 minutes then lower the heat to 375°F (190°C). Cook for another 17 minutes per 1lb (450g) for rare beef and add another 15 minutes for medium or 30 minutes for well done.

BASTING
While the beef is cooking, baste at least three times to keep it moist. Take the pan out of the oven, tip the juices to one end and spoon over the meat.

STANDING
When the beef is cooked, cover with foil and let it stand for at least 10 minutes to enhance its flavor and make carving easier.

JUICES
Stick a skewer into the middle of the meat to find out if it's cooked. If the juices are clear, it's well done; pink indicates medium and red shows it's rare.

HOW TO CARVE A CUT OF BEEF

Meat is made up of thousands of tiny strands of muscle, and the way you carve it can determine how tender or tough the meat turns out. Carving is an art that can easily be mastered, provided that you have a suitable sharp knife and some practice! Let the meat "rest" for at least 10 minutes before carving.

INDISPENSABLE THINGS

- Cooked cut of beef
- Carving knife
- Sharpening steel
- Carving fork with guard
- Board or spiked plate

KNIFE & FORK

The blade of the carving knife should be slightly flexible. Sharpen the knife each time it is to be used for carving, so that it will cut straight through the meat instead of sawing and tearing. You also need a carving fork with a guard, in case the knife slips.

FLAT SURFACE

Stand the meat on a flat slip-proof surface, such as a wooden board or on a plate with spikes to hold it in position. Remove any string and/or skewers that might be in the way.

CARVING

You'll find it much easier to carve standing up. Create a flat bottom by slicing away one end of the roast. Cut even-sized slices across the grain of the meat to shorten the fibers and make the meat seem more tender.

HOW TO MAKE CHOCOLATE SOUFFLÉ

Impress your friends with this fabulously easy and delicious chocolate dessert. The perfect soufflé should be light, crisp on top and slightly moist in the middle. This soufflé may shrink a little on its journey from oven to table, but it won't collapse. Use good-quality chocolate, but note that chocolate with a high content of cocoa solids (over 55 percent) will make the soufflé too bitter. This recipe makes one large soufflé to serve 6, or 4—6 individual ramekins, and you can make it an hour or two ahead, unbaked, and keep in the refrigerator until ready to go.

INDISPENSABLE THINGS

- 4oz (115g) dark chocolate
- Melted butter, for greasing
- ¼ cup superfine sugar
- 4 large egg yolks
- 5 large egg whites
- Pinch of salt
- Confectioners' sugar, for dusting
- Baking pan
- 3 bowls
- Saucepan of hot water
- Wooden spoon
- Soufflé dish or individual ramekins
- Whisk
- Metal spoon
- Butter knife

1 Preheat the oven to 400°F (200°C) and put in the baking pan to heat up. Break the chocolate into a heatproof bowl and melt it over a saucepan of simmering water, making sure the bottom of the bowl doesn't touch the water. Let stand until the chocolate is just soft, which will take about 5 minutes.

2 Remove the chocolate from the heat and beat with a wooden spoon until smooth and glossy. Let the melted chocolate cool slightly. Meanwhile, grease the soufflé dish lightly and sprinkle with a little of the superfine sugar.

3 Separate the eggs into two bowls. Stir the rest of the sugar and four of the egg yolks into the chocolate. Whisk the egg whites with the salt until they form stiff peaks. Then, using a metal spoon, fold them gently into the chocolate mixture.

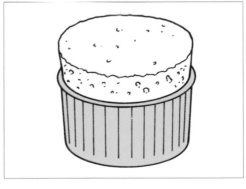

4 Fill the soufflé dish or individual ramekins until they are nearly full. Take a butter knife and pull it across the top of the dish so the mixture is completely flat. Wipe any splashes off the outside of the dish, or they will burn while cooking.

5 Place on the baking tray in the oven and bake for about 20 minutes, until the soufflé rises and puffs up. It should have risen by about two-thirds of its original height and wobble when moved, but be set on top. Serve straight from the oven, dusted with confectioners' sugar, accompanied by chocolate sauce or whipping cream.

HOW TO MAKE A SPONGE CAKE

Successful cakemaking is extremely satisfying, but it requires strict attention to detail. All ingredients should be at room temperature when you start. Careful measuring, precise oven temperatures and timing are also crucial to success. A cake should be baked as soon as it is mixed and you should never open the oven door until at least three-quarters of the cooking time has elapsed, because the temperature will drop suddenly and the air in the cake will contract, causing the cake to sink. For a really easy recipe, just put all of the sponge ingredients in a food processor and blend.

INDISPENSABLE THINGS

- Oil, for brushing
- 1 stick/8 tablespoons butter or margarine
- 1/2 cup superfine sugar
- 2 medium eggs
- Vanilla extract
- Generous 1/2 cup self-rising flour
- 1–2 tablespoons hot water or milk
- Jelly
- Whipped cream
- Confectioners' sugar, for dusting
- 2 x 6-in. (15-cm) cake pans
- Wax paper
- Wooden spoon
- Large mixing bowl
- Strainer
- Butter knife
- Wire rack

1 Assemble all your ingredients and utensils and preheat your oven to 400°F (200°C). Line the base of each cake pan with a disk of wax paper and lightly brush the sides with oil.

2 Cream the butter until light in color, then beat in the sugar, a little at a time, and beat until the mixture has a mousselike consistency. The creaming incorporates air and is the secret of the sponge's lightness.

3 Mix the eggs together in a separate bowl and gradually beat into the creamed mixture a little at a time. If the mixture begins to curdle, simply sift in some of your flour and stir it, then continue.

4 Sir in a few drops of vanilla extract. Fold the sifted flour into the mixture. You should have a mixture that drops off the spoon easily, but if the consistency is not right, add a little hot water or milk.

5 Divide the mixture into the two cake pans. Push the mixture toward the edges of the pans and smooth out the tops with a butter knife. Put the cakes into the oven for 20 minutes.

6 If the sponges are cooked, they will have come away slightly from the sides of the pan and, when you gently press the top of the cakes, they will spring back. If they are not ready, give them another 3–5 minutes but no longer. When the sponges are cooked, turn them out on to a wire rack and peel off the wax paper. Let cool, then sandwich together with a layer of jelly and whipped cream. Dust the top with confectioners' sugar.

HOW TO MAKE A BLT

A BLT is an irresistible combination of bacon, lettuce and tomato between two pieces of bread. This delicious sandwich is really simple to make, and the trick is to use good-quality ingredients and get the balance between them just right. The BLT is known and loved throughout the world, but is generally regarded as an American classic. The world's biggest BLT was assembled in Sonoma County, California, in 2003, and was 104 ft. (31.6m) long and covered an area of almost 100 square feet (9.7m2).

INDISPENSABLE THINGS

- 4 slices smoked or unsmoked bacon, preferably dry cured
- 2 slices bread, lightly toasted
- 2 lettuce leaves, washed
- 1 firm tomato, sliced
- Mayonnaise
- Paper towel
- Butter knife

A PRACTICAL HISTORY OF THE SANDWICH

John Montague, the 4th Earl of Sandwich, was an 18th-century English aristocrat whose name is immortalized in this humble snack. History records him as an inveterate gambler who preferred playing cards to eating his dinner. Snacks of meat served between slices of bread satisfied his hunger and enabled him to stay longer at the card table. The less colorful account is that he was a hard-working peer who didn't have time to stop for lunch, so ate a meat-and-bread snack at his desk. Whatever the truth, this type of fast food soon became very popular among the English gentry and later among the whole of society.

TOMATO

Use a firm, ripe tomato, cut into thick slices and sprinkled lightly with salt. Many prefer a beefsteak variety for its firm flesh and fewer seeds—this makes the BLT a seasonal treat. Arrange the slices of tomato so they overlap slightly.

BREAD

This can be white, whole wheat or sourdough, according to preference, but it's best to go with something that tastes mild and that doesn't compete with the flavor of the bacon (this rules out rye bread and wholemeals). It is usually lightly toasted.

BACON

This is regarded as the magical ingredient that transmutes a basic sandwich into gold. Many would argue that standard supermarket bacon just isn't good enough, but whatever type you use, fry until crisp, then place on a paper towel to blot up excess grease.

LETTUCE

You will need a couple of leaves of a crisp, bland variety—romaine, Boston or iceberg are all perfect. Strong-tasting lettuces change the nature of the BLT.

MAYO

Use good-quality mayonnaise, but not too much, or it will mask the other flavors. Spread this on both slices of bread using a butter knife, and dab it on instead of rubbing it in.

HOW TO MAKE A MARTINI

This legendary cocktail is a drink long associated with sophistication, glamor and power. Aficionados included Ernest Hemingway, Winston Churchill, Frank Sinatra and, of course, the ultrasuave fictional James Bond, although he used vodka and gin. In a classic martini, you need only three things: gin, dry vermouth and an olive or two. Other alcohols, garnishes and methods can be used for different variations, but to a purist, they wouldn't be considered true martinis.

INDISPENSABLE THINGS

- Cocktail shaker
- Long-stemmed, cone-shaped cocktail glass
- Crushed ice
- Few drops to ½fl oz (15ml) dry vermouth
- 2fl oz (60ml) good-quality dry gin
- Angostura bitters (optional)
- Olives or twist of lemon, skewered on a toothstick

A PRACTICAL HISTORY OF THE MARTINI

There are as many supposed origins of the martini as there are ways to make it, but the first written reference to a martini is found in the *Bon Vivant's Companion: Or How to Mix Drinks* (1887), a bartender's manual that lists sweet vermouth among the ingredients. The martini rose in popularity in the United States during the Prohibition period of the 1920s, when gin was quick and easy to produce, but was of such poor quality that it needed the addition of vermouth to disguise its taste.

1 For absolute purists, everything should be at room temperature before you make the cocktail. However, many favor storing the gin in the freezer to make it syrupy, although this will result in a blunter, more oily taste. Never put vermouth in the freezer because it will partially freeze, ruining its taste.

2 Add plenty of ice to the cocktail shaker to chill and blend the ingredients. Add the vermouth—from a few drops to a full shot, according to taste. Some prefer just to roll the vermouth around a chilled cocktail glass to form a coating, then tip out the vermouth. This makes a dry martini.

3 Place the gin in the cocktail shaker and stir for 20 seconds, or shake vigorously. Shaking will make the gin temporarily cloudy, and some people believe this technique bruises the gin. Strain into the glass and add a dash of Angostura bitters, if desired. Garnish with the olives or lemon twist.

INDISPENSABLE VARIATION

There are countless variations on the classic cocktail:

- A Vodka martini uses vodka instead of gin.

- A Gibson is a classic martini garnished with cocktail onions instead of olives or a lemon twist.

- Adding a dash of olive brine creates what is known as a dirty martini, and takes the edge off the harshness of the gin.

HOW TO OPEN A CHAMPAGNE BOTTLE

The secret of opening a champagne bottle without injuring your guests or showering the contents around the room is to make sure the wine is well chilled before opening and then to simply twist the bottle, instead of pulling on the cork. The best serving temperature is around 45°F (7°C). If you put your hand on the bottle, it should feel very cold, not just cool—champagne that is too warm will foam and spill when you open the bottle.

INDISPENSABLE THINGS

- Bottle of champagne
- Kitchen towel
- Champagne glass

1 Never use a corkscrew on a champagne bottle because the contents are under pressure and may explode. Hold the bottle upright and remove the foil and wire cage.

2 Drape a kitchen towel over the top of the bottle. If the cork pops before you're ready, the towel will stop it from flying off and will also catch any wine spills. Grip the cork between fingers and thumb. Using your other hand, turn the bottom of the bottle until you hear a soft "pop."

3 Remove the towel and cork, and pour a little champagne into a champagne glass. Wait for the foam to subside, then top up with more champagne until the glass is two-thirds full.

HOW TO MAKE AN OIL & VINEGAR DRESSING

An oil and vinegar dressing not only livens up salads, but also adds zing to pasta, fish and vegetables. Simply put all the ingredients in a screw-top jar, shake until well blended and drizzle over your dish. An oil and vinegar dressing will keep in the refrigerator for up to three days, but is best made fresh. It is an unstable emulsion and will separate after an hour—in this case, simply shake again to recombine.

INDISPENSABLE THINGS

- 6 tablespoons olive oil
- 2 tablespoons vinegar
- 1 teaspoon Dijon mustard
- Salt & pepper

OIL

The ratio of 3 parts oil to 1 part vinegar is usual, although less oil is used if a milder acid than vinegar is substituted. The better the quality of oil, the better the taste—use extra-virgin olive oil. Don't be afraid to experiment with different flavored oils, such as garlic-infused oil.

VINEGAR

Any good-quality vinegar will do. Red or white wine vinegar is the norm, but try balsamic or tarragon vinegar for a different taste. Vinegar can be replaced with another acid, such as lemon or orange juice.

MUSTARD

Add a small amount of Dijon mustard to act as an emulsifying agent and bind the oil and vinegar together. Powdered mustard would add flavor, but does not emulsify the ingredients.

SALT & PEPPER

Add salt and pepper—sea salt and freshly milled black pepper, if possible—according to taste.

HOW TO CHOP ONIONS SO YOU DON'T CRY

Onions make you cry because, when you cut them, you break apart cells that combine with enzymes to release gases that are dissolved by the water in your eyes. Oxygen in the air converts the dissolved gas into sulfuric acid, so your eyes form tears to wash the acid away. Try these indispensable tips for chopping onions without tears.

INDISPENSABLE THINGS

- Onions
- Sharp knife
- Swimming goggles or a mask
- Water
- Chewing gum

KEEP THEM COLD

Chilling is supposed to change chemical compounds in the onion, reducing the amount of gas that they release.

ABSORB THE GASES IN WATER

Cut the onions in a bowl of water, under running water or near a cloud of steam (from a kettle). Alternatively, chew gum to produce saliva in your mouth, which will reduce the virulence of the sting.

EFFECTIVE CUTTING

Use a sharp blade to chop an onion to minimize cell damage, and cut it quickly to reduce the time gases have to reach the eyes. Cut the root off last because it has the highest concentration of enzymes.

PROTECT YOUR EYES

Use swimming goggles or a mask with tight-fitting seals to prevent gases from entering the eyes. This is always effective.

HOW TO CRUSH GARLIC WITHOUT A PRESS

The cut of garlic affects its flavor, and crushing garlic releases more of its aromatic oils than simply chopping or slicing it. Garlic presses are effective, but fussy to clean, so try these easy methods instead. To begin, take a clove of garlic and strip off its papery covering.

INDISPENSABLE THINGS

- Garlic cloves
- Wide-blade knife
- Cutting board
- Paper towels
- Food can (unopened)
- Pestle and mortar
- Wooden spoon

KNIFE
Position the garlic clove flat on a chopping board with the hollow side facing downward. Place a knife with a wide blade flat over the garlic, being careful not to touch the sharp edge of the blade. Press down strongly with the palm of your hand.

PESTLE & MORTAR
Crush the garlic clove in a porcelain pestle and mortar – wood and stone versions absorb the scent of garlic and can taint the flavor of anything else you crush in it.

SPOON
Place the garlic clove on a cutting board. Use the back of a spoon to press down and apply pressure in order to crush the garlic.

CAN
Wrap the clove of garlic in a piece of paper towel. Place on the cutting board, then whack it with the bottom of an unopened food can.

HOW TO SET THE TABLE

Planning a formal dinner party and need a reminder of how to set a table? Fear not—it's fairly straightforward. The basic rule is: cutlery is placed in the order of use; that is, from the outside in toward the plate. A second rule, with a few exceptions is: forks go to the left of the plate and knives and spoons go to the right. Cups and saucers are placed near the knives or can be brought out after the meal. Finally, decide on a seating plan, and, if you want, put out cards with place names.

INDISPENSABLE THINGS

- Tablecloth
- Napkins
- Bread plates with butter knives
- Dinner plates
- Salad plates or soup bowls
- Water glasses
- Wine glasses
- Liqueur glasses
- Salad or fish forks
- Dinner forks
- Dessert forks
- Salad or fish knives
- Dinner knives
- Soup or melon spoons
- Dessert spoons

PRACTICAL TIP

It's a good idea to wear cotton gloves when handling silver cutlery to prevent the oils and acids in your skin from tarnishing the utensils. Rubber gloves contain sulphur that makes silver tarnish, so don't wear these when handling it.

GLASSES

Set out glasses in order of use above the knives. Usually this means placing the water glass to the left, then to its right the red wine, white wine and liqueur glasses.

TABLECLOTH

If you use a tablecloth, it should, of course, be spotlessly clean, ironed and with the middle crease arranged so that it runs in a straight line down the center of the table.

NAPKINS

Napkins can be folded and placed at the side, on the plate, under the forks or inside one of the glasses, depending on your preference.

CUTLERY POSITION

The placement of cutlery is always guided by the menu, working from the outside in. Cutlery should be about 1/2in. (12mm) away from the plate or each other, and should also be lined up evenly from the bottom ends. Each course should have its own utensils. Place forks to the left and knives to the right.

PLATES

Dinner plates need to be centered in front of each chair. Soup bowls or salad plates sit on top of each dinner plate. The bread plate should be placed to the side. Alternatively, bring out appropriate plates for each course and place on top of the dinner plate (which acts as an underplate).

KNIVES

Knives should be placed with their cutting edge toward the dinner plate—except the butter knife, which should be laid flat on a bread plate.

SPOONS

Place soup or melon spoons to the right of the knives. The dessert spoon lies at the head of the plate, centered above it.

HOW TO SERVE WINE

Serve wine like a professional with these simple tricks of the trade. Stemmed glasses are extremely important, because the stem enables the wine to be held without the palm of your hand heating it up too much. The shape of a glass can also affect the taste of the wine.

INDISPENSABLE THINGS

• Opened bottle of wine
• Wine glass

STILL WINE. Pour still wines slowly toward the center of the glass. Fill up to just below the widest section, so that the guest can swirl the wine to release the aroma without risk of spillage. Finish pouring the wine, tilting the tip of the bottle upward and slightly rotating your hand, so that the wine doesn't drip.

RED WINE. The best red wine glasses have a large round bowl, which gives the wine a greater surface exposure. Swirling the wine around in the glass aerates it and helps to remove sediment.

WHITE WINE. Tulip-shape glasses that narrow at the rim are best for white wine because this helps to preserve more of the chill that enhances the wine.

SPARKLING WINE. Flute-type champagne glasses are ideal for sparkling wines because they provide a central point from which bubbles can rise. Hold the glass at an angle and pour the wine against the side, like a beer.

IN THE YARD

Make the most of your outdoor space with
this indispensable guide to plant growth
and maintenance. Covering everything from
potting your plants to making a cold frame
or a compost pile, these clear instructions
will guide you effortlessly through the
practical tasks needed to help
your plants flourish.

HOW TO DOUBLE DIG

This is an excellent way of cultivating soil for the vegetable plot. The deeper the planting soil, the deeper the roots can go, which leads to stronger plants and a higher yield at harvest. Hard work but straightforward, double digging usually needs to be done only once. Remember that you have two layers to work: the top layer dug with a spade and the bottom layer dug with a garden fork. The best time to do it is in fall and early winter, when the ground is moist, but not waterlogged or frozen. It then has time to settle before planting in spring.

INDISPENSABLE THINGS

- 2 stakes
- String
- Wheelbarrow
- Spade
- Fork
- Compost (rotten vegetable matter, about 1 bucket per 10 square feet (1m²)

PRACTICAL TIP

Make sure that you don't overdo it—you need a strong back for double digging and you don't have to do all your digging in one day.

1 Make sure your bed is free of weeds, and mark out the area you are going to dig with a piece of string stretched between two stakes (5 x 20ft./1.5 x 6m is ideal). Begin at one end of the bed and dig a narrow trench, about 12in. (30cm) wide and 12in. (30cm) deep, along the length of the bed, placing the excavated soil in a wheelbarrow.

2 Work a garden fork into the floor of the trench, and work it around to loosen the subsoil. This is why it's called double digging, because you're digging twice the depth of usual digging. Continue until the soil at the bottom of the trench is loosened. Add compost and fork in.

3 Dig a second trench directly next to the first. Place the excavated topsoil into the first trench you dug and enrich with compost. Loosen the soil at the bottom of the second trench with the garden fork and add more compost.

4 Dig a third trench next to the second trench. Backfill the second one with the excavated topsoil and enrich with compost. Loosen the soil at the bottom of the third trench with the garden fork and add compost. Continue this process until you have double dug the whole bed. Fill the last trench with the soil in the wheelbarrow. You'll end up with a raised bed because you have incorporated organic matter and broken up the soil.

HOW TO PLANT A SEED

Starting plants from seed is a great, inexpensive way to grow vegetables, herbs and flowers. Read the instructions on the seed pack first to see if they require any special treatment—some seeds need soaking before sowing.

INDISPENSABLE THINGS

- Seeds
- Seed tray
- Growing medium
- Spray mist bottle
- Plastic bag or plastic wrap
- Light source
- Fertilizer

1 Premoisten the growing medium with a small amount of tepid water. Fill the seed tray with soil (about two-thirds full), but do not pack the soil down hard.

2 Plant your seeds shallow, not deep. Sprinkle tiny seeds on the surface. Spray the soil surface with water to settle the soil firmly over the seeds, but do not saturate it.

3 Cover your seed tray with plastic wrap or put in a plastic bag to keep the soil evenly moist while the seeds germinate. Place the seed tray in a warm location somewhere that won't be in direct sunlight.

4 When the shoots appear, remove the plastic and place in direct sunlight. Water as needed and add fertilizer. Once there are a few leaves and the seedling is about 2in. (5cm) high, transplant into individual pots.

HOW TO REPOT A PLANT

If your indoor potted plants appear to be stunted, deformed, pale and dull, or top-heavy, the reason for this is that they may be pot-bound and need to be moved to a larger pot. Pot-bound roots have outgrown their container and are starting to circle around the inside or poke out the drainage holes in search of more growing room.

INDISPENSABLE THINGS

- Plant
- Plant pot
- Soil mix

1 Take the plant out of its pot and knock off any old soil. Unwind circling roots and cut off any that look rotted or that need to be pruned back.

2 Choose a new pot that is only about 1–2in. (3–6cm) larger in diameter than the old one. Don't get too big a pot, because it will hold more soil and more water than the plant can use, which can lead to rot.

3 Put a few inches of new soil mix in the bottom of the new pot, put the plant into the pot, and see if the level is high enough. The plant should be about 1in. (2.5cm) below the top of the pot.

4 Fill in around the roots with soil, tapping it down lightly with your fingers. Water the plant moderately.

HOW TO TAKE CUTTINGS

This is an easy way to increase the number of your plants in your yard. Cuttings can be taken from stems, roots or leaves on some plants. Those taken from new shoots will root easily in spring to provide new plants for flower beds or pots. Alternatively, take cuttings of your favorite plants in late summer, keep them indoors in the winter, and plant outside in the spring. Always take cuttings in the morning, when the plants are at their freshest.

INDISPENSABLE THINGS

- Sharp knife or pruners
- 4-in. (10-cm) pot
- Soil mix
- Hormone rooting powder
- Dibble
- Spray mist bottle

1 Choose healthy, nonflowering shoots to use for cuttings. Use a clean sharp knife or pruners to cut them from the parent plant. Cut below a single leaf joint or pair of leaves, aiming for a cutting of 3–4in. (7–10cm) long. Remove any leaves from the bottom half of the cutting.

2 Fill a 4-in. (10cm) pot with soil mix. Dip the bottom of each cutting into hormone rooting powder to promote root development. Carefully tap off any excess liquid or powder. Use a dibble to make holes in the soil mix.

3 Insert the bottom of the cutting into the soil mix and firm in. Where possible, try to position cuttings so that their leaves don't touch each other. Water with a spray mist bottle, and label the pot so you know what the cuttings are.

4 Cover the pot with a clear plastic bag and place the pot indoors out of direct sunlight. Mist regularly to keep the soil mix moist. Remove the bag once a day and shake out excess water to prevent it from becoming too humid inside. The cuttings should root in six to eight weeks. When the roots appear at the bottom of the pot, plant the cuttings singly in pots of the same size.

A PRACTICAL HISTORY OF PLANT PROPAGATION

The Greek philosopher and disciple of Aristotle, Theophrastus (37I–c.287 B.C.E.) wrote *Enquiry into Plants* and *On the Causes of Plants*, two large botanical treatises that describe starting new plants from seeds and cuttings. The cuttings that he had most success with were actually rooted suckers that were separated or divided from the mother plant. The Romans worked out that using thin sheets of mica (glass) helped produce heat for protecting plants, encouraging them to grow. Ancient Chinese gardeners were also skilled in different methods of plant propagation.

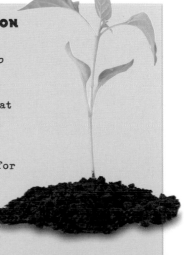

HOW TO CHOP LOGS

Chopping wood for your fire can be a potential disaster, but with a little preparation and knowledge, you can safely produce a stack of logs. Always wear safety equipment, always place your log on a stable platform and always make sure there are no bystanders or pets in the vicinity so they won't be hurt by flying splinters. Your goal is to hit the log directly in the center: a glancing blow may result in injury to yourself, so aim carefully. Never use a dull or damaged ax, and don't attempt to chop logs at all if you have a back problem.

INDISPENSABLE THINGS

- Pile of logs
- Saw
- Hand ax
- Safety glasses
- Safety boots
- Chopping block

👉 PRACTICAL TIP

Look after your tools and they'll last longer. When you've finished using the ax, lightly oil the blade to prevent rust and put a cover over it for safety reasons and to help keep it sharp.

SAFETY EQUIPMENT

This woodcutter should be wearing safety goggles to protect his eyes from flying splinters. Safety boots with steel toes are also recommended—the ax might miss the wood and hit your foot instead.

AX

Use a hand ax with a sharp edge. Make sure that the head of the ax is attached securely to the shaft, otherwise the blade may fly off while you chop.

LOGS

Throw the log away if you find any metal, such as old nails in it. Damp logs are much more difficult to chop, as are logs with knots in them. If the log you want to chop was cut at an angle, it won't rest on the chopping block, so first you need to saw the ends off straight.

ACTION

Plant your feet firmly on the ground, shoulder-width apart to balance your weight. Place one hand at the end of the ax handle and hold tight close to the ax head with the other. Raise the ax in an arc over your shoulder. Aim carefully for the center, swing hard and follow through to force the ax head right through the log and embed itself in the chopping block.

CHOPPING BLOCK

Place the log upright on a chopping block, such as a large tree stump. The log has to be on a solid surface in order for the force of your ax to split it. The chopping block provides a solid base and raises the log so that your ax will meet it squarely.

TAPPING

If your ax doesn't chop the wood in half with the first hit, tap the ax (now embedded in the log) on the chopping block until it makes its way down the grain and splits the log in two.

HOW TO MAKE A TRELLIS

A trellis is nothing more than a frame for supporting plants, but it can range in size from a mere backdrop to a container to an elaborate structure running the length of a wall. Design a trellis to accommodate the climbing plant you have in mind—some vines will grab on to any surface; bushier plants may need to be tied onto a trellis. You'll get the best results from natural-born climbers, such as cucumbers, beans, squash, peas and tomatoes. If your soil is dry and hard, deeply water the day before you plan to build the trellis to make it easier to drive the poles or stakes into the ground.

INDISPENSABLE THINGS

- Bamboo, tree branches or broom handles
- Garden twine, raffia or cloth
- Spade
- Wooden mallet
- Wooden posts
- Wire, string or netting
- Staple gun

PRACTICAL TIP

Trellised plants can lose moisture quickly because they are exposed to wind and sun. Put a mulch on top of the soil to retain moisture and water regularly—the easiest way to do this is to entwine a drip tubing system through the trellis.

TEPEE TRELLIS

1 Tepee trellises make excellent supports for beans, peas and tomatoes, and for heavily fruited crops, such as melon and squash. You will need three to six poles of equal length—bamboo, branches or broom handles. Choose thin ones for lightweight plants and stouter ones for heavier crops.

2 Use garden twine, raffia or strips of cloth to tie poles together near the top. Pull the poles into a tight bundle, wrap the twine around the bundle a few times and tie it snugly. Weave the twine in and out of the bundled sticks and make sure it's sturdy, stable and secure.

3 Prop the tepee over the planting area. Push the poles about 1ft. (30cm) into the ground. Leave one area of the tepee plant-free so you can harvest produce easily. For a larger crop, space the poles in two rows and then place bamboo poles horizontally between them to add extra support.

FENCE TRELLIS

1 To make a fence trellis, dig two holes 24in. (60cm) deep and 10ft. (3m) apart. Use a mallet and drive a wooden post deeply into each hole. Tamp in with soil. Place other posts in between where needed.

2 Wrap wire or string tightly around one stake, then run it to the other fence post, wrap it around and tie it tightly. Wrap more wire horizontally around the posts at regular intervals, and vertically between the wires. Or attach mesh netting, using a staple gun.

HOW TO MAKE A BIRD BOX

This cheap and easy project is a great way of attracting birds into your yard. Specially constructed bird boxes imitate the cavities in trees and can be a real help to birds when rearing their young. Only make a perch if it is intended for house sparrows, because they will sit on it and peck at other birds using the box. Locate your bird box in a northeast facing spot, high up in a tree or building away from predators, strong sunlight and wind. Avoid placing near other bird boxes, tables or feeders.

INDISPENSABLE THINGS

- Wood, 1/2 x 6 x 60in. (15 x 150 x 1,500mm)
- Pencil and ruler
- Saw
- Hammer
- Galvanized 3/4in. (20mm) nails
- Sealant
- Drill with cutting bits
- Hinge
- Screws
- Screwdriver
- Hook-and-eye fastener
- Linseed oil

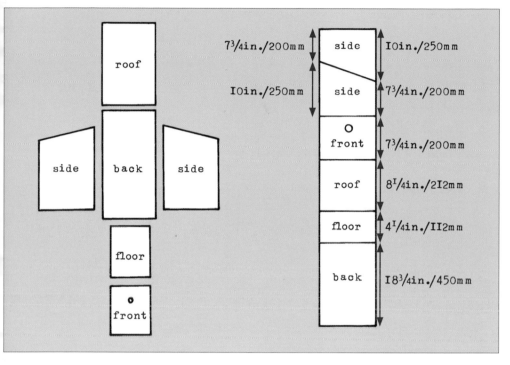

side	10in./250mm
side	7³/₄in./200mm
front	7³/₄in./200mm
roof	8¹/₄in./212mm
floor	4¹/₄in./112mm
back	18³/₄in./450mm

7³/₄in./200mm
10in./250mm

1 Any wood will do, but exterior-grade plywood is best. Mark out the six sections of the bird box with a pencil and ruler to the dimensions shown above, and write the name of each panel onto the marked-out wood to save confusion later. Where possible, try to ensure that the grain will run vertically in the finished box because this will help drainage.

Cut out the panels of wood. Make a small hole in the floor to let liquid waste drain. The hole size for the entrance is important because some birds will oust others if they can get into the box. For wrens, nuthatches and chickadees, make a 1¹/₄-in. (32-mm) hole; for woodpeckers and tree swallows, make a 1³/₄-in. (45-mm) hole; for Eastern bluebirds and house finches, make a 2-in. (50-mm) hole; for a purple martin, make a 2¹/₂-in. (70-mm) hole. Nail the sides, back and floor together. To make it waterproof and windproof, seal the sides with sealant.

FINISHING TOUCHES

Attach the top to the sides of the box with a hinge so that it can be opened, and add a hook-and-eye fastener to keep it shut. You don't need to paint the box—in fact, some colors are known to scare birds off. A coat of linseed oil will keep the wood from drying out, but avoid wood preservatives because they can be poisonous to wildlife. Clean out the box every year, 2—3 weeks after birds have fledged (October—November). Remove any old nests or bedding and rinse out the box with boiling water to kill parasites. To avoid poisoning the birds, do not use any pesticides or flea powder.

HOW TO PLANT A WINDOW BOX

A window box is a great way to brighten up the exterior of your home. Most plants will thrive in containers if they are given the correct soil and watering conditions. A simple but effective design is to choose one type of plant that grows up, one that trails down and one bushy type to fill in the middle. Water your window box frequently to keep it moist, usually once a day during summer and fall. Use liquid fertilizer once every two weeks when plants are established, and deadhead when necessary.

PRACTICAL TIP

Flowers in window boxes grow away from the window, but if you want them to grow vertically instead of outward, turn your window box around every few days (obviously you can't do this if it's secured to the wall!).

INDISPENSABLE THINGS

- Window box
- Clean broken earthenware for the bottom
- Soil mix, moistened with warm water
- Plants of your choice

LOCATION

Before buying, consider how the box will be secured. Is the sill wide and strong enough for the box to sit securely? If in doubt, the box should be attached to the wall. Window boxes can be attached to walls facing any direction, but south and west-facing boxes require more watering. North-facing boxes will need shade-tolerant plants. If your box is in a very hot location, insert styrofoam tiles along the front to keep the inside cool.

CHOICE

There are a number of store-bought window boxes available, from simple plastic trays to metal, terra-cotta and ornate wood, but keep in mind that metal boxes may become too hot. Choose a window box that will blend in with your house wall— the more natural looking, the better. Measure the windowsill before buying a window box to make sure it will fit.

LENGTH

For the best results in a window box garden, the box should be at least 3–4ft. (1–1.25m) long but not more than 6ft. (2m). Any larger, and it will be too heavy to suspend and secure properly, and it will be very difficult to lift. Choose a container with good drainage holes and cover the holes at the bottom with a layer of pieces of broken earthenware.

PLANTING

Fill the container to three-quarters full with soil mix. Before planting, arrange the plants while they're still in the box, to see how they will look best. Take into account structure, color and foliage texture. Place taller plants in the middle and trailing plants, such as ivy, along the edge. When you're happy, knock them out of their pots and plant them at around ¾in. (2cm) below the rim. Firm in and water.

HOW TO MAKE A COLD FRAME

A cold frame is a bottomless box with a see-through lid, used to protect tender plants throughout the winter months in cold regions and to extend the growing season. Relying solely on the heat and warmth of the sun, a cold frame costs nothing to use and very little to build. The size of the frame depends on the size of the window(s), but do not make your cold frame so wide that you cannot easily reach the plants at the back, especially if you're growing vegetables. A maximum width of 3—4ft. (I—I.25m) is about right for most people to reach the back for weeding or harvesting their produce.

INDISPENSABLE THINGS

- Old window
- Heavy-duty hinges
- Tape measure
- Lengths of wood
- Saw
- 2-in. (50mm) stainless steel screws
- Phillips screwdriver
- Wood glue
- Hook-and-eye closure
- Paint

1 Before building a cold frame, choose a good location. You need a site that receives an ample amount of sunlight each day; one where you can butt the cold frame up against an existing structure to provide protection from winds and rain; and one with good drainage to allow water to flow away from the cold frame.

2 The top of most cold frames made at home are old windows (the glass lets in sunshine), so the dimensions of the frame depend on the size of the window you use. You will need to hinge the window, so buy some heavy-duty hinges. You will need to build your frame to fit your window, making sure that the back is higher than the front.

3 Measure the window's side length. Draw a line that length from top to bottom of a plank. Saw along this to make the angled top pieces. Cut 2 planks the same length as the flat edge of those angled top pieces to form the box sides and another 3 the same as the front length of the window (1 to make the front and 2 to make the back of the frame).

4 Glue the pieces of wood together and screw together at the joints for extra support. Place the old window over the top and attach with hinges on the back. If wind is likely to blow your window top open, add a simple hook-and-eye closure to the front.

5 Paint the outside of the frame to make it weatherproof. You'll also want to include a way to keep the window open for ventilation during mild days when the temperature reaches above 45°F (7°C). A spare piece of wood can be used as a prop.

HOW TO PRUNE A ROSEBUSH

It is hard to kill a rose with pruning. Like a bad haircut, most mistakes will grow out quickly and it is better to prune than to let roses grow rampant. No pruning results in a mess of tangled stems bearing only a few flowers.

INDISPENSABLE THINGS

- Pruners
- Loppers for longer stems
- Thick gloves (preferably long ones)

WHY

Roses need pruning to promote new growth, increase air circulation, shape the plant and remove dead, damaged or diseased stems

WHEN

Modern hybrids need regular deadheading to promote continuous flowering. Give a hard pruning in the spring, when the leaf buds begin to swell on the rose plants. Rosebushes that flower only once, such as ramblers and Old Garden Roses, need a light pruning in summer after flowering and when the blooms have faded.

HOW

Using clean, sharp tools, begin pruning from the base of the plant. Make a clean cut at a 45-degree angle, about ¼in (5mm) above a new, outward-facing bud.

INDISPENSABLE ROSES

Napoleon Bonaparte's first wife, Josephine, established a famous rose garden at Malmaison, in France. Apparently, she liked to wander around with a rose, which she would hold near her mouth when conversing to conceal her rotten teeth.

HOW TO WATER A HOUSEPLANT

Most houseplants require a thorough soaking and then to be left alone until they almost dry out. Stick a small knife in the compost: if it comes out dry with no soil particles attached, then your plant needs watering. If the soil is very dry, leave the pot in an inch of water for 30 minutes, until the top of the soil is moist.

INDISPENSABLE THINGS

- Houseplant
- Tap water

LOCATION

A plant in a warm bright room requires more water than the same plant in a cool dark room.

SEASON

Most plants grow faster in the spring and summer than in the fall and winter. The faster a plant grows, the more water it needs.

POT

Plants in small pots dry out faster than those in large ones. A plant in a porous container, such as terra-cotta, will dry out faster than the same plant in a metal or plastic one.

WATER

Tap water is fine, but leave it in a pitcher for 30 minutes so any chlorine evaporates and it reaches room temperature (if water is too cold, the roots can't absorb it).

METHOD

Water thoroughly from the top until the water comes out the drip holes. This leaches out salts that have built up in the soil from fertilizers.

HOW TO MAKE COMPOST

Compost is used to feed and nourish the soil to help you grow healthy plants. To make your own compost, just provide the right ingredients and let nature do the rest. The finished product should be dark, crumbly and sweet smelling. For best results, use a mixture of green and brown ingredients. Do not compost meat, fish, dairy products or cooked food (these will attract vermin), cat litter, diapers or weeds with seed heads. You will know that your compost pile is right if it becomes hot in the middle—this is important to sterilize the compost and kill off any pathogens that cause disease.

INDISPENSABLE THINGS

- Compost container
- Water

BROWN INGREDIENTS
- Cardboard (cereal boxes, egg cartons, toilet rolls)
- Wood shavings
- Prunings
- Fallen leaves

GREEN INGREDIENTS
- Grass clippings
- Vegetable trimmings
- Cut plants and flowers
- Tea bags
- Coffee grounds
- Vegetarian pet manure and bedding

INGREDIENTS

Green compost ingredients are those rich in nitrogen, and include urine, so yes, you can urinate on the compost pile! A 2008 report from the Oregon State University Extension Service found that coffee grounds increased the heat of the compost pile, killing off pathogens and weed seeds and having much the same effect as manure.

FIRST STEPS

To start your compost, place a few woody plant stems or small twigs at the bottom of the container to improve the air circulation and drainage. Collect enough materials to make a layer of at least 12in. (30cm) in the compost container. Turn the compost every few weeks to keep things decomposing.

MAINTENANCE

Brown compost ingredients are rich in carbon. Roughly 40 percent of the average garbage can contents are suitable for composting, so it helps to cut down on landfill, too. Continue to fill the container as and when you have ingredients. Remember that a thriving compost pile needs water—it should remain damp, but not be dripping wet. If you do not get enough rainfall, pour a bucket of water over it once a week to keep things decomposing.

LEAVE TO MATURE

When the container is full—which it may never be because the contents will sink as it composts—or when you decide to, stop adding any more. If the lower layers have composted, use this on the garden. Mix everything else together well. Add water if it is dry, or add dry brown material if it is soggy. Replace in the container and leave to mature. This can take from a couple of months to a year.

HEALTH & BEAUTY

LOOKING AFTER CLOTHES

They say you shouldn't judge a book by its cover, but that's nonsense. Everything about your appearance—from the buttons on your coat to the shine of your shoes— speaks volumes about who you are. This chapter tells you how to use your clothes to show off your best side.

HOW TO MEND A HOLE IN YOUR POCKET

There's a hole in your pocket. You know there is because every time you put away some loose change, it gushes from your pants like a small win on a slot machine. Fortunately, the repair job is quick and easy. If the seam has come apart, turn the pocket inside-out, remove any loose threads and sew. If there's a hole in the fabric, then you can patch it. For the quickest fix, turn the pocket inside out and sew right across it. You'll end up with a smaller pocket, but it will take barely a minute to ensure your cents look after themselves.

INDISPENSABLE THINGS

- Patch or spare pocket
- Pins
- Needle
- Thread

👉 PRACTICAL TIP

Put together a mini sewing kit so that you have the basics on hand. You need a variety package of needles (a needle threader will save you fuss); sharp scissors; all-purpose thread in black, white and a few basic colors; bonding glue for superfast hemming repairs; safety pins for emergencies; and all the spare buttons that came with your clothes.

1 Find some fabric that is the same weight as the pocket. Cut a patch to cover the hole, leaving a ¾-in. (2-cm) edge all the way around. Turn the pocket inside out, then lay the patch over the hole so that the fabric is right-side up. Pin around the hole, turning under the edges of the patch as you go.

2 Sew the patch into place by hand, using a simple stitch (you'll need to backstitch if the fabric is heavy). If using a machine, tack the patch into place first. Place the foot over the beginning of the tack line. Use a zigzag stitch to sew all around the pocket (pivoting at the corners), making sure that you don't sew through it.

ALTERNATIVELY, if the hole is in the base of a pocket you can simply fold up the pocket to cover the hole. Pin into place, then handsew unless using a machine. Stitch right across the pocket, through both sides at once. This method will make the pocket shorter than before.

ANOTHER REPAIR OPTION if the hole is at the base, is to use the bottom of a pocket from discarded pants to cover it (the fabric should be the same weight). Cut the repair pocket so it will reach over the hole, then slip over the pocket to be fixed. Pin and handstitch into place, or use a machine as in step 2.

A PRACTICAL HISTORY OF POCKETS

The word pocket is related to "pouch," and also to the defunct word "poke," which meant "sack" (as in "pig in a poke"). Herein lies a clue to the origin of the modern pocket. It began life in the Middle Ages as a detachable money bag that was kept, for maximum safety, inside the clothes. In later centuries, as clothing technology improved, pants were provided with a convenient tailored slit, so that people could reach their money without undoing their belt. From there it was a short step to stitching the little pouch (or "poke-ette") permanently and invisibly into the fabric of a man's pants.

HOW TO SEW ON A BUTTON

Buttons can come off even the most expensive item of clothing, and nothing looks less stylish than a gaping shirtfront or a flapping sleeve. If you have an amenable grandmother to act as your personal seamstress, all well and good. If not, then it pays to know how to do this job yourself. The key thing is to make sure that you do not sew on your button either too loosely or too tight.

INDISPENSABLE THINGS

- Thread matching the fabric or button
- Needle
- Scissors
- Matchsticks (head removed)
- Spare button (two or four holes)

A PRACTICAL HISTORY OF BUTTONS

The Amish of Pennsylvania don't use buttons because buttons aren't mentioned in the Bible. But buttons were part of tailoring technology well before New Testament times, and were known to the Romans. The buttonhole, on the other hand, was not conceived until the 14th century—and it revolutionized fashion by making it possible to cut clothes to fit a shapely body. Buttons became a status symbol, an early form of bling (another reason the godly Amish are opposed to them). Horn or clay buttons gave way to sparkling bijoux of gold, silver or glass. Mass-produced buttons arrived with the Industrial Revolution. For a time, clothes and even boots were festooned with so many rows of buttons that they couldn't be fastened by hand—hence, the invention of the button hook.

☛ INDISPENSABLE WARNING

If you are sewing a button onto a jacket made from heavy fabric, use a thimble to protect your finger when pushing the needle through.

1 Cut a thread 18–24in. (45–60cm) long and slip through the eye of the needle. Pull the ends together and tie in a double knot. Cut off the loose ends.

2 Line up the button with the other buttons and with the buttonhole. Insert the needle through the fabric and up through one of the button's holes and pull the thread through.

3 Place a matchstick across the button. Push the needle into the hole opposite the one you started with and through the fabric. Hold the matchstick as you pull the thread down, anchoring the button on the fabric.

4 Repeat the stitch to secure the button. If you have a four-hole button, do the other side, again using two stitches. Then push your needle through the fabric and pull the thread up between the fabric and button.

5 Remove the matchstick. Wind the thread around the thread between fabric and button three times (up to six if the material is thick). This creates a "shank," which raises the button away from the fabric for easy fastening.

6 Now loop the thread around the shank again, but this time leave it loose. Pass the needle through the loop and pull the thread taut to create a knot. Repeat, then cut the thread close to the shank.

HOW TO WASH CASHMERE

Your cashmere sweater may say "dry clean only," but that's often the manufacturer's lawyer talking—if the label says hand-wash and you plunge the sweater into boiling hot water, you'll be demanding a refund. Most cashmere garments (not quite all of them) can be washed, and if you do it right, they will actually last longer than if you clean them chemically. And washing is cheaper than dry cleaning, so you will not only preserve your cashmere, but you'll also save cash.

INDISPENSABLE THINGS

- Special mild detergent
- Tepid water
- Two towels

INDISPENSABLE WARNING

Be very careful when washing a cashmere sweater: if you make any mistakes, then you could shrink or damage the item. Expensive cashmere may be dry cleaned as a safeguard.

CASHMERE CLEAN

Use a special mild detergent to clean cashmere. Ordinary detergent is too harsh and can destroy the natural oils in cashmere. Add the soap to water that is just warm (not hot) and swish around to distribute. Submerge the sweater, then gently squeeze the suds through it

SOAKING

Do not rub, twist or stretch the garment in any way. Soak for 10 minutes, then rinse carefully in cool, clean water; repeat until the rinse water is clear.

STORING CASHMERE

Your cashmere is delicate, so treat it carefully. Wash and dry it before storing in a garment bag. Use cedar balls or lavender to keep moths away—because moths love cashmere.

SQUEEZE DRYING

Very gently squeeze out the excess water. Lay a clean towel flat on the floor, then place the garment on top. Very carefully roll it up, pressing with the palms of your hands to squeeze the water into the towel. Reshape the garment and dry flat on another towel or drying rack, away from direct heat or sunlight. Do not dry cashmere on a line; it will pull out of shape. Never tumble-dry cashmere.

STAIN REMOVAL

If your garment has a grease stain, then it is best to take it to the dry cleaners; rubbing the cashmere will harm it.

IN THE MACHINE

Some cashmere can be washed in a machine (check the care label). Always fasten any buttons and turn the item inside out first. Place in a cotton pillow case, and select the wool cycle on your machine. Again, use a special mild detergent. Select a very gentle, short spin before drying flat.

HOW TO IRON A SHIRT

Let's face it: shirts need ironing. Resign yourself to spending 5 minutes on each one. The upside is that you'll soon be good at it—and there is real satisfaction in a perfectly pressed shirt. For that brand-new crispness, invest in some spray starch: hang up the shirt, fasten the top button and lightly spray before ironing. A word of warning: always iron in a clean place. There's nothing worse than realizing that you have just dragged a spotless white sleeve through the cat's litter tray.

INDISPENSABLE THINGS

- Steam iron
- Ironing board
- A shirt
- Hanger

🖎 PRACTICAL TIP

If your shirt is very creased, use a spray mist bottle to spray it lightly with water. Roll up the shirt and wrap in a towel for 10 minutes so that the dampness spreads to every part of the shirt. Then iron as instructed.

Heat the iron to the right temperature (check the manufacturer's label). If you are ironing linen or cotton, you'll need the steam function, so fill the iron with water. Start with the collar. Open it out flat, then position it underside-up on the ironing board. Iron from each point into the center. Turn it over and do the other side.

Pull one shoulder of the shirt onto the tapered end of the ironing board, so that the back yoke is on the ironing board. Smooth it out and then press. Do the same on the other side.

Open the cuff and press first the inside, then the outside. Lay the back of one sleeve on the board and smooth it flat. Press, working from the shoulder down to the cuff. Do the front of the sleeve in the same way. Repeat the process on the other sleeve.

Next do the button-side front panel. Slip the sleeve into the tapered end of the ironing board and press the top section first. Then move the panel so that it is flat on the board and press the remainder. Be careful around the buttons.

Iron the back of the shirt, working from the shoulder to the hem. Then do the remaining front panel.

Place on a hanger, making sure that the shirt is hanging straight with the sleeves over the front of the shirt. Button the first and third buttons, and hang in your wardrobe, leaving plenty of space around it.

HOW TO MEASURE YOUR BRA SIZE

Ladies—if you are wearing a bra that's the correct size, then you're in a minority. As many as 8 out of 10 women are in the wrong one. We spend fortunes on our underwear, but when it comes to bras, we have a one-size-fits-all mentality, often 34B. Generally speaking, we overestimate the band size (the numerical part) and underestimate the cup size (the alphabetical part). Wearing the right bra can make you stand better, look taller and appear slimmer.

INDISPENSABLE THINGS

- Soft tape measure
- A non-padded, comfortable bra

A PRACTICAL HISTORY OF BRAS

In ancient Crete, women wore a garment that lifted bare breasts out of clothing—the antecedent of every support bra. The first modern bra was invented by Mary Phelps Jacob, an American debutante. She wanted an undergarment that was lighter than a corset that would not show through her fitted evening gown. Her solution was two silk handkerchiefs attached to ribbon. Bras in the 1920s flattened the breast, to suit the fashion for a boyish figure. The first bras to support the bust and enhance a woman's natural curves were created by Ida Rosenthal, a Russian-American immigrant at the end of the decade. With her husband, she founded the bra company Maidenform, and introduced the concept of cup sizes.

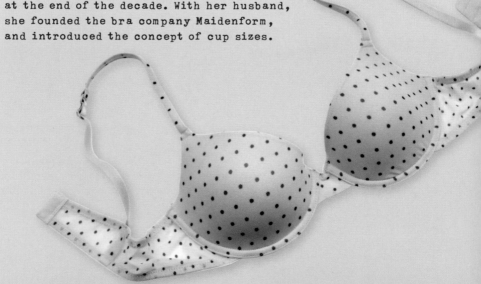

INDISPENSABLE BRA CALCULATOR

Measure (in inches) just under your breasts, keeping the tape close-fitting and level all the way round. To get your bra size, add 4 to an even measure, 5 to an odd one (32, 34 and so on). Next, measure all around your body at the fullest part of the breasts—ideally wear a comfortable non wired bra while doing this and do not squash the breast. To find your cup size, subtract the first measurement from the second. If the difference is 0, you're an A-cup; I inch less, AA cup; I inch more, B cup; 2 inches, C; 3 inches, D; 4 inches, DD; 5 inches, E; 6 inches, F; 7 inches, FF; 8 inches, G.

HEALTH & BEAUTY

CHECKING THE CUPS
There should be no bulging flesh (indicating cups that are too small) or wrinkling fabric (too big). Underwiring should curve around the breasts, and the center of the bra should lie flat against your body.

TRYING ON
...ting a bra is an inexact science, but it gives you a rough idea of ...at size to select. Enlist the help ...a professional fitter in the store ...ou can. Because manufacturers use different cuts and fabrics, you'll need to try on a number of bras to find the perfect fit.

CHECKING THE BAND
The back of the band should be level with the front; if it is riding up, the bra is probably too big. Make sure the band fits snugly without leaving a red mark.

FINAL FIT
Slip the straps off your shoulders—the bra should stay put if it fits and gives the right support. Stretch up your hands and move around to check the fit. Check your new bustline under your clothing to ensure you have a smooth line.

HOW TO POLISH YOUR SHOES

It is said that you can tell a lot about a person by their shoes. It was long held, for example, that only a shady character would wear brown suede around town. It is certainly true that the state of your shoes sends a message. Scuffed, worn shoes say that you don't care much about yourself; well-maintained, polished shoes spell high self-esteem. But whether you believe in footwear psychology or not, you should polish your shoes regularly, simply because they'll last you much longer.

INDISPENSABLE THINGS

- A pair of shoes
- Old newspaper
- 2 fine-bristled boot brushes
- Shoe polish to match the color of your shoes
- Soft cotton cloth

A PRACTICAL HISTORY OF SHOE SHINING

Dubbin—a mixture of tallow (animal fat) and oil—has been used since the Middle Ages to make shoe leather soft and waterproof. In the 18th century, the fashionable had their shoes shined with polishes incorporating beeswax or lanolin, which gave a better sheen. Blacking—made from soot—was incorporated to give color. The world's best-known shoe polish—Kiwi—comes from Australia. It was first sold in 1904 and was named in honor of the Scottish maker's New Zealander wife. Kiwi became one of Australia's most successful exports. Its popularity took off during World War I, when the pleasing little disc-shaped cans were used as barter by British troops.

1 Clean any dirt off the shoes using warm water. Let the shoes dry. Cover the floor with old newspaper to protect it from polish. Remove laces from light-colored shoes.

2 Rub a fine-bristled boot brush over the polish. Then brush over the shoes, applying it as evenly as you can (be sparing with the polish; you need only a fine layer).

3 Put the shoes to one side for five minutes to let the polish sink in. Then rub a second boot brush all over the shoe, using a brisk back-and-forward motion. This will remove any excess polish and give your shoes the first layer of shine.

4 Take a damp cotton cloth and wrap tightly around the index finger, holding the rest tightly in your palm—the cloth over your fingertip should be smooth.

5 Apply a little polish to the cloth, then rub into the shoe using small circular movements. Dampen the cloth and reapply polish as necessary. Work from toe to heel and then back down the other side, not forgetting any hard-to-reach areas such as around the stitches. Spend as long as you like to get the desired sheen—the more time you spend, the higher the sheen will be.

PRACTICAL TIP

Always use one brush to put polish on and one to brush it off; do not mix them up.

HOW TO TIE A BOW TIE

If you want to wear a bow tie, you must know how to tie one. A clip-on bow tie is a sartorial abomination that instantly marks you out as a know-nothing arriviste. People think that tying a bow tie is fiendishly difficult, but that is a myth spread about by the dinner jacket-wearing elite. The fact is, tying a bow is no harder than tying your shoelaces. Yet it is a skill that, once mastered, immediately marks you out as a gentleman.

A PRACTICAL HISTORY OF TIES

Neckties and bow ties alike are descendants of the cravat. These knotted kerchiefs came into fashion in the 17th century, when they were worn by swashbuckling Croatian mercenaries in the service of France (the term "cravat" is derived from the French word for "Croat"). Then as now, the cravat was worn inside the shirt. In later centuries, it migrated to the outside of the collar, and necessarily became a thin strip of colored material. It is impossible to say why the bow tie became a more formal item than the necktie, but the practical advantage of the bow is that it does not dangle, hence its popularity with surgeons.

1 Place the tie around your neck so that one end (A) hangs lower than the other end (B). Then cross the longer end (A) over the shorter one (B), keeping the crossover close to your neck.

2 Take the longer end (A) through the loop to make a simple knot and hold it up and out of the way. Leave end B dangling down.

3 Now bend end B over itself. Holding it between your thumb and index finger, place the loop in a central position between the points of your shirt's collar—this is where the knot of the bow tie will be.

4 Now drop end A over both the crossover you made in step 1 and over the front of end B. It should hang down vertically.

5 Hold the double-ended B with one hand while you fold end A over itself as shown. Then slide the loop you have formed with end A behind loop B, as shown—this is the tricky part, but it gets easier with practice.

6 Pull gently on each loop at the same time to tighten the knot—then adjust to straighten. When you want to untie the bow, pull on the tails.

HEALTH & BEAUTY

HOW TO WEAR A SUIT

To wear a suit well, you must first buy a suit well. Above all, it has to fit. This may seem obvious, but men are just as vain as women, and it is all too easy to buy the suit that fits the shape you would like to be. Nothing looks worse than a pair of formal pants that cut into the gut like cheesewire or a jacket that gapes like the jaws of a yawning hippo. So be honest with yourself—or better, take advice from a tailor or an honest friend.

INDISPENSABLE THINGS

- Formal suit
- Tie
- Shirt
- Polished shoes

CONSERVATIVE COLORS

For a business suit, you can't go wrong with black, but other subdued colors are acceptable: charcoal gray, navy blue, dark shades of brown. A pinstripe looks good if it is subtle; if it is too strong you will look like a zebra. Striking colors (powder blue, white, shades of yellow) are all right if you are a children's entertainer, but not otherwise.

STAND TALL

You will naturally be more conscious of your posture when in formal wear, which is good. Hold your head high, pull back your shoulders, and when you walk, walk purposefully. These things will make you look better and will show off your clothes to the best advantage.

SHIRT & TIE

Shirt and ties are a besuited man's chance to show off his plumage. A splash of color looks good. The shirt should generally be plain and contrast with the suit: go for pale pinks, lilacs and blues. Ties should match in a contrasting way: say, maroons and purples with an unobtrusive pattern. Ties depicting phalanxes of flying pigs are permissible on the first day back at work after the Christmas holidays, but at no other time.

ARMS & SLEEVES

Sleeve-length is vital to the overall look. The cuffs of your shirt should protrude about an inch (2.5cm) from the end of your sleeve. The best way to make certain that they do is to wear a formal shirt when you go to buy your suit. Cufflinks are a classy touch that separates the CEO from the office assistant.

LOSE YOUR KEYS

Your suit is not a backpack, so don't treat it like one. Don't fill your pockets with car keys, cell phones, loose change, breath mints—they will ruin the look. If you must have your wallet with you, make sure it as slim as can be, and keep it in your inside jacket pocket.

LEGS

If your legs on your pants are too long you will look sloppy. If they are too short, you will look like your mom bought your suit before your last growing spurt. The hems of the legs should rest lightly on your (highly polished) black shoes—with no bunching.

HOW TO PUT A CREASE IN A PAIR OF PANTS

No matter how casual a man's style, there will come an occasion—his wedding or a vital job interview—when he needs to put a crease in his pants. Pressing pants is a skill, like shaving, that every man should learn. And, as with shaving, when it goes wrong it looks terrible. The common pants pressing gaffs are the zigzag crease, the multiple crease and the off-center crease. All of them are sartorial disasters, to be avoided at all costs. Here is how to go about getting the perfect crease.

INDISPENSABLE THINGS

- Pair of formal pants
- Steam iron
- Ironing board
- Spray mist bottle
- Water
- Paper bag

A PRACTICAL HISTORY OF IRONS

Vikings used flat stones to press and pleat their cloth. In the Middle Ages, similar tools were known as slickstones or sleekstones. "Shee that wanteth a sleek-stone to smooth hir linnen, wil take a pebble," wrote the Elizabethan dramatist John Lyly. About that time, blacksmiths began to make "flat irons"—out of iron. You needed a pair to get the work done: one in hand and the other on the stove. It was hot, difficult work, and you had to keep the iron scrupulously clean to avoid marking the cloth. Ironing became easier once electric irons came into use—too easy for some. Hence, the new sport of extreme ironing, in which people take an ironing board to some remote location such as a mountain top and do a little ironic ironing outdoors.

THE POSITION

Hold your pants by the hems, and match up the inner and outer seams of both legs exactly. Then lay them on the ironing board, positioning one leg over the other. Put your hand in the pocket of the top leg, and extend your finger to the farthest corner; it should end exactly at the intended crease.

GETTING THE CREASE

Fold the top leg neatly out of the way, and smooth the bottom leg so it is perfectly flat. Dampen the intended crease by spraying with water, then lay a paper bag over the top and press hard; start at the hem and continue up the leg. If there are no pleats, fold the top section of the upper pant leg back so that you can do the crotch area. Then flip the pants over so that you can do the other leg.

PLEATS

If your pants have pleats, iron your creases only as far as the end of the pleat. A single pleat should line up with the trouser crease; if you have a double pleat, the inner one should align. Pleats shouldn't have the razor sharpness of a crease; use the iron to press the material in between the pleats rather than pressing down on them.

HANGING

If you are not wearing your pants straight away, slip them onto a wooden (not wire) hanger and place in the closet with plenty of space around them.

HOW TO PACK A SUITCASE

It's a good idea to travel light, and not just because of strict airline rules on baggage. Dragging a suitcase the size of a refrigerator behind you is a nuisance—to you and to everyone in your path. So pack clothing that you can layer and concentrate on interchangeable outfits: you want pants that work with several tops. Above all, do not pack too many shoes. Check that the clothes you are taking match your plans. If you are spending a week on the beach, leave your tuxedo at home. You always need less than you think you do, so leave the just-in-case items at home. Squashed clothes become creased clothes, which is why the best packers are utterly ruthless.

INDISPENSABLE THINGS

- Suitcase
- Vacation clothes
- Toiletries and other items
- Plastic bags
- Colored ribbon
- Tissue paper

PRACTICAL TIP

Tissue paper will help stop your clothes from wrinkling. Place a sheet in between each layer, and place another at the back of shirts or jackets before folding. A large ball of crumpled tissue paper inside the collar of a shirt will help protect it from crushing.

BELTS & UNDERWEAR

Snake a thick belt around the inside edge of your suitcase to stop it from getting crushed. Coil thin belts, placed in a bag, and tuck inside a shoe. Underwear can be rolled, bagged and placed in shoes or used to fill gaps in the case. If you have underwired bras, first place something soft in the cup—other underwear or crumpled tissue paper—and then fold.

IDENTIFICATION

Tie a piece of colored ribbon around the handle of your suitcase so you can spot it easily on the baggage carousel. And put your name and address inside; use the luggage label for only your name and flight details.

ROLL OR FOLD?

Roll T-shirts and use them to fill gaps in your suitcase. Carefully fold shirts and blouses: first fold in the sleeves from a point a couple of inches in from the seam, then fold up the bottom of the sleeves and shirt and finally bring the top and bottom together to make a neat rectangle.

HEAVY ITEMS

Pack heavy, nonbreakable items, such as shoes or books, against the base of your suitcase (at the wheel end). This will stop them from pushing your clothes down and creasing them while you are carrying or wheeling the suitcase. Put shoes into a plastic bag if they are dirty, and always wear your heaviest pair on the plane.

TOILETRIES

Wrap all your toiletries in heavy, sealed plastic bags. Pack the smallest size possible to save on weight and space—decant shampoo and liquids into refillable plastic travel bottles. Do not fill bottles to the very top.

STACKING YOUR CLOTHES

Put the heaviest items, such as your jeans and sweaters, at the bottom of the suitcase, follow with jackets and dresses, and place folded shirts and delicates on top. If you have more than one pair of pants, lay them so that the top ends are at opposite sides of the case; this avoids layering one bulky waistband over another.

HEALTH & BEAUTY

HOW TO REMOVE A BLOODSTAIN

For some reason (maybe Lady Macbeth is to blame) blood is thought to be the indelible stain. In fact, blood is easy to remove if you get to it quickly; and there are ways to get rid of dried blood, too. The one thing to avoid is chucking your clothes in the wash without treating the stain first—once hot water hits the protein in blood, the stain will indeed set permanently.

INDISPENSABLE THINGS

- Cold water
- Liquid detergent
- Household ammonia
- Salt

👉 INDISPENSABLE WARNING

Use these tips on washable items. For dry clean only items, blot the bloodstain with a paper towel and take to the cleaner's straight away.

OUT & ABOUT
If you can't whip off your shirt and wash it straight away, spit on the stain and rub in. The enzymes in saliva help to break down the proteins in blood.

INSTANT ACTION
Wash out a bloodstain as soon as possible using cold water and liquid detergent.

PERSISTENT STAINS
If the stain persists, rub a little salt into the spot (but don't rub woollen items).

OLD STAINS
If the bloodstain is old or stubborn, soak the clothing for 20 minutes in a large bowl of cold water with 3 tablespoons of household ammonia. Then launder as usual.

LOOKING AFTER YOU

Your body is a well-oiled machine—but
it is possibly not quite as well-oiled as
it should be, or once was. This chapter
shows you how to keep your physical
self from going slightly rusty, and
also how to maintain a shining mind
and a gleaming spirit.

HOW TO SHARPEN YOUR MEMORY

The brain is a muscle, so the more you use it, the fitter it gets. There are all kinds of mental push-ups and intellectual aerobics that you can do to make your brain bulge like a Schwarzenegger bicep. This is almost literally true; in taxi drivers, the part of the brain that deals with spatial knowledge is often larger than in other people. The memory is the part of the mind that is most likely to grow weak with age; the best way to stop this from happening is to give it a daily workout. Use it or lose it.

A PRACTICAL HISTORY OF MEMORY TRICKS

The earliest memory feat was performed by Simonides of Ceos, who lived in the 5th century B.C.E. He had left a banquet just before the roof collapsed, killing everyone inside. The bodies were crushed beyond recognition, but Simonides was able to recall who sat where. This led Simonides to develop a method in which physical spaces (loci) are used to remember things. Dominic O'Brien, eight times winner of the World Memory Championship, has used a similar technique to memorize the order of IO shuffled decks of cards in the space of an hour. Even an elephant might struggle to match that feat of memory.

INDISPENSABLE THINGS

• Attention to detail

USE THE LOCI METHOD

To remember a series of things, bring to mind a familiar building (such as your house). Mentally place a visual reminder for each item in different rooms or areas (the more striking the image, the better). You could have a statue of the Madonna in the hallway (to remind you to call your mother), a flaming Olympic torch on the mantelpiece (to tell you to pay the gas bill). Take a mental stroll through the house when you need to remember what you have to do.

BREAK IT DOWN

Mentally divide a string of numbers down into chunks: so the six-digit number 775362 is more easily recalled as 77 53 62.

THINK VISUAL

Striking mental images can help you recall names or foreign words. For example, if you are introduced to a Mr. Appleton, picture him sitting in a bathtub of apples, with a ton weight falling on his head.

REPEAT IT

If you know that there is something you want to remember, such as an address, repeating it out loud several times will make it easier to recall later on.

USE MNEMONICS

These handy devices are useful for remembering lists. For example, the six strings of a guitar are tuned to the notes EADGBE, which can be remembered using the phrase "Even after dinner, greedy boys eat."

HOW TO DO THE PERFECT SIT-UP

For toning the abdominals, there is nothing better than the old-fashioned sit-up. It requires no special equipment, but will rapidly build core strength if done properly and regularly. You should notice the results within weeks. You will look trimmer around the midriff and will feel fitter and more powerful. But it's essential to do it right, or you risk hurting your back and neck. The key is to make sure that your abdominals are doing the work, not your neck or back muscles.

INDISPENSABLE THINGS

- A carpeted or padded floor, or exercise mat
- Warmed-up muscles
- Your physician's permission, if in any doubt

INDISPENSABLE WARNING

Sit-ups should be practiced with caution, especially if you have lower back problems. Stop if you feel any pain. If you feel strain in the neck or back, then stop and reassess your technique. Seek medical advice if the pain persists. If sit-ups feel too difficult, try alternative forms of abdominal work.

1 Lie on your back on the floor. Bend your legs so that they form a right angle at the knee, and so that your feet are resting flat on the floor, shoulder-width apart. Don't anchor your feet under a piece of furniture; you'll work the hip flexors and leg muscles rather than the abdominals.

2 Place your hands by your ears, or cross them over your chest. If you are a beginner, you'll find it easier to keep your arms by your side. Never lace your hands behind your head.

3 Slowly squeeze your abdominal muscles to bring your head, then shoulders and then trunk off the floor—work very slowly. Exhale as you come up to help the abdominal muscles contract. Be sure to keep your neck straight and relaxed.

4 Once you reach a point where your trunk is at an angle of 30 degrees to the floor, hold this position for a few seconds, and then slowly lower yourself back down. Breathe in as you come down. Keep your feet flat on the floor throughout.

PRACTICAL TIP

Do a few sit-ups at a time. Build up the number you do very gradually, as your fitness improves. It's more important to do a few sit-ups well than to do a lot with a poor technique.

5 Pause *before* your shoulders and head touch the floor, and raise yourself up for the next sit-up. Remember to exhale as you come up and inhale as you come down.

HEALTH & BEAUTY

HOW TO GO JOGGING

Jogging is no more or less than a good walk sped up a little. It is one of the simplest and most satisfying forms of aerobic exercise you can do—just put on your shoes and go. The main difference between jogging and running is attitude: when you run you want to be faster than the rest. But when you jog you are running against no one but yourself—the ideal noncompetitive sport.

INDISPENSABLE THINGS

- **Running shoes**
- **A little motivation**
- **Your physician's permission, if in any doubt**

GET GOOD SHOES

You can run in any old clothes, but you must invest in proper running shoes. They aren't cheap, but you do not have to spend a fortune. Go to a specialty running store, and take advice from a knowledgeable salesperson. As with car tires, you can't go wrong if you choose a well-known, respected brand, as long as they fit properly.

🐾 INDISPENSABLE WARNING

Always take medical advice before starting any strenuous form of exercise. Warm up before your run, and cool down afterward.

TAKE RESTS

Don't jog every day—your muscles need time to recover. Aim to run three or four times a week. If you are training for a race, you should "go long" once a week—that is, increase the time or distance of your longest run. If you are struggling on a jog, there is no shame in stopping and resting. The runner's mantra is "train, don't strain."

DRINK WATER

You should be thoroughly hydrated before you set out to jog. Drink several glasses of water in the hour or two before you start. Have another drink when you return. If you are running for more than half an hour, take a bottle of water with you.

GO SLOW

If you have never run before, or if you have not run for some months, then take it very easy to begin with. For a first outing, 10 minutes (with rests if need be) is long enough. When jogging you should never be so out of breath that you can't hold a conversation.

FIND A BUDDY

Motivation is hard to find. It is too easy to find an excuse to take a day off. So find yourself a running buddy and make a definite date. Then you can't dodge your appointment with the sidewalk, and the companionship will make your run more fun.

DON'T HURT YOURSELF

Most runners get slight pains from time to time. You will soon learn to tell the difference between a wholesome muscle ache and a genuine hurt. Don't try to "run off" an injury; you will only make it worse and put yourself out of action for a long stretch.

HEALTH & BEAUTY

HOW TO PRACTICE YOGA

Yoga is not just exercise for New Age hipsters. It's great for strengthening muscles and improving flexibility. When it comes to all-round bodywork, yoga is unbeatable. The best way to learn is in a class with an experienced teacher—you want someone who practices what they preach. There are various forms to choose from. If you want to work up a sweat, try astanga vinyasa. If gentle stretches are more your thing, seek out a scaravelli or viniyoga class. However, the correct mental attitude is as important as the physical pose. Yoga is not a competitive sport—you get no extra points for best downward dog pose.

INDISPENSABLE THINGS

- "Sticky" yoga mat
- Comfortable clothing
- Bare feet
- Your physician's permission, if in any doubt

PHYSICAL POSTURES

Don't expect to get into demanding poses right away—it can take years to master advanced ones such as the lotus. Never force your body farther than it wants to go; with regular practice, your muscles will gradually become more supple.

BREATHING

Breathe deeply and smoothly, through the nose. Try to coordinate your breath with your movements.

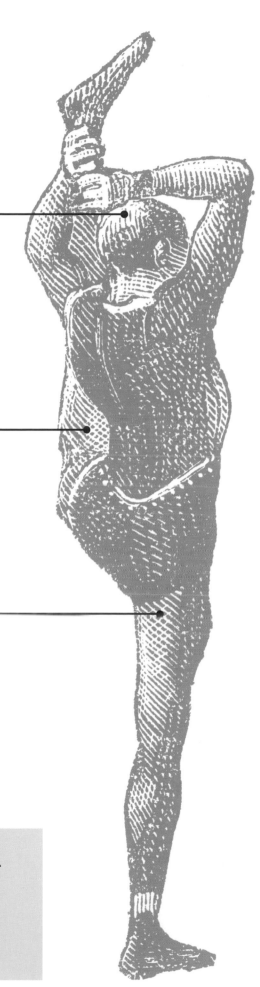

AWARENESS

Yoga integrates body and mind, and it is important to approach it with concentration and a calm mental attitude. Don't measure yourself against other people in your class; yoga is designed to help develop an accepting, nonjudgmental, state of mind.

WHERE TO PRACTICE

All you need is a quiet space, free from clutter. Make sure you have enough room to stretch out without knocking into anything. Avoid doing yoga directly under the sun or next to a heat source.

WHEN TO PRACTICE

You can do yoga at any time of day. Many yogis opt for mornings, when the mind is alert and stiff muscles benefit from stretching, but you may find an evening session more practical. Wait two hours after eating a meal before practicing yoga, and visit the bathroom before you start.

☞ PRACTICAL TIP

There are many different styles of yoga—go to a few classes to find a teacher and style that suit you. It's best to settle on one type of yoga and stick to it, rather than to keep changing.

HOW TO DO A HEADSTAND

The headstand has so many benefits that it is known as the king of postures (the elegant shoulder stand is the queen). It increases the flow of blood to the head, revitalizing body and mind. It also relieves back strain, promotes good circulation and encourages deep exhalation. It's also a great posture for improving sleep and concentration.

INDISPENSABLE THINGS

- **Patience**
- **Concentration**

STARTING OUT

A STRONG BASE
You don't have to be especially strong to do a headstand. The key is to create a tripod with your two elbows and clasped hands at the center—and to conquer any natural fear of being upside down. Learn the pose in slow and easy stages, under the guidance of an experienced teacher. It is best practiced at the end of a yoga session.

AN EASIER OPTION
Try doing a headstand in the corner of a room; press the backs of your hands into the corner and let each hip touch the walls.

☞ INDISPENSABLE WARNING

Discuss with your physician and a yoga teacher whether or not this pose is suitable for you. Headstands should not be practiced by people suffering from high blood pressure, eye, heart, neck or back problems, by women who are pregnant or menstruating, or by those suffering from a headache or migraine.

1 Kneel down and clasp each elbow with the opposite hand—the elbows should be shoulder-width apart. Release your hands and place them on the floor with your fingers interlocked.

2 Place the crown of your head on the floor so that your little fingers are touching the back of your head—your hands and elbows should form a triangle.

3 Straighten your knees, pushing up on the balls of your feet and lifting your hips. Keep your thighs, knees and heels together, and walk your feet in until your neck and back form a straight line—this is a good place for beginners to stop.

4 Breathing out, bend your knees in toward the chest and slowly lift your feet off the floor. Bring your heels toward your buttocks, keeping your knees bent. Push your elbows down to the floor and lift your shoulders away from it. Stop here if you cannot do a full headstand.

5 If you feel able, straighten your legs so that the soles of your feet (not your toes) face toward the ceiling. Press down into the forearms, and take a few slow breaths (gradually build the time you spend in the pose as you practice).

6 Come out of the pose slowly, reversing the sequence of going into it. To counterstretch the spine and normalize the circulation, kneel with your buttocks resting on your feet, your forehead on the floor and your arms by your sides (child's pose). Rest here for a minute or so.

[☞] PRACTICAL TIP

If you feel yourself start to topple, drop your feet so that they hit the floor first.

HOW TO DO TAI CHI

Tai chi may look balletic, but every move is derived from the kind of punches and parries practiced by martial artists, such as Bruce Lee and Jackie Chan. Tai chi moves are performed in a strict sequence (the "form"). The "walk" is a simple meditative exercise that can easily be done at home. Keep a sense of softness in your posture—there are no tensed muscles in tai chi. Keep the mind concentrated, and breathe rhythmically and smoothly.

INDISPENSABLE THINGS

- Loose comfortable clothing
- Shoes with thin, flexible soles (such as lightweight sneakers)
- Your physician's permission, if in any doubt

INDISPENSABLE WARNING

Be careful not to twist your knee in a different direction to the rest of your leg, or to bend it farther than the toe. Tai chi is not suitable for people with knee problems.

START

Put your feet together, toes forward. Shift your weight onto the left foot, lift the right one and move it out to the side so that your feet are parallel, shoulder-width apart and your weight equally balanced.

RAISE LEFT FOOT

Stand tall and breathe. Bring all of your weight onto the right leg. Raise up the heel of your left foot, leaving your toes resting on the ground for a moment.

SHIFT WEIGHT

Step forward with your left foot, maintaining an upright posture as you do so. Place the left heel on the floor, and then roll down the rest of the foot. Keep your weight on the back leg

A PRACTICAL HISTORY OF TAI CHI

The founder of tai chi was a monk named Chang San Feng, who was born in China in 1247. His inspiration came from watching a snake fight a crane, where each animal used its natural movement to evade the other.

HEALTH & BEAUTY

WEIGHT ON LEFT

Now slowly bring your weight onto the left leg, letting the left knee bend slightly while you straighten the right one. Do not lean forward.

FORWARD

When all of your weight is on the left leg, step forward with your right foot, heel first. Remember to keep your weight on the back leg.

REPEAT

Repeat for 10 minutes or so. You can also try stepping backward, in which case you should place the toes of the leading foot on the ground first, instead of the heel.

HOW TO JUMP ROPE

Jump rope is not just for little girls. It's a great all-round sport for grown-ups: good for cardiorespiratory fitness, suppleness, endurance, balance and coordination. And it will help trim hips, thighs and buttocks. The world's greatest boxers—including three-time heavyweight champion Lennox Lewis—routinely jump rope in their training. However, don't think you can take the nearest child's jump rope. You need a rope that is the right length for your height. Jumping with a rope that's too short is as pointless—and potentially damaging—as running a marathon in shoes that are too small.

INDISPENSABLE THINGS

- Jump rope
- Sneakers
- Floor with some "give" in it
- Plenty of space
- Your physician's permission, if in any doubt

INDISPENSABLE WARNING

Always take medical advice before beginning any strenuous form of exercise. Start slowly, and be sure not to trip over the rope (which is easy to do if you are not concentrating). Keep sessions short at first and build them up gradually as your fitness improves.

HEALTH & BEAUTY

YOUR ROPE

To ensure your rope is the right length for you, stand on the center and pull the handles upward—they should reach underarm height when the rope is taut. Any longer, and you'll need to shorten it (most good ropes are adjustable).

BASIC TECHNIQUE

Have your feet slightly apart and drop the rope behind you. Bring it over your head and, when it gets to your feet, jump over it. Bend at the ankles rather than the knees as you jump, and keep your jumps low. Watch that you don't lean forward (your back should be straight), keep your elbows close to your body and turn the rope smoothly.

BURN RATE

A 10-minute jumping session will burn between 70 and 110 calories, depending on your weight and on how much you exert yourself. One study found that a 10-minute session of jumping rope gave as many health benefits as a 30-minute run.

SKIPPING TRICKS

Once you have mastered the basic technique, try some jumping tricks. Try going backward (back jump), using alternate feet to jump the rope (speed step), using one foot for several jumps and then the other (hop jump), crossing your hands as you bring the rope over (the crisscross), or alternate between one jump with the legs apart and one with the legs together (jack jump).

HOW TO SHAPE YOUR EYEBROWS

A well-defined eyebrow is a thing of wonder—provided that it matches its neighbor, of course. Your brows are no less expressive and personal a feature than your mouth or your eyes. And, like your mouth and your eyes, they will benefit from a little cosmetic attention. Shaping your eyebrows will enhance your good looks—but don't overdo it, because pencil-thin lines give your face a mean, cruel look. Tweeze cautiously and sparingly (and definitely leave waxing to the professionals).

INDISPENSABLE THINGS

- Washcloth
- Cotton ball
- Witch hazel
- Eyebrow brush or clean, old mascara wand
- Eyebrow pencil
- Tweezers with slanted ends
- Magnifying mirror

1 Wash your face, then place a warm washcloth over your eyebrows for a minute, to help soften the hair follicles. Wipe a cotton ball soaked in witch hazel over the brows (repeat this regularly throughout the plucking process). Brush the hair of your eyebrows up and out, using your brush.

2 Assess the natural shape of your eyebrows in the mirror—it's best to follow this closely. Take an eyebrow pencil and hold it vertically at the side of your nose. Your eyebrow should start at the point where it intersects with the pencil—make a dot with an eyebrow pencil as a guide.

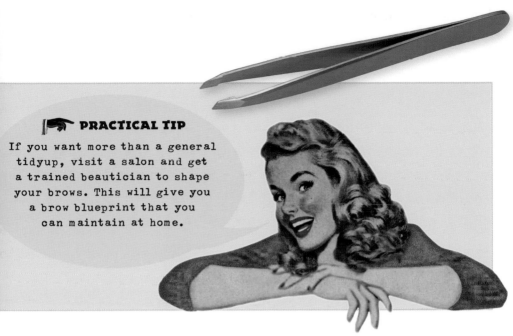

PRACTICAL TIP

If you want more than a general tidyup, visit a salon and get a trained beautician to shape your brows. This will give you a brow blueprint that you can maintain at home.

3 Remove any hairs that are between your nose and the dot. Use two fingers to keep the skin tight, and remove the hairs in the direction they are growing, using small sharp movements. Remove one hair at a time, then do the other side.

5 Now remove any other hairs that are obviously outside the natural curve of your brows. Always pluck from below, not above. It's best to pluck a few hairs from each brow at a time, alternating between them in order to keep the shape symmetrical and avoid overplucking.

4 Take your pencil again and angle it from the outside edge of the nostril to the outer corner of the eye and beyond. The point where it hits the brow marks the end of your eyebrow. Again, make a dot and then remove any hairs beyond this point, being sure to pluck the hair in the direction it is growing.

6 Wipe with the cotton ball again, to soothe any redness and swelling. To finish, use your pencil to fill in any gaps, using small light strokes, then brush again.

HOW TO LOSE WEIGHT

Sad to say, there are no miracle diets. To lose weight you must use up more calories than you take in. The best way to do this—the only sensible way—is to eat a healthy balanced diet and to exercise regularly. Faddy diets don't work; 80 percent of dieters end up fatter than they started. So take your time, and slim down slowly. You will be healthier and fitter, you will probably live longer—and you know what?—you will be an altogether happier person.

☞ INDISPENSABLE WARNING

Always check with your physician before embarking on a major change in your diet or starting a new exercise regime. Check that you really are overweight before starting a weight-loss program.

INDISPENSABLE THINGS

- Your physician's permission, if in any doubt
- Willpower
- Patience

GET ACTIVE

Regular exercise will help you to reach and maintain a healthy weight. Ideally, you should spend 30 minutes a day doing something that makes you slightly breathless and sweaty. Brisk walking is a good way to start. Be gradual about the way you build up the amount and the intensity of the exercise that you do.

EAT SMALL

Using a smaller plate at mealtimes can help you monitor how much you eat. Eat slowly, chewing each mouthful, so that you savor your food and notice when you are getting full (it takes 20 minutes for your body to signal that it has had enough). Be particularly careful when you eat out and cannot control your portion size.

EAT WELL

Eat a balanced diet: plenty of fruits and vegetables, as well as fiber-rich whole grains, legumes, lean meat and low-fat dairy products (ask your physician to refer you to a nutritionist if you need help with this). Choose healthy snacks, such as raw nuts or plain homemade popcorn, rather than potato chips and cookies. Avoid prepared meals—even those labeled "low fat" can be loaded with sugar.

HEALTH & BEAUTY

DRINK LESS, DRINK MORE

Alcohol and sugary drinks are high in calories—so cut them out. Drink plenty of water instead (8 cups/2 liters) a day is the optimum). Hot (sugar-free!) drinks can make a good alternative to a snack. Try green tea; it is tasty and healthy and there is some evidence that it can help boost the metabolic rate and so help you burn calories faster.

TAKE YOUR TIME

Don't expect to lose weight quickly. Aspire to lose no more than 1lb (0.5kg) a week. Watch yourself when you reach your target weight; this is the time when most people relax their regimen and backslide.

HOW TO GET A SIX-PACK

The six-pack has become the very cipher of sexiness for the modern man. But this wedge of abdominal muscle only looks like a six-pack—the bottom of a pack of beer cans—when it is highly developed and not hidden below a layer of fat. This means that acquiring one is much easier for younger adults and more challenging for those with a few years' indulgence under their belts. So leaner-bodied guys should concentrate on muscle-building exercises, while those carrying a few extra pounds must be sure to also eat healthily and do plenty of cardiovascular exercises if they want that washboard stomach.

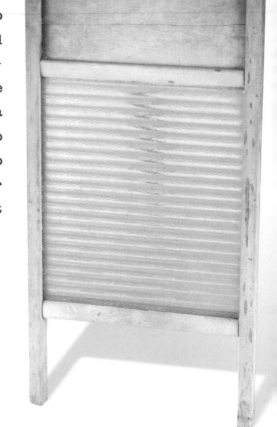

INDISPENSABLE THINGS

- Your physician's permission, if in any doubt
- A healthy diet
- Dedication
- Basic level of fitness

A PRACTICAL HISTORY OF MUSCLE BUILDING

Bodybuilding goes back to ancient times. The Egyptians used stones as weights to develop their muscles, and dumbbells dating from the 11th century have been found in India. In the late 19th century, strongmen showed off their prowess alongside bearded ladies at traveling shows. Later, men began "sculpting" the body into an aesthetically pleasing form (the first body-building contest was held at London's Royal Albert Hall in 1901). The idea that every man can (and should) aspire to a muscle-bound physique was popularized by Charles Atlas. His advertisements, describing the transformation of a "97-pound weakling" into a muscleman, ran from the 1940s until the late 1970s.

☞ INDISPENSABLE WARNING

Always consult an expert before doing strenuous exercise. Abdominal exercises such as sit-ups should be practiced with caution, especially for those with lower back problems. A gym will advise you on which exercises are best for you and will help you with your technique.

MUSCLE BUILDING

A muscular body burns calories faster than a flabby one. To build muscles, combine weight training with regular cardiovascular exercise, such as running, jump rope or squash. You need to do cardiovascular exercise for at least 20–30 minutes before you start to burn fat.

HEALTHY DIET

Losing fat is essential so your toned muscles won't show through a layer of blubber. Eat a healthy diet that is low in fat, drink plenty of water and exercise regularly. To shed fat, you need to be burning more calories than provided in the food you eat.

TARGETED EXERCISES

Sit-ups, crunches and leg lifts help tone the abdominal muscles. But researchers at San Diego University say the best six-pack exercise is the bicycle move. To do this, lie with your lower back pressed to the floor and bent knees raised to a 45-degree angle. Put your hands behind your ears so that your elbows point at your feet, then "bicycle" your legs so that your elbows hit the opposite knee. Breathe steadily throughout the exercise.

HOW TO GET A CLOSE SHAVE

Designer stubble is so 1990s; beards really only suit saints and sea captains; moustaches of any kind are the hallmark of foreign despots. So let's face it: 99.9 percent of men look best without facial hair. But even a clean-shaven face will not look good if the job is not done well, or if the process causes cuts and soreness or razor burn. To get a really pleasing, close shave, you need to take some time and care. You also need to go down the wet route; electric razors just don't measure up.

A PRACTICAL HISTORY OF THE RAZOR

If you find shaving boring, spare a thought for our prehistoric ancestors. Contrary to popular belief, they were not all beardies, but actually went to the trouble of shaving with flints, clam shells or sharks' teeth. One of the benefits of the Bronze Age was the invention of the metal razor. Blades made of copper or gold were used in India and Egypt 6,000 years ago. Steel "cut-throat" razors were produced in Sheffield, England, in the early part of the 19th century, but the safety razor with disposable blades was not mass-produced until the beginning of the 20th century. Its inventor was the magnificently named King Camp Gillette.

INDISPENSABLE THINGS

- Flannel
- Basin of hot water
- Shaving foam and brush, or other shaving lubricant
- Nondisposable razor
- Mirror
- Towel
- Aftershave balm

1 Take a hot shower—this will soften your stubble and open up the pores, making shaving much easier. If that isn't possible, wash your face with warm water and then hold a warm, damp washcloth over the bearded part for a minute or two.

2 Fill the sink halfway with hot water, wet your face and apply your lubricant. If using shaving cream, lather it up and apply with a shaving brush in circular strokes to make a thick, even layer. Alternatively, use shaving foam or gel. Don't skimp or you risk razor burn.

3 Take your razor, making sure that it is clean and sharp (a blunt razor is more likely to give you a nick or cause ingrown hairs). Use one hand to pull the skin taut as you shave. Start with the sides of the face, using long, smooth strokes, working in the direction of the hair growth. Do not press down.

4 Rinse your razor in the basin after every stroke. Shave your moustache, chin area and neck, continuing to scrape the razor along the grain.

5 If you need a closer shave, wash your face, reapply your lubricant and then shave again, this time against the direction of the hair growth. Once your shave is complete, splash your face with clean, cold water, then pat dry with a towel. Apply a good-quality aftershave balm.

☞ PRACTICAL TIP

Change your blade at least once a week to be sure of a close shave.

HOW TO HAVE PERFECT NAILS

You may not be that worried about your nails, but be sure that other people will be. Dirty, bitten and torn nails are instant turn-offs—they tell other people that you don't care about yourself. But overembellished nails are just as woeful. As ever in matters of taste and fashion, simplicity is the best policy. Short and rounded nails will always look good so long as you keep up the maintenance. Chipped nail polish looks worse than no nail polish.

INDISPENSABLE THINGS

- Hand and nail cream
- Rubber gloves
- Emery board
- Cuticle stick
- Base coat
- Nail polish
- Top coat
- Nail polish remover
- Cotton swab

☞ PRACTICAL TIP

Always wear rubber gloves when you are doing household chores—cleaning chemicals can weaken your nails. If you are digging or trying to pry off a lid, use an appropriate implement—never your nails.

CARING FOR CUTICLES

It's best not to cut your cuticles. Soak your hands before pushing back the cuticles using a cuticle stick.

SHAPING THE NAIL

Be sure to keep your nails filed to the same length; it looks odd when one nail is shorter than the rest. Use an emery board to shape (not a metal file), filing in one direction rather than going back and forward. Keep the nails short and naturally rounded—square-ended or long nails are out.

WHICH COLOR?

Dark colors on long fingernails can look vulgar. Generally speaking, the darker the color, the shorter the nail should be. If regular maintenance isn't your thing, go for clear nail polish (chips won't show) or use a buffer instead.

HEALTH & BEAUTY

PUTTING ON THE POLISH

Rinse and dry your hands, then apply an undercoat. This will provide a smooth surface for the polish (it will also stop your nails from yellowing from frequent polishing). Paint one central strip, from base to tip, then work out to the sides. Let dry before applying a second coat. Paint on a top coat to make your nails super-glossy and to seal in the color. A fresh application of top coat every couple of days will help keep your nails looking good.

CORRECTING MISTAKES

If your polish goes onto the skin, dip a cotton swab in nail polish remover and run down the sides of your nail to remove.

BASIC MAINTENANCE

Moisturize your hands and nails often—whenever you wash them and always before bed. It's a good idea to keep some cream by the kitchen sink, in the bathroom, in the glove compartment of your car and by your bed so that you never forget. Keep your nails out of very hot water altogether.

HOW TO GET RID OF PIMPLES

A zit raises its ugly head just when you are about to go on a big date. It's not the end of the world, but it feels like it. The temptation to squeeze a pimple is almost overwhelming—but resist. A burst pimple may well look bigger, redder and altogether worse (not to mention the fact that it may get infected). There are better ways to make a pimple go away—or at least to render it invisible for the duration of a movie or a romantic dinner.

☞ INDISPENSABLE WARNING

Seek medical advice if you have frequent outbreaks of pimples because this may indicate you have acne or another skin condition.

INDISPENSABLE THINGS

- Mild cleanser
- Toner
- Soap
- Concealer
- Face powder
- Phone number of a dermatologist

☞ PRACTICAL EMERGENCY TIP

If your skin breaks out before a huge and immovable event—say, your wedding day—see a dermatologist. Possible treatments include injecting the skin with diluted cortisone.

HEALTH & BEAUTY

AVOID MAKEUP

Go bare-faced to promote healing—foundation clogs up your pores, so it will keep the pimple from drying out. If you can't face the day without makeup, remove it as soon as you get home. High-factor sunscreens are also bad for people who have frequent breakouts (you may want to consider wearing a hat that shades your face instead).

STAYING PIMPLE-FREE

Pimples can break out at times of hormonal activity, such as the end of the menstrual cycle. They're also more likely to occur when you are stressed. Eating a good balanced diet, getting plenty of sleep and drinking plenty of water will help to keep the skin clear. But don't worry about eating the occasional bar of chocolate—it's not true that sugary, fatty foods cause acne.

HIDE THAT ZIT

Dab a little oil-free, antibacterial concealer on the pimple and pat with powder. Wear a bright red lipstick or dramatic eye makeup to draw attention to all the fabulous things that happen on your face. Any zit is, after all, going to be much smaller and less interesting than your fascinating mouth or your luminous eyes.

KEEP CLEAN

Good hygiene is the best way to speed healing. Wash your face twice a day with a gentle cleanser, rinse well, pat dry, then follow with toner. Don't put moisturizer on a pimple. Be sure to wash your hands often, and avoid touching your face as much as possible. Tie back long hair to keep it off your face, and change your pillow case regularly.

HOW TO GIVE UP SMOKING

Smokers are masters at ignoring bad news. Somehow the fact that a cigarette habit can give you cellulite or even gangrene in no way detracts from the sublime pleasure of lighting up. However, there is no doubt that smoking is becoming less glamorous. It is not just that so many people object; the fact is there is nothing cool about huddling in a doorway in the rain taking furtive drags from a damp cigarette. It really is time to give it up.

INDISPENSABLE THINGS

• Willpower

COMMIT

Set a quit date, and stick to it. Work out when your cravings are likely to be strongest, and have a strategy in place to beat them—for example, if you always light up after dinner, have a mint instead.

KNOW YOURSELF

Before you quit, work out why you want to stop— health, money or to improve your sex life. A good reason is a powerful motivator.

A PRACTICAL HISTORY OF SMOKING

It's been known for years that smoking is bad for you. In 1604, within a generation of tobacco arriving in Europe, King James I of England described it as "a custom loathsome to the eye, hateful to the nose, harmful to the brain, dangerous to the lungs." However, for centuries, people smoked for the good of their health. In the 17th century, tobacco was believed to protect against plague—and boys at Eton College in England were beaten for not smoking their pipes. In 1950, scientists proved the link between lung cancer and smoking. The cigarette habit has been in long, slow decline ever since.

GET HELP
You don't have to do it on your own. Join a stop-smoking group or get some one-on-one counseling—see your physician for a referral. Call a stop-smoking phoneline, too (get details from your physician or on the Internet).

EXERCISE
If you are worried that your weight will balloon, kick-start your exercise program. Going out for a run is a great way to divert those cravings into something truly health giving.

GET DRUGS
Nicotine Replacement Therapy (NRT) has been shown to double your chances of quitting. You can get NRT over-the-counter or in prescription form in gum, patches, lozenges or nasal spray.

REWARD YOURSELF
Quitting is a hard job, so book yourself a facial as a treat, or buy some new CDs—your reward will be practically free if you take into account the money you are saving on cigarettes.

HOW TO MEDITATE

If everyone meditated, the world would probably be a much happier place. Meditation is not a way to do nothing—sitting completely still for even a few minutes can be a detox for the mind. There are no guarantees when it comes to meditation, but it is likely that practicing stillness on a regular basis will make you less stressed, more relaxed—and just possibly enlightened. One study found that regular meditators needed to visit their physician less frequently than nonmeditators—which is probably the reason many physicians recommend it.

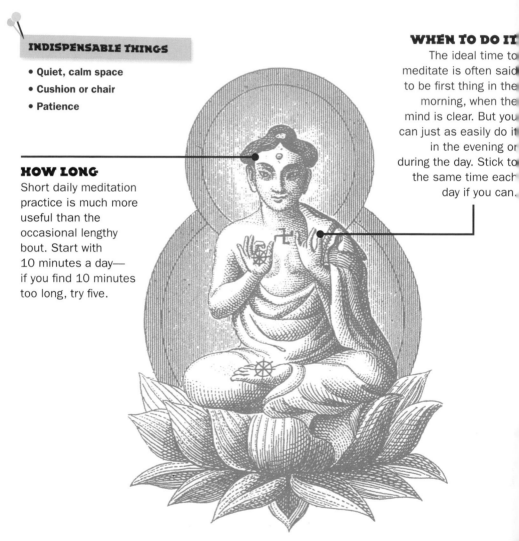

INDISPENSABLE THINGS

- Quiet, calm space
- Cushion or chair
- Patience

WHEN TO DO IT

The ideal time to meditate is often said to be first thing in the morning, when the mind is clear. But you can just as easily do it in the evening or during the day. Stick to the same time each day if you can.

HOW LONG

Short daily meditation practice is much more useful than the occasional lengthy bout. Start with 10 minutes a day— if you find 10 minutes too long, try five.

🐘 INDISPENSABLE WARNING

If you have experienced mental illness or recent emotional problems, talk to your physician before practicing meditation. It is advisable to learn meditation under the guidance of an experienced and reputable teacher. Be wary of self-styled "gurus" and cults.

BASIC TECHNIQUE

Close your eyes. Focus your attention on your breath, either noticing the sensations when it passes in and out of the nostrils or the rise and fall of your chest (stick to one or the other focus; do not switch between them). Don't try to breathe more deeply or regularly; this should happen naturally as you relax. Every time you notice yourself thinking (or falling asleep), gently bring your attention back to your breath.

MENTAL ATTITUDE

Meditation is a technique to enable you to notice the mind's activity without judging it. So don't be hard on yourself if you are distracted—it's normal to lose your focus many, many times. Practicing meditation in a group, under the guidance of a good teacher, will help enormously with concentration and motivation.

SITTING POSITIONS

The lotus is the traditional pose for meditation—but it suits only those with years of yoga behind them. Less-experienced meditators should sit on a cushion on the floor or on a chair with a straight back (both feet flat on the floor). The important thing is to keep your back straight and shoulders relaxed, and to be comfortable enough to maintain your pose.

HOW TO DO YOUR EYE MAKEUP

They say that the eyes are the window of the soul, which means that eye makeup is "window dressing." Skillfully executed eye makeup can make your eyes look bigger, brighter and more beautiful. But you need to get the basic colors right. The salesperson at the cosmetic counter is a good person to ask—but check that you like her makeup first. And be prepared to invest in a decent set of brushes because you need the right tools to get a good result.

INDISPENSABLE THINGS

- Selection of eye makeup brushes
- Light, medium and darker eye shadows
- Shimmer shadow
- Mascara
- Concealer
- Eyeliner

PRACTICAL TIP

A lot of women try to match their eye shadow to their eye color, but you get a more interesting and vibrant effect if you go for contrast. If you have green eyes, purple shades, such as violet, look beautiful. For blue eyes, browns and golds are a good choice. Brown-eyed women should try blue or greenish hues. If you are using eyeliner, make sure it complements the eye shadow—plum for violet, chocolate for brown and dark green for green shades.

1 Use an allover shadow brush to apply a light neutral color over the entire lid of the eye. You can also use a sponge-tip applicator (often supplied free with an eye shadow) to do this.

2 Brush a medium-tone shadow over the part of the lid that covers the eyeball. Again, you can use a sponge-tip applicator for this, but a contour brush works best. Blend the colors where they meet.

3 Now use a fine smudge brush to apply dark shadow along the lash line, blending it into the mid-tone. Apply under the bottom lashes, too.

4 Then use a small shadow brush to apply a small amount of light-tone shimmer shadow to the brow bone. This will help the eyes to appear brighter.

5 Apply mascara to the tips of both upper and lower lashes (your lashes will look better if you curl them first). Use repeated light brushstrokes to extend the lashes and build up the color.

6 Finally, apply concealer to any dark areas under the eyes. Use your finger to blend the concealer in well.

HOW TO CLEAN YOUR TEETH

You would think that everybody brushes their teeth often enough to know what they are doing. However, the very fact that we do it so frequently means that few of us give it the attention it requires. Brushing your teeth should take at least two minutes if you do it properly—the chances are you spend barely 30 seconds. The consequences of inadequate brushing are various and horrible—tooth decay, gum disease and bad breath. So whatever else you do, be sure to go the full I20 seconds to keep the tooth fairy from your door. And don't forget to floss.

INDISPENSABLE THINGS

- Soft-bristled toothbrush
- Fluoride toothpaste
- Dental floss

PRACTICAL TIP

Some people find that their gums bleed when they start to floss. This usually means that t' gums are inflamed, and it shoul stop happening if you floss regularly and in the correct way. If the bleeding continues longer than a week or two, see your dentist for advice.

1 First clean the outsides, then the insides of the teeth, using small circular movements. It helps to angle the brush against the gum line at about 45 degrees. Make sure you brush along the gum line, because this action stimulates blood flow to the gums.

2 Clean the insides of the upper and lower middle teeth by tilting the brush vertically so that you can reach them. Finally, brush along the biting surfaces, using a back-and-forth motion.

3 Clean your tongue using your brush or a special tongue cleaner—this will help get rid of bacteria buildup and freshen your breath. Rinse your mouth, drawing the water through your teeth.

4 Take a 18in. (45cm) length of floss and wind it around the middle finger of each hand. Use your thumbs and index fingers to hold the floss taut, leaving yourself about 1in. (2.5cm) in between to work with.

5 Gently guide the floss up around the tooth and under the gum line, in a smooth circular movement. Gently rub down the tooth a few times. Clean between all your teeth, remembering to do both sides. Wind the floss along so that you use a clean piece each time.

6 Give your mouth a good rinse, drawing the water through your teeth, to wash away any dislodged food particles.

HEALTH & BEAUTY

HOW TO BLOW-DRY YOUR HAIR STRAIGHT

If you were blessed with straight hair as an infant, the chances are you spent your childhood longing for waves and ringlets. For grown-up women, however, curls are out and stick-straight is in. According to one survey, two-thirds of us prefer our hair to be sleek and smooth. If you don't want to shell out for hair straighteners, then blow-drying is the best way to straighten your hair. You'll need time and patience—it takes about 30 minutes—and also a good hair dryer to get a perfect flat-iron style.

INDISPENSABLE THINGS

- Damp, just washed hair
- Wide-tooth comb
- Hair dryer with nozzle
- Heat protectant
- Straightening balm
- Large hairdressing clips
- Thick round brush

A PRACTICAL HISTORY OF HAIR

Hair—especially women's hair—has always had deep cultural significance. In many ancient cultures, long hair with vibrant color was considered beautiful for a very sound anthropological reason. It advertised youth, and it proclaimed that the woman in question had enjoyed uninterrupted good health over an extended period. Blonde or brunette, a good head of hair was a visual indicator that the woman in question was a safe prospect as a mate. All the vast resources of modern beauticians and stylists— their many chemicals and coloring agents, their multifarious creams and conditioners—are aimed at evoking that same subliminal and primeval human response to an eye-catching set of locks.

1 Comb your hair with a wide-tooth comb. Roughly dry under a cool dryer while running your fingers through it—you want to get it about 80 percent dry before you start straightening. Apply heat protectant and straightening balm, according to the manufacturer's instructions.

2 Divide your hair into several sections. Clip the sides and front of your hair on top of the head, leaving the back loose. Take a small section of the loose hair at the back in order to style it.

3 Use your brush to lift the hair at the roots and then pull it down to the ends at the same time as you dry it. Hold the hair dryer nozzle about 4in. (10cm) away from the hair, and direct the air *down* the shaft to encourage it to lie flat (don't let the dryer get too close).

4 Now do the upper side. Again, use your brush to pull the hair straight as you dry it, keeping the tension as even as possible. Keep the dryer moving to avoid burning the hair, and try not to overdry any areas.

5 Make sure the hair is completely dry before moving on to the next small section of the back. Once you have done the back of the hair, do the sides, followed by the bangs and crown.

HOW TO DO A PUSH-UP

Push-ups are a way of using your body as a kind of dumb-bell. Every time you do a push-up you are lifting part of your own weight, and at the same time building the "Popeye" muscles—your biceps and triceps. The push-up also works the chest, shoulders and abdominal muscles—and builds overall upper body strength. It's a great exercise to do if you are into racket sports, because it helps you to get more power into every shot. And if a full push-up is too difficult, try the bent-knee version. It's sometimes dubbed the "girl's push-up," which is a chauvinist's way of saying it's a good option for beginners.

INDISPENSABLE THINGS

- A carpeted or padded floor (or "sticky" yoga mat)
- Comfortable, unrestrictive clothing
- Warmed-up muscles
- Your physician's permission, if in any doubt

☞ INDISPENSABLE WARNING

Stop immediately if you feel any pain, and seek medical advice if the pain persists.

FULL PUSH-UP

1 Lie face down on the floor. Put your hands on the floor, either side of your chest and slightly farther apart than your shoulders, with fingers facing forward. Keeping your feet slightly apart, place them so that the toes and the balls of your feet are on the floor.

2 Raise yourself up until your arms are straight, breathing out as you do so. Keep your abdominals pulled in. Your neck, back and legs should form a straight line (or "plank")—do not push your buttocks in the air or arch your back. Hold this position.

3 Now slowly lower your chest to the ground by bending the arms until the elbows form a right angle and your chest is about 2in. (5cm) from the floor. Breathe in as you come down.

4 Repeat up to 10 times, working slowly and concentrating on your technique rather than on speed. Pause for a moment between each push-up. Stop if your lower back starts to sag or you get tired. Over time, you can build up the number of push-ups you do in each session.

BENT-KNEE PUSH-UP

1 Lie on the floor, with your hands either side of your chest, fingers facing forward and elbows bent. Bring your feet off the floor, bending your knees to form a 45-degree angle.

2 Breathing out, raise yourself up until your arms are straight. Keep your back and neck in a straight line and pause for a moment. Breathe in as you lower yourself back until your chest is about 2in. (5cm) from the floor. Pause and repeat.

HEALTH & BEAUTY

HOW TO IMPROVE YOUR POSTURE

Your mother was right when she told you to sit up straight. Most of us have faulty posture, and 9 out of 10 people have back problems at some point in their lives. This is the inevitable result of years spent hunched over laptops or slouched on couches—or else, more actively, carrying babies on one hip or lopsidedly toting bags of schoolbooks or heavy shopping bags. You can add inches to your height, improve your health and even boost your confidence in an instant—simply by holding yourself properly.

INDISPENSABLE THINGS

- Body awareness

BE SPINE FRIENDLY

Stand so that your spine tends toward its natural curve. This means keeping your head upright, relaxing your shoulders, pulling the blades in and down the back, pulling in your abdomen, keeping the hips level and tucking in the tailbone.

SEE AN EXPERT

The Alexander Technique, a way of learning how to get rid of harmful tension in your body, specifically targets your posture. It's best taught on a one-to-one basis. For more details, check it out on the Internet.

GO EAST

Try Eastern forms of exercise, such as yoga and tai chi. They work on the whole body, so they naturally improve your posture. You may notice a difference in the way you stand after a few sessions. Pilates incorporates elements of yoga, and is known to encourage good postural habits. Or try dance—you don't often see a ballerina with a hunchback.

START AT THE TOP

Where the head leads, the rest of the body will follow. Jutting out the chin like a sergeant major will pull your spine out of its optimal position. So, keep your head erect with your chin parallel to the floor and your neck soft—you'll feel the rest of the spine lengthen below. A good tip is to imagine there is a string attached to the center of your crown, helping to lift you into an upright posture.

CHECK YOURSELF

Don't get stuck in the same pose for long periods— get in the habit of checking your posture and adjusting it regularly. If you use a computer, make sure you have a proper chair and that you keep both feet flat on the floor, knees slightly apart. Don't cross your legs; it twists the spine. Get up and walk around at regular intervals.

SHOE SENSE

Ladies, lose the high heels. They push the spine out of alignment. Wear comfortable shoes with a low heel.

HOW TO SLEEP BETTER

One in three people has trouble sleeping. If you are one of them, take heart from the fact that most sleep problems are treatable. The key is not to spend your evenings worrying about things that are vexatious to the spirit. Don't exercise at night, drink a lot or watch too much television. You need to get yourself in the mood for sleep.

INDISPENSABLE THINGS

- **A good mattress (less than 10 years old)**
- **Enough covers**

SET A ROUTINE

Going to bed and getting up at the same times every day—including weekends—helps set your body clock for good, regular sleep. So resist the lie-in.

STAY WARM

Keeping warm will help you to drop off. Make sure you have a decent quilt or enough blankets. Having a warm bath an hour or so before bedtime can soothe you into a state of sleepiness.

☞ INDISPENSABLE WARNING

Seek medical advice if you constantly feel tired, or if you have trouble falling asleep on a regular basis.

EAT WELL, BUT NOT TOO WELL

Avoid a heavy meal before bedtime. Coffee late at night is another mistake, as are black tea, chocolate and cola. Try an old-fashioned mug of hot milk with some toast—carbs help trigger the release of serotonin which makes you drowsy.

LOOKING AFTER A BABY

Most of the complicated items that you have in your home come with an instruction booklet—except babies. The only way to learn how to manage one is to manage one. This chapter points you in the right direction with insider secrets, and with handy tips to help you avoid the rookie errors.

HOW TO HOLD A BABY

All new parents worry that they are going to drop their little darling—but they almost never do. The key things are to support the baby's head, since the neck muscles are too floppy to do the job themselves, and to keep the baby close to you so that he or she feels secure. Ignore grandmothers who warn you not to "spoil" your baby by cuddling. Scientists have confirmed what mothers instinctively know: babies need bodily contact to help them grow, sleep better and be happy. It even strengthens the immune system and helps with brain development. A cuddled baby is a more clever, contented baby.

INDISPENSABLE THINGS

• A baby

1 Make your baby aware of your presence by talking softly and offering gentle touches before you pick him or her up. Lean toward the baby, and slide one hand under the neck and head.

2 Now place your other hand under the lower back and buttocks. Slowly bring the baby toward your chest before you start to sit up (your baby feels more secure held against your body, so limit the amount of time he or she is suspended in midair).

3 Keep your hands in position as you support your baby upright against your chest, with his or her head on your shoulder. Once you get the hang of carrying your baby, you'll be able to use your elbow to support the buttocks, while the hand of the same arm keeps the head in position.

4 Another good position is the cradle hold. Keeping your hand under the baby's buttocks and lower back, gently bring the head to rest on the upper part of your forearm. Keep the baby close to your body, and place your spare hand on the baby's hip and thigh.

HEALTH & BEAUTY

A PRACTICAL HISTORY OF HOLDING

Many babies born in the first half of the 20th century were raised according to the childcare theories of Truby King. Babies were not comforted when they cried—this "weakened the character"—and they were fed on a strict every-four-hours regimen. In the 1960s, a more compassionate approach was advocated by Benjamin Spock, who urged parents to follow their instincts above all. "You know more than you think you do" was his mantra. Jean Liedloff, writing in the 1970s, went further. Having observed the practices of Amazonian peoples, she proposed that mothers hold the baby continuously, day and night, for the first six months.

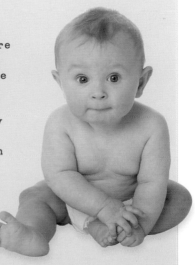

HOW TO CHANGE A DIAPER

A baby has its diaper changed some 4,000 times, so every parent is an expert in the end. Babies don't enjoy having their clothes removed—it makes them feel unsafe—so work as swiftly as you can. Have everything at hand, but out of baby's reach. Changing diapers can be fun, a time when you deepen your bond through singing or chatting, and through the sublime knowledge that you are meeting your child's needs. That's during the day; at night, the last thing you want is playtime. Learn to change diapers in dim light, avoid eye contact—and keep quiet.

INDISPENSABLE THINGS

- Clean changing area
- Changing mat or towel
- Washcloth or cotton balls
- Warm water
- Diaper rash cream (if needed)
- Clean diaper (plus liner if using a cloth diaper)
- Clean clothes if necessary
- Diaper bag (if using disposable diapers) or lidded diaper bucket (for cloth ones)

PRACTICAL TIP

It's better for a young baby's skin to clean up with water rather than wipes. If you prefer to use wipes, choose a brand that is free from alcohol or fragrance. Don't use talcum powder because the baby may inhale it.

INDISPENSABLE WARNING

Never leave your baby on a raised diaper-changing surface unattended. Keep one hand on the baby to prevent him or her from rolling off.

1 Wash your hands, then place your baby on a flat changing surface. Put a towel under the baby to keep him or her warm. Take off the baby's lower clothing, then unfasten the diaper.

2 Lift up the baby's ankles with one hand. Wipe away as much as possible of any liquid stools, using the front of the diaper. Remove the diaper, folding it in half and place out of reach. If changing a boy, place a dry washcloth over his penis: baby urine can travel far.

3 Using a washcloth or cotton balls dipped in lukewarm water, clean the area thoroughly, including the leg creases. Always wipe a girl from front to back.

4 Pat the diaper area dry with a clean towel or washcloth; this will help to prevent diaper rash. If the skin is sore, apply a thin layer of diaper rash cream.

5 Open out a clean diaper, and lay it under your baby's buttocks, level with the waist. Fasten (make sure a boy's penis is tucked down first). Fold the front of the diaper clear of the cord, if your baby is newborn.

6 Wash your hands and dress your baby. Clean the area and dispose of the diaper and washcloth/cotton balls. Wash your hands one last time.

HOW TO STOP A BABY FROM CRYING

Babies cry—it's what they do. Until they acquire the power of speech, yelling their heads off is their only way of communicating. So the key to stopping a baby crying is to figure out what is bugging the little tyke and deliver it as quickly as possible. And don't worry if your baby's crying stresses you out—you are biologically programmed to feel unhappy if your special boy or girl is unhappy. The good news is that most crying has a limited number of causes. If you know what they are, then you are already halfway to having a contented baby.

INDISPENSABLE THINGS

• Love

☞ INDISPENSABLE WARNING

Always seek medical advice if your baby's cry is unusual or persistent, with no clear cause.

CHECKLIST

Babies generally cry for a reason, and it is likely to be one of these: hunger, gas, discomfort (from a wet diaper, feeling too cold or too warm, or from clothing that is too tight), overstimulation or loneliness. Get in the habit of running through a mental list of possible causes. It is amazingly easy to forget the diaper, which is the most obvious cause of all.

BABY-WEARING

Hold your baby as much as possible. Studies have found that babies who are carried often tend to cry less. Limit the time your baby spends in the stroller, bouncy chair or car seat, so that he or she gets plenty of human contact.

CHANGING PLACES

Babies often cry when they are in a place that is too busy, such as a shopping center or a family party. Going somewhere quiet, and holding your baby close (skin to skin if possible) may help him or her calm down. Fresh air sometimes has a soothing effect

COMFORT

The idea that you spoil a baby by responding to his or her cries is a myth that refuses to die. You are likely to soothe a baby much more quickly if you respond straight away to any sign of distress—and he or she is more likely to grow into a happy, secure child.

STOPPING THE CRYING

To soothe a baby, hold him or her securely. Gently rock or sway your baby, while shushing calmly in the ear (this replicates the motion and sound of being in the womb). If your baby is still distressed, try putting him to the breast for a short comfort feed to settle him, (or offer the crook of your clean little finger if you are not breast-feeding).

HOW TO GET A BABY TO SLEEP THROUGH THE NIGHT

There is no easy way to make a baby sleep through the night, no matter what your grandmother says. What is more, every baby is different. Some little angels naturally go eight hours from a young age, but many others don't. One survey found that less than one-quarter of some babies were sleeping through the night at the age of 10 months. So, to some extent, your child's sleeping habits are out of your hands (which, when you think about it, is a kind of comfort for stressed-out new parents). Nevertheless, there are ways of promoting good bedtime routines and "sleep hygiene."

INDISPENSABLE THINGS

- Patience
- Calm
- Love

☞ INDISPENSABLE WARNING

Always put your baby to sleep on his or her back, with the feet at the foot of the crib. This is known to reduce the risk of Sudden Infant Death Syndrome (SIDS). Make sure that the baby doesn't get too hot, use lightweight covers (not quilts) and keep extraneous objects out of the crib (crib bumpers, toys, pillows, etc.).

SLEEP ENVIRONMENT

Make sure the bedroom is conducive to sleep: dark, quiet and reasonably warm (60–65°F/16–18°C). Blackout blinds can be very useful. It's best if your baby shares your room until the age of six months.

FILL THE TUMMY

A baby sleeps better after a good feed. If giving a bottle, wake your baby to feed at your bedtime. If breast-feeding, "cluster-feed" in the evening. Many nursing mothers find that the baby feeds almost constantly from late afternoon to bedtime.

LEARNING TO SLEEP

Teaching your baby to drop off alone can take time. Ideally, put him or her in the crib while awake, but sleepy. It can help to provide gentle sound, such as a musical mobile, ticking clock or a recording of white noise (such as a vacuum cleaner or washing machine). Stay close by and pick up your baby if he or she becomes distressed. Never leave a young baby (under six months) to cry.

SWADDLING

Many babies like the security of swaddling. Use a lightweight sheet or swaddling cloth. Swaddling may not be suitable in hot weather; ask your physician for advice.

BEDTIME

When you feel it is time to establish a bedtime, follow a fixed routine each evening. Keep the hour before bedtime calm. Do one or more of the following: warm bath, massage, pajamas, story, song, rocking or cuddling, feed, cleaning teeth, stroking time in the crib. Stick to the same order of events each night.

HOW TO BABYPROOF A HOME

Babies and toddlers possess irrepressible curiosity. They seem instinctively drawn to everyday objects that—in their little hands—suddenly become perilous: the hot cup of coffee on the kitchen table, the electrical outlet with its three fascinating holes, the scissors in the sewing basket... As a parent, you must get into the habit of scanning every room you enter for danger. And don't think babyproofing once is enough. Every day, and every stage of development, gives your baby new opportunities to seek out danger, thus scaring the daylights out of you.

INDISPENSABLE THINGS

- **Common sense**
- **A small measure of paranoia**

TOYS

Pay attention to the age ranges given on toy packaging—they are there for safety reasons. Don't give children under three anything with long strings or small parts. Check secondhand toys very carefully; they may not conform to today's stringent safety standards.

YARDS

Ponds in the backyard are pretty, but highly dangerous. The only really safe option is to fill it in. At least, place a secure fence around it, and cover it with mesh. Drain paddling pools and turn them upside down after use. Lock away garden chemicals and tools.

BAGS

Rummaging through a purse is a favorite baby activity. Don't keep medication or anything sharp—such as nail clippers—in yours.

STAIRS

Fit safety gates at the top and bottom of the stairs once your baby is getting ready to crawl. Don't wait until he or she has started. Check the banisters: they should be vertical and spaced no more than 4in. (10cm) apart.

FURNITURE

Put away light pieces of furniture that an adventurous baby could pull over. Fit corner covers on the sharp edges of coffee tables and similar pieces. Secure freestanding bookshelves to the wall.

FIRE

Fit smoke alarms on every floor, and a carbon monoxide alarm near the furnace. Switch off appliances at the wall when not in use, and use outlet covers. If you have a fireplace, make sure you use a secured fire guard when it is in use (and while the ashes are still warm).

HEALTH & BEAUTY

GENERAL SAFETY

Fit childproof locks to kitchen drawers and cabinets, and store cleaning products, medication and other dangerous items out of reach. Always cook with the pan handles turned inward.

WINDOWS

Make sure all windows are locked. Never leave an upstairs window open if your child can reach it, and do not place low items of furniture nearby.

ELECTRICAL CORDS

Watch out for trailing electrical cords, and keep them safely tucked away. Always keep your iron and the cord well out of reach (it's best to iron when your children are safely tucked up in bed).

HOW TO CLEAN A BABY

Little babies can be as slippery as an oiled fish. Getting one in and out of the bath can be tricky. Fortunately, you don't have to do it every day. The latest thinking holds that it is better for a baby's skin if you wait a few weeks before giving the first bath. Thereafter a couple of baths a week is sufficient. Daily "topping and tailing"—cleaning the messy ends with cotton balls—is a perfectly adequate way to keep your baby clean between baths.

INDISPENSABLE THINGS

- 2 towels
- Cotton balls
- Bowl of cooled boiled water
- Clean diaper

👉 PRACTICAL TIP

Keep the room warm and your baby covered. If your baby is less than 10 days old, you'll need to wipe around the bottom of the umbilical cord—check with your midwife or physician how to do this.

1 Undress your baby down to his or her diaper and undershirt, and cover with a towel. Dampen a cotton ball and wipe one eye from the bridge of the nose outward. Clean the other eye in the same way, using a fresh cotton ball.

2 Wipe the baby's face using more damp cotton balls. Clean around the ears (but not inside them), and wipe the folds of the neck. Pat dry. Then clean the hands and under the arms in the same way.

3 Now take off the diaper and wash the diaper area, making sure that you clean all the folds around the groin and legs. Wipe from front to back, and do not pull back the labia or foreskin. Pat dry, then put on a clean diaper and dress your child.

HOW TO BATHE A BABY

Don't expect your baby to enjoy a long soak. Young babies are often freaked out by being stripped and placed in water. The key is to hold them securely, talk in a reassuring way, and, above all, keep bathtime brief. Babies are incapable of regulating their own body temperature, so it's vital that both the room and the bathwater are comfortably warm.

INDISPENSABLE THINGS

- Towel (preferably hooded)
- Cotton balls
- Cooled boiled water (for eyes)
- Baby bath or washing-up bowl
- Warm water
- Clean diaper
- Clean clothes

☞ INDISPENSABLE WARNING

Never leave a baby alone in the bathtub. Always test the water temperature with a bath thermometer, and with your elbow or wrist (both are more sensitive to heat). It should be comfortably warm, not hot.

1 Undress your baby to the diaper, wrap in a towel and wash eyes and face as described opposite. Hold over the bathtub, supporting the back, neck and head with one arm and hand. Use the other to gently rinse the baby's hair with water. Pat it dry.

2 Remove the diaper, then place the baby in the bathtub (clean the diaper area first if soiled). Hold the baby's upper arm with your hand, using your wrist to support the head and neck; use your other hand to support the buttocks. Use this hand to splash the baby's body once he or she is safely in the bathtub (repeating this keeps your baby warm).

3 Lift the baby out in the same way and wrap in a towel, making sure you cover the head as well as the body. Cuddle, then pat dry, making sure all the creases are dry. Put on a clean diaper and clothing.

HEALTH & BEAUTY

HOW TO TAKE A TODDLER ON A PLANE

For an adult, international air travel is a joy and a thrill. For an adult with small children, international air travel could be a nightmare. There's almost no way to make an airplane journey with toddlers or babies a restful, happy experience. The most you can hope for is to get to your destination with your sanity intact. The key to this is to take an armory of items designed to distract, pacify and otherwise relax your little traveling companions.

INDISPENSABLE THINGS

- Toys, books and DVDs
- More toys
- Edible treats
- Infinite patience
- Spare clothing (you and child)
- Diapers and changing paraphernalia

RESIGN YOURSELF

You are not going to get to read that novel, or watch the movie. For you, the entire journey is a cramped and rather long-winded nursery session. You might as well come to terms with that fact while you are still on the tarmac.

BE PREPARED

A selection of toys to keep your child amused is essential hand luggage: crayons, coloring pages (printed from the Internet), sticker books and finger puppets are excellent light options. It's a good idea to wrap up toys and produce them at intervals (say, one an hour). Pack a special soft toy or comfort object in case your child wants to sleep.

SEATING PLAN

Book a window seat, and ideally a seat for your toddler. Take along an airline-approved car seat to strap him or her into.

BEFORE THE FLIGHT

Talk to your child about what to expect in the days before the journey. An "at the airport" book will be invaluable—most children will enjoy the anticipation beforehand and then spotting things featured in the book once they get to the airport. Take the pre-boarding option if you can, so that you can get settled more easily.

STORY TIME

Take a judicial mix of long-term favorites and exciting new books to read to your children. A good book is worth its weight in gold, because it can buy you half an hour's peace and quiet. Storybooks loaded onto an MP3 player will prove a welcome diversion, while a portable DVD player and selection of DVDs is a godsend for long flights.

THINK SNACKS

Pack your own food for the children rather than rely on the in-flight meal. Give them familiar picnic food, but be prepared to suspend all normal nutritional rules during the journey.

HEALTH & BEAUTY

HOW TO BREAST-FEED

Breast-feeding is the best and most natural way to feed
your baby, but from a mother's perspective, breast-feeding
is also a skill that takes time to get right. Fortunately,
you won't be short of practice. Tiny babies feed a lot
(ignore anyone who says, "Surely he can't be hungry again
already?"). The most important thing is to let the baby
feed whenever and for as long as he or she wants. Some
kind of routine will gradually develop after the first six
weeks. And remember to drink plenty of water and to eat
plenty of healthy food yourself: you need 500 extra calories
a day when you're breast-feeding.

INDISPENSABLE THINGS

- Time
- Patience
- Cushions, pillows or
  breast-feeding cushion

PRACTICAL TIP

Seek help from a breast-feeding
counselor if you feel you are
struggling with breast-feeding,
or contact a breast-feeding
support organization, such
as the La Leche League.

1 First, find a comfortable position to feed your baby. Keep your back straight and use cushions to support your back and arm. This is the traditional cradle position, in which the baby lies along your arm, head just below the crook, buttocks in your hand.

THE CROSS-CRADLE is wonderful for new mothers, because it is easier to maneuver the baby into the right position. The baby's head is in your hand, buttocks in the crook of your arm; you feed from the opposite side as you hold the baby. Use your spare hand to support the breast.

THE FOOTBALL HOLD is good for newborns, twins, as well as women who had a cesarean section. You feed from the same side as you hold the baby (keeping him or her away from any scar). The baby's head is in your hand, back along your arm, legs resting on a pillow.

THE LYING-DOWN POSITION is great for night-time feeds. Face the baby and cradle with your lower arm. You'll need pillows to get comfortable. Put them behind your back and between your knees, as well as one behind the baby to keep him or her close.

2 Hold the baby on his or her side, so that the head and back form a straight line, the tummy toward you and the nose opposite your nipple. Brush the baby's top lip with your nipple if he or she doesn't open the mouth. Wait until the mouth opens really wide.

3 Draw the baby's shoulders toward you so that the chin approaches the breast first. Once latched on, the mouth should be wide, nose almost touching your breast. If it hurts for more than a few seconds, slip your little finger into the baby's mouth to release the hold and try again.

HOW TO GIVE A BABY A BOTTLE

The bottle-feeding family has to be super-organized—nobody wants to be holding a screaming baby at 3 a.m. while waiting for the sterilizer to ping. Plan ahead, and you will save yourself a lot of grief. The great convenience of bottles is, of course, that both parents can share the feeding. A young baby will develop a secure attachment with whoever is meeting his or her needs, so even if Mom is the main provider, Dad can put in occasional guest appearances. Drinking milk and cuddling are a baby's greatest pleasures, so feeding your child is the best way for you to bond.

INDISPENSABLE THINGS

- 6 wide-necked bottles
- 6 nipples
- Bottle brush
- Sterilizing equipment
- Infant formula milk
- Cooled, freshly boiled water
- Bowl of hot water

GIVING FORMULA

Hold your baby so that the upper body and head are upright (a 45-degree angle is comfortable). Sit quietly and make plenty of eye contact. If you can, loosen your own clothing and place the baby against your chest for some skin-to-skin contact. Do not prop a bottle up so that your baby can feed himself or herself—there is a risk of choking.

HOW MUCH, HOW OFTEN?

Be guided by your baby's appetite rather than a rigid schedule. Feed your baby when he or she seems hungry, and let the baby decide how much milk to take. A feeding pattern will naturally emerge over the weeks—and your baby won't be miserable in the meantime.

STERILIZING

Your baby's bottles and nipples need to be well washed and sterilized before use. Use a bottle brush to clean thoroughly, turn the nipple inside out, then sterilize in a steam unit or by boiling in a large lidded pan for 10 minutes (leave the lid on until you are ready to make up the bottles; they won't stay sterile once you remove it).

WHICH NIPPLE?

Choose a nipple with an orthodontic shape to help protect your baby's teeth. Make sure that you get the right flow rate for your baby (newborn, slow, medium or fast). Too fast a flow, for example, will rush your baby. He or she is likely to take in more air, leading to painful gas. Check nipples regularly and discard them at the first sign of wear.

MAKING THE FORMULA

Always measure the water first then add the powder according to the manufacturer's instructions. You'll need recently boiled water, cooled to room temperature. Mix in the bottle, shake to combine, then keep in the center of the refrigerator until needed. Warm by standing the bottle in a bowl of hot water, and shake a few drops on your wrist to check the temperature. Do not heat in a microwave: this can cause "hot spots" in the milk. Discard undrunk milk after 1 hour.

HOW TO INTRODUCE SOLID FOOD

Giving solids is fun, but many people start too early. The latest scientific thinking suggests that it is better for your baby if you wait until six months, when a baby's digestive system can handle mashed-up versions of many "adult" foods (so no messing about with purées). Also the "tongue thrust reflex"—which makes babies poke food straight out of their mouths—will have disappeared. Waiting that bit extra makes weaning more straightforward.

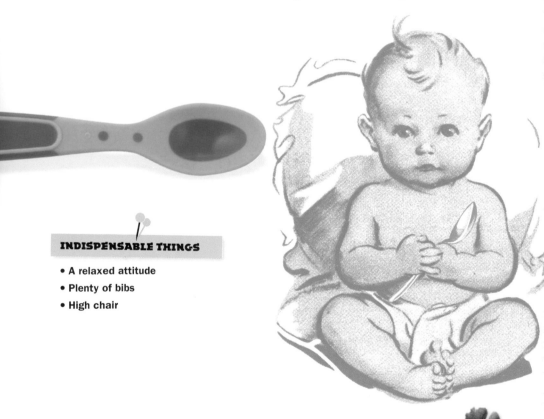

INDISPENSABLE THINGS

- A relaxed attitude
- Plenty of bibs
- High chair

☞ **INDISPENSABLE WARNINGS**

It's advisable to introduce common allergenic foods—eggs (well-cooked yolks only), dairy products, soy, cereals that contain gluten (wheat, rye, barley, oats), fish and so on—one at a time from the age of six months and to start with a small amount. If there is a family history of allergies or allergic conditions (hay fever, eczema, asthma), introduce solids very carefully and do not give your baby peanuts or sesame seeds for the first three years. Always read labels carefully to check for nut content. See your physician for individual advice. Do not give honey or shellfish to children under one year of age, or whole or chopped nuts to children under five.

HOW TO DO IT

Start by offering small amounts, and let your baby decide whether to take it. Gradually build up to several meals a day. Never force a baby to eat—he or she gets most of the nutrition necessary from formula or breastmilk.

DON'T RUSH IT

Generally a six month old will show great interest in food and may try to grab food out of your hand. But don't worry if your baby isn't interested yet; some babies do not start eating until later in the year.

WHAT TO GIVE

A six-month-old baby can eat most grown-up things, but should not be given very spicy, oily, salty or sweet foods. Start with some low-allergen foods, such as slivers of ripe pear or cooked carrot puree, and then progress to chicken, legumes, grains and other foods (appropriately prepared and cut). Give fresh homemade foods rather than store-bought food.

HEALTH & BEAUTY

FINGER FOODS

Good chewing foods include cooked carrots cut into sticks; slices of toast; banana cut into long fingers; cooked green beans; rice cakes; and slices of broiled polenta. Later on, try strips of chicken, sticks of cheese, cooked haricot beans, and so on. Stay close in case of choking.

DRINKS

Don't cut back on milk in order to get your baby to eat more food. Stick to sips of water with mealtimes if your baby seems thirsty, rather than giving diluted juice (which is bad for the emerging teeth).

STARTING EARLY

All the advice here is for healthy babies of six months. If you want to start your baby on solids earlier, talk to your physician. Many foods—including bread—should not be given because of the risk of allergies. No baby should be given solid food before the age of four months.

HOW TO READ A BEDTIME STORY

Babies can't read—but they love books and stories long before they can follow what is happening on the page. To a six month old, a tale told out loud is like a favorite piece of music, which is why they are happy to hear the same story again and again. Daily story times will help your baby come to see books as an inexhaustible source of knowledge and pleasure. The habit of reading is one of the best gifts you can give your child.

INDISPENSABLE THINGS

- Time
- Fun books

HOW TO READ

Get comfortable together. Read slowly and expressively, using different voices for different characters. Point out things in the pictures. Be enthusiastic about the things that grab your child's attention. Give the child plenty of time to look at the images.

GIVE CHOICE

Let your child choose the bedtime story. Don't worry if he or she picks the same one day after day. It may be dull for you, but children enjoy repetition and learn from it. He or she will eventually want to move on to something new.

BOOKS FOR TODDLERS

Young toddlers enjoy stories featuring familiar objects and activities. Older ones appreciate books about counting, colors and shapes as well as those with simple stories they can learn by heart.

BOOKS FOR BABIES

Small babies like brightly colored picture books. The best are made from cloth or board, and can be safely chewed.

HOW TO MAKE PLAY DOUGH

All children are natural-born potters and sculptors. Many children, for example, love fashioning little men out of play dough, smashing them flat with a tiny fist and then rolling out arms and legs and torsos all over again. There is no need to buy commercial model clay. Making your own play dough is cheaper, and it is more fun for your child. The dough will keep for a month or so in a sealed plastic bag or container (store it in the refrigerator).

INDISPENSABLE THINGS

- Plain flour
- Cream of tartar
- Table salt
- Cooking oil
- Food coloring
- Saucepan
- Rubber gloves

BASIC RECIPES

Place ¾ cup (125g) all-purpose flour, 1 tablespoon cream of tartar and ¼ cup (60g) table salt in an old saucepan, then pour in 1 cup (125ml) water and 2 teaspoons of oil. Stir over a low heat for a few minutes, until the mixture forms a ball of dough that pulls away from the sides of the pan. Cool before using.

ADDING COLOR

Divide the dough into several large balls. Put a few drops of different food coloring onto each batch—the more you put on, the brighter the hue—then work into the dough. Wear rubber gloves to prevent your hands from getting stained.

GOOD CLEAN FUN

Get your children to play on a wipe-clean mat. A blunt children's knife, cookie cutters and a toy rolling pin are all good utensils.

☞ INDISPENSABLE WARNING

Homemade play dough is high in salt, so don't let your child eat it. Keep it out of pets' reach.

TRAVEL & SPORTS

ON THE ROAD

Driving a car is one of the great pleasures
of our age——as is riding a bike. However,
it can turn into a disastrous experience
if you're not well prepared. Here are
some essential tips on how to keep your
wheels turning smoothly.

HOW TO PARALLEL PARK

Are you one of those annoying people who whizzes up to a parking space and backs into it perfectly, in one neat, flowing move? If so, then you won't need to read this. However, if you're you one of those people who always goes into the space at the wrong angle and ends up either driving over innocent pedestrians or needing a gangplank to get from the car to the sidewalk, then read on. Here are five simple steps to ease the pain.

INDISPENSABLE CHECKS

- Check for oncoming cars
- Check your rearview mirror
- Check for pedestrians

PRACTICAL TIP

First practice somewhere there aren't any other cars, using traffic cones if you have them.

1 First find a suitable parking space. Ideally, it should be about 5ft. (1.5m) longer than your car—and certainly no less that 2ft. (60cm) longer. Signal and place your car level with the car parked in front of the empty spot and about 2ft. (60cm) away from . Keep your signal lights on.

2 Take your time. Check your mirrors. If there are other cars approaching, let them pass before you start your maneuver. When you are ready, put the engine into reverse and start backing into the space. Look over your shoulder and turn the wheel as far as it will go toward the curb.

3 Straighten the wheel once the rear edge of the driver door is level with the bumper of the other car. You should be at 5 degrees to the curb and about 3ft. (1m) way. Your passenger door should be about in. (15cm) from the car in front. If you're too lose too soon, try again.

4 Back into the space until your front bumper is clear of the rear bumper on the car in front. Then turn the wheel as far as possible away from the curb and continue reversing until your car is in the space. Imagine the whole maneuver as an "S"—and watch out for the car behind!

5 Straighten the wheel and move your car forward until you are centered in the space. Ideally, you should be 6–8in. (15–20cm) away from the curb. State laws vary, with some states requiring you to park no more than 12in. (30cm) from the curb, while other states allow as much as 18in. (45cm). Either way, practice makes perfect.

HOW TO CHANGE GEAR

"Gears? What are they?" If you're used to driving an automatic car, that may well be your attitude. But not all cars are automatic and, particularly if you're driving in Europe, you may find yourself having to change gears in the old-fashioned way. The good news is that it's not as difficult as it sounds. In fact, you might find yourself enjoying the human/machine symbiosis so much you won't want to go back to your pig-headed automatic.

INDISPENSABLE CHECKS

- **Use a low gear around corners**
- **Never "ride" the clutch**

GEARS

Remember: Low gears (1–3) provide maximum acceleration at low speeds; high gears (4 and 5) provide more speed but less acceleration.

1ST GEAR

1st gear is used for starting off, maneuvering and negotiating hazards.

2ND GEAR

2nd gear is used for going downhill, gaining speed after starting off and negotiating hazards, such as junctions.

4TH GEAR

4th gear is used at speeds of over 30mph (48kph), when there are no hazards to negotiate.

3RD GEAR

3rd gear is used to gain speed going uphill and negotiating hazards at speed. It can also be used to give better control going down steep hills and going around bends.

5TH GEAR

5th gear is used at high speeds on highways to improve fuel efficiency.

REVERSE GEAR

Reverse is a low gear, like 1st gear, used to maneuver backward at slow speeds.

GEAR PATTERNS
It's important to memorize the gear pattern. Most cars have an H-shape diagram on the gearshift handle to show the position of the gears. The position of the reverse gear varies from car to car, and you will probably have to either push the gear lever down or lift it up in order to engage in reverse. This is to prevent you from accidentally going into reverse while driving.

CLUTCH CONTROL
The tricky part is using the clutch to transfer from one gear to another. Push the clutch pedal all the way down and select the gear you want (1st gear if starting on level ground or uphill; 2nd gear if starting downhill). Put your foot on the accelerator and increase the pressure as you release the clutch. Imagine you are transferring the weight from one foot to the other. If you are starting from a standstill, you'll need to release the brake as the clutch engages. Listen to the engine: if it starts to falter, it needs more fuel, so press down on the accelerator (not too much). If it starts to "race," it's got too much fuel, so ease off the accelerator (that's better). Once the gear is properly engaged, release the clutch completely and away you go. Practice in a safe place until you are familiar with the "friction point" of the clutch—that is, the point at which the engine starts to engage.

WHILE YOU WAIT
Never "ride" your clutch while stopped at traffic lights. It wastes fuel, pollutes the atmosphere and damages the clutch mechanism. Put on the brakes and change into neutral.

HOW TO CHECK YOUR OIL & WATER

Just because you have your car serviced every few months doesn't mean you can ignore it the rest of the time. Basic maintenance, such as checking the oil and water levels, should be as routine as vacuuming the carpet. Not only can it help you catch a problem before it becomes serious, but it will also familiarize you with the inner workings of your car. And that's a lot more empowering than ending up on the side of the road with a steaming engine, waiting for the tow truck to come.

INDISPENSABLE CHECKS

Monthly checks:

- Engine oil level
- Engine water/coolant level
- Transmission oil level
  (on automatic cars)
- Brake fluid level
- Power-steering fluid level
- Tire pressure and condition
- Windshield wiper fluid level
- Windshield wiper condition
- Lights

PRACTICAL TIP

Look closely at the oil on the dipstick. If it's jet black, it's time to change the oil; if it's brown/black, then it's OK. If it's streaked with white, like coffee, then you've got a problem. Take your car to a mechanic to be checked.

CHECKING THE OIL LEVEL

1 Park your car on level ground, and make sure that the engine is warm but not hot. Locate the dipstick. It will be sticking out the side of the engine and probably have a red handle. If you can't find it, refer to the owner's manual.

2 Pull the dipstick out and wipe it clean on of any oil residue with a dry, lint-free rag. Push it all the way back into place.

3 Pull the dipstick out again and check that the oil level is in between the "maximum" and "minimum" marks. If it's low, you'll need to fill up with the recommended grade of oil (refer to your manual or ask at a garage).

4 Locate the oil tank lid and pour in about 2 pints (1 liter) of oil. Check the level on the dipstick before adding any more. It's better to pour in a little at a time than to overfill the tank. When the level is correct, close the lid and reinsert the dipstick.

CHECKING THE WATER LEVEL

1 Locate the plastic coolant reservoir (not to be confused with the windshield washer fluid or the brake oil reservoir). Wait for the engine to cool before opening the lid.

2 Check the coolant level is between the "maximum" and "minimum" marks. If it's low, fill up with the recommended mix of water and antifreeze (usually 1:1, but refer to your manual or ask at a garage).

HOW TO TOW A VEHICLE

Even the best-made car is likely to break down sometimes. If you belong to a road service organization, such as AAA, it should be able to help you out. If not, it will work out a lot cheaper to persuade a friend to tow your car home to a garage or, if all else fails, to the junkyard!

INDISPENSABLE THINGS

- Strong rope, cable or chain
- Secure tying point

BE VISIBLE
Switch your emergency lights on and make sure you have an "CAR IN TOW" sign visible behind the car that is being towed.

TOW POINTS
Use a sturdy rope, cable or chain no longer than 15ft. (4.5m) to attach the front of the broken-down car to the rear of the tow car. Do not attach the rope to the bumpers! Most cars have built-in tow points specially made for the purpose. If your car doesn't, attach the rope to the undercarriage.

NEUTRAL
Make sure the car being towed is in neutral.

STEADY SPEED
Drive the tow car as smoothly as possible to avoid the rope "snatching." Keep your speed below 45mph (72kph) because the effective load greatly increases above this speed. Keep the tow rope taut to prevent sudden jerks that might break it.

ROPES
Tow ropes with hefty metal hooks at either end are sold at most auto stores. If you're using plain rope, make sure it's strong enough and that the knots at either end are secure. If the tow rope is more than 5ft. (1.5m) long, you must ensure it is clearly visible to other drivers by attaching a rag to the middle of it.

TOWING RULE
Both drivers must be fully qualified and both cars must be legally on the road with functioning lights and brakes, for example. You are only allowed to tow a car on a highway for the minimum distance necessary to reach a place of safety. Some states require breakaway brakes

HOW TO PUSH START A CAR

Dead battery? Fear not, you can still get going by push starting your car. The idea is to get some momentum going by pushing the car down a hill and then engaging the engine to get it spinning. Put your foot down on the accelerator and, brrrm, off you go! However, don't try this on an automatic car—it only works on cars with manual transmission.

INDISPENSABLE THINGS

- A willing helper or two (don't try this on your own)
- Level or downhill road

ENGAGE

When the car is moving at a fair speed (at least 3–5mph/5–8kph), signal to your helper(s) to stand aside and engage the clutch. As soon as the engine starts, press your foot down on the accelerator to rev it up. You can then either continue driving as usual or stop and run the engine in neutral for a few moments to make sure everything's working properly.

DOWNHILL

If possible, position the car so that it's pointing down a hill, or at least on level ground. Switch the ignition on, and make sure all electrical accessories are switched off. Put the engine in 1st or 2nd gear, depress the clutch pedal fully with your foot and then release the brake.

PUSH

Once you've released the brake, signal to your helper(s) to push the back of the car with all their might. Don't try pushing the car on your own and jumping in to push start it; people have been run over doing this. Find someone to help. And remember, the faster the car is going, the more likely the engine is to start.

FIND THE SOURCE

Make sure you find the source of the problem. If it's because the lights were left on overnight, you can recharge the battery by driving the car around for about 25 minutes. If the battery goes dead repeatedly, it probably means that it needs replacing or there's a problem with the car's alternator or possibly the fan belt.

HOW TO CHANGE A TIRE

Thump-a-thump-a-thump-a-thump! Believe it or not, many people don't realize right away that they've got a puncture. If you're driving along and the steering becomes erratic and the car starts to bump on the road more than usual, then you've probably got a flat. Slow down immediately, switch on your emergency lights and pull over somewhere safe. The sooner you stop, the less damage there'll be. And ladies, don't bother asking a fella to help. This is one you can do yourselves, honest!

INDISPENSABLE THINGS

- Spare wheel
- Jack
- Wrench
- Large screwdriver (optional)

1 Park the car on level, firm ground, preferably with the punctured tire facing away from the road, and well clear of any traffic. Set your emergency triangle about 100ft. (30m) behind the car. For a manual, put the parking break on. If you've got an automatic, put it in "Park." Switch off the engine.

2 Check that you've got all the tools you need (see list on page 186). They'll probably be in the trunk with the spare wheel. If you can't find them, refer to the owner's manual. Get down on your knees and find the nearest jacking point. Make sure the jack fits and take a couple of turns with the handle.

3 Before jacking up the car fully, loosen the wheel's nuts slightly. If a hubcap or wheel cover is fitted, use the flat end of the wheel wrench or a large screwdriver to pry it off. Fit the wrench to one nut at a time and break it loose by turning it firmly counterclockwise. If you can't turn it by hand, use your feet.

4 Once you've loosened all the wheel nuts (not too much), use the jack to lift the side of the car until the punctured wheel is raised off the road. Now loosen the nuts completely and put them in a safe place. Remove the faulty wheel and put it in the trunk of the car.

5 Line the spare wheel up with the bolts and lift it into place. You may need to raise the car a little more with the jack to give sufficient clearance. Starting from the bottom, tighten the nuts first by hand, then with the wrench. Don't fully tighten them yet.

6 Let the car down fully and remove the jack. With the wheel held in place by the weight of the car, tighten the nuts as firmly as possible by hand. Start with any nut, then tighten the one opposite and finish the rest. Replace the hubcap or wheel cover and put away your tools. Don't forget to get the puncture mended!

TRAVEL & SPORTS

HOW TO HOOK UP JUMPER CABLES

A less stressful alternative to push starting a car with a dead battery is to connect it to another car. The idea is that you use the power from another car's battery to fire your engine. A set of jumper cables can be bought from any automobile parts store. Finding a friend who will donate their car for a few minutes might be a little harder.

- A donor car
- Jumper cables

RED CABLE

With both engines switched off, connect one end of the red cable to the positive terminal (marked with a "+") of the dead battery. Then connect the other end to the positive terminal of the donor battery, making sure you don't let it touch either car on the way.

POSITION THE CARS

Position the donor car so that the batteries are close together—but not so close that the cars touch, because this will create sparks.

BLACK CABLE

Connect one end of the black cable to the negative terminal (marked with a "−") of the donor battery and the other end to any exposed metal part of the other car (such as a bolt or metal bracket). This is safer than connecting it directly battery-to-battery.

START THE ENGINE

Once the leads are connected, start the engine of the donor car and run it at a fast idle speed. Let it run for a minute or so before starting the engine of the other car. Let your engine run for a few minutes before switching off the engine of the donor car and disconnecting the cables in exact reverse order.

HOW TO FIX A SQUEAKY FAN BELT

Does your car sound like it's got a squeaky mouse under the hood? Sounds cute, doesn't it? Trouble is, it's probably the fan belt squeaking, which could signal problems further down the line. In any case, the novelty is liable to wear off, and pretty soon you'll be thinking of ways to get rid of the mouse. Here's some tips on how to do it.

INDISPENSABLE THINGS

- Lubricant (talcum powder, wax, soap)
- New fan belt

TOO OLD?

Fan belts also squeak when they're old and the rubber has become hard, cracked or frayed. If that's the case, you'll need a new one. It's easy enough to do yourself, with the help of a car repair manual, or your local mechanic should be able to fix it in a jiffy.

TOO LOOSE OR TIGHT?

A squeaking fan belt usually means it's either too loose or too tight. Use the owner's manual to locate the fan belt, and press it (with engine switched off) to check how much "play" it has. It should have about 1in. (2cm)—much more or much less and you should have it adjusted.

LUBRICATE

A temporary solution is to rub some lubricant on the inside edge of the fan belt. What lubricant? Well, suggestions range from talcum powder to candle wax, but most mechanics will tell you to steer clear of oil because this will only encourage the belt to slip. Our advice? A good old-fashioned bar of soap.

TRAVEL & SPORTS

HOW TO SERVICE A BICYCLE

Riding a bike with squeaky brakes, rusty chain and jumping gears is not much fun. On the other hand, paying for someone to repair it can cost more than the price of a new bike. The solution is to service your bike yourself. Just a few minutes a month of washing off the mud and oiling the moving parts can save you hundreds. Even adjusting the brake pads isn't that difficult, once you know how.

👉 PRACTICAL TIPS

Keep your bike running smoothly by washing it whenever it becomes dirty to prevent any buildup; wiping all exposed metal with an oily rag, using bike oil (not WD-40); keeping your tires pumped up to avoid excess wear; and servicing it regularly.

INDISPENSABLE THINGS

- Pump
- Chain lubricant
- Cloth or rag
- Bike oil
- Spray lubricant
- Wrench or hex key

1 Check your tire pressure once a week. Squeeze the sides of the tires. If they squeeze together easily, the tire needs pumping up. Don't squeeze the outer face, because that is more rigid and will disguise low air pressure.

2 Check what type of valve your bike has. A Presta valve is very slender and has a locknut, which will need to be undone before you start pumping. A Schrader valve looks like a car tire valve and doesn't need unlocking. Pump the tires up until the sides are firm, but not rock hard. If you pump them up too much, they may burst.

3 You should oil your chain once a month. Most experts advise against using spray oils, such as WD-40, and recommend specially made chain lubricant. Turn the pedals backward and apply the lubricant until the chain is covered in a thin layer. Wipe off any excess with a rag.

4 Oil the joints of the front and rear gear mechanisms (known as derailleurs). Oil the brake and gear cables, changing gear and applying the brakes to expose more cable. Use a special spray lubricant (not WD-40) that can be sprayed into the cable housing. Wipe off any excess with a rag.

5 Brakes become less effective in time, because cables stretch and brake pads wear down. Most bikes have an adjusting barrel between the brake lever and the cable housing and/or between the brake and the cable housing. Turn either one counterclockwise to increase brake tension.

6 Check that the brake pads are at the right height. They should touch the rim of the wheel, not rub on the tire or hang over the rim. Ideally, the leading edge (nearest the front of the bike) should be "toed," or angled slightly in, to prevent squeaking. Use a wrench or hex key to adjust accordingly.

TRAVEL & SPORTS

HOW TO FIX A BICYCLE PUNCTURE

You can go for years without a puncture, and then get three in a row. However, that's no excuse to forget your bike in the garage! With just a few basic tools, you can mend it and be back on the road in no time. It's cheaper than taking it to the bike shop—and so much more satisfying. Mending a puncture is also an excellent way to familiarize yourself with your bike and check that everything is functioning properly—from the brakes to the ball bearings.

INDISPENSABLE THINGS

- Spanner (possibly)
- Pen, lever or wrench
- Pump
- Bucket of water
- Puncture repair kit: rubber patches; rubber vulcanizing solution (glue that sticks rubber together); small piece of sandpaper

☞ INDISPENSABLE WARNING

Don't forget to reconnect the brakes before you ride off.

1 Take off the wheel. Release the brakes by squeezing the pads together and unhooking the cable. Turn the bike upside down. If it is fitted with quick-release wheels, simply open the lever and lift the wheel out. If the bike doesn't have quick-release wheels, use a wrench to undo the nuts on either side of the axle.

2 Let all the air out of the tube. Insert a lever between the rim and the tire, pry the tire away from the rim and hook the end of the lever onto a spoke. Repeat this process with another lever and keep on going until you can pull the tube out. Be careful not to pinch the tube with the levers.

3 Pump up the tube and listen for escaping air. If that doesn't work, feed it into a bucket of water and watch for bubbles. Mark the leak with a pencil and roughen the area with sandpaper. Once the tube's dry, apply a thin layer of glue and wait until it's touch-dry. Peel off the protective film on the patch and press it into place.

4 To reinstall the tube, inflate it slightly to prevent it from getting pinched. Insert the valve into its hole and slide the tube into the rim. Push the tire bead over the edge of the rim with your thumbs, starting at the valve and working your way round. Only use a lever if you have to. Once the tire is in place, refit the wheel and pump the tire up to normal pressure.

A PRACTICAL HISTORY OF WHEELS

The earliest depiction of a wheeled vehicle is on a vase dating back to c.3500 B.C.E. The oldest wheel in existence was discovered in Slovenia and is thought to be at least 6,000 years old. The first "modern" bike was the Rover Safety Bicycle created by English inventor John Kemp Starley in 1885. Some 1.4 billion bikes are now in existence. The inventor of the modern automobile was Karl Benz, who patented his first combustion engine in 1879 and his first car six years later. There are currently more than 590 million cars in the world.

HOW TO KEEP THE KIDS ENTERTAINED ON A LONG CAR JOURNEY

Computer games and iPods have taken much of the stress out of long car journeys with the kids. However, even those can lose their interest after a while—and, besides, family activities are so much more fun.

INDISPENSABLE THINGS

- **Puzzle books**
- **Plenty of snacks**
- **Music compilation**
- **Note pad and pens**
- **Regular stops**
- **Patience of a saint**

SONGS
You can't beat a good sing-along to lift the spirits. Print out the lyrics of old favorites from the Internet before you leave, or make a CD compilation. Even teenagers can't stop themselves singing along to ABBA!

WORD ASSOCIATION
Someone says a word, the next person says the first word it brings to their mind and so on around the car. For example, "White," "Black," "Knight," "Sword." Players can challenge if the association isn't clear.

MAPPING
Before you leave, print out a map of your route and highlight the major towns you'll be passing through for the kids to cross out as you drive past. Better still, write a list of place names for them to check off.

ALPHABET GAMES
Take turns to compile a list of shopping items using words starting with the letters of the alphabet. For example, one persons says, "I went to the grocery store and bought apples," and the next person says, "I went to the grocery store and bought apples and bananas," and so on.

LICENSE PLATE GAM
Get your children to writ down the letters of license plate and to mak as many words as possib out of them (for exampl "POR" becomes "pork "export," and so or For older kids and adult see who can be the fir to think of a word—th sillier the bette

FUN & GAMES

Wouldn't life be boring if we just sat
around all day working and watching
television? Learning to have fun is one
of the most important life skills. And
it's no good saying you don't know how
to sail a boat or do an ollie or play
roulette—we'll show you how.

HOW TO ROW A BOAT WITH ONE OAR

You've taken your girl/boyfriend for a row on the lake to impress them with your rowing prowess. Halfway across, you lean over to give him/her a romantic kiss. Mmmwaah! When you open your eyes, one of the oars has slipped into the water and is drifting toward the duck pond. Without hesitation, you swing the remaining oar over the back of the boat and save the day by practicing your newly acquired art of sculling. He/she is duly impressed, you row back to shore and live together happily ever after.

INDISPENSABLE THINGS

- Oar
- Relaxed wrists

☞ PRACTICAL TIP

Rowing with two oars? Easy! Hold the handles so the blades are a hand's width above the water. Lean forward and dip the blades in the water. Push your body back and pull the oars toward you. Lift the blades out of the water and repeat!

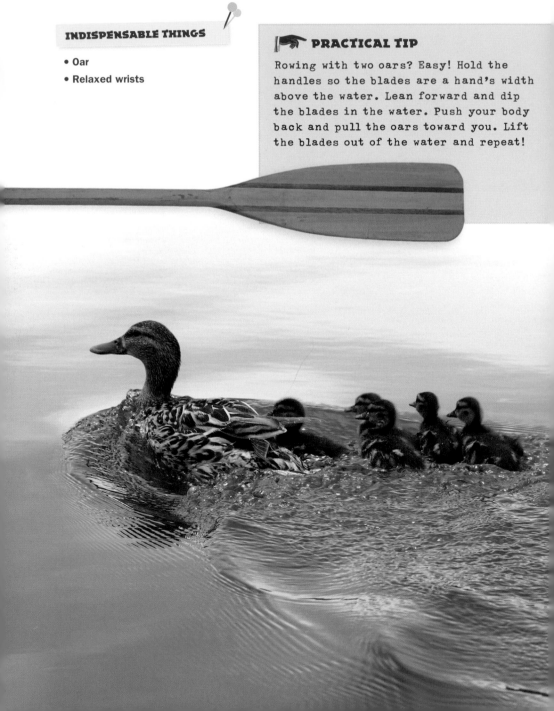

MOVING THE OAR

As you move from left to right, your hand makes a figure-eight movement, with the blade of the oar moving like the tail of a fish. It's one of those things that's more complicated to explain than it is to do. Everything will become clear once you have an oar in your hand.

HEAVY & NARROW

The best boat for sculling is heavy and narrow. A light boat (such as an inflatable dinghy) provides too little leverage, and the back gets thrown from side to side.

ADVANTAGE

Sculling has several advantages over rowing with two oars. For starters, the oar never comes out of the water, which means there is less wind resistance when you row into a strong wind. If towing another boat, it also provides a steady pull and prevents the rope jerking suddenly.

NOTCH

With luck, the boat will already have a notch cut into the back that the oar will fit into. If not, hopefully you planned in advance and have fitted an extra oarlock (the metal crutches that hold the oars) where the notch should be. It will need to be offset if you use an outboard engine.

SWEEP & PIVOT

Note how the depressed, or deepest, edge of the blade cuts a path in the water. As you reach the end of that sweep, push your wrist downward and your knuckles up, and push the oar to your left. Again, note how the deepest edge of the blade cuts the water. When you reach the end of that sweep, pivot the oar back to its original position and repeat the process.

ANGLING

Run the oar over the back of the boat and into the water at an angle of about 45 degrees, resting it in the notch. Facing the back of the boat, grip the handle with your right hand, wrist raised, knuckles down, elbow slightly lowered. Lever the oar against the notch by pulling it firmly to your right.

HOW TO SAIL A BOAT

Oh no! The captain's fallen over the side, the mate's in bed with dysentery and the deckhand fell in love with a *señorita* and jumped ship. There's only you left to sail the boat safely back to port. Mustering all your courage, you lick your finger and stick it up in the air. The air cooling one side of your finger instantly tells you which way the wind is blowing, and you're ready to take command. "Splice the mainbrace!" you shout, as you grab the helm.

☞ PRACTICAL TIP

Check that you know the direction of the wind . . . it's usually at right angles to the waves.

INDISPENSABLE THING

• A steady wind

1 Make sure the boat is pointing into the wind. For example, the "pointy" front end of the boat should point in the direction the wind is coming from. This is like being in "neutral" and means that when the sails are raised, the boat won't go running off.

2 Uncover the mainsail and find the halyard. The mainsail is the big sail attached to the back of the mast, and the halyard is the rope that hoists the mainsail to the top of the mast. Check the sail is unhindered and pull it up as far as it will go.

3 On most modern boats, there is a sail attached to a roller at the front of the boat. This is called the genoa, and it's controlled by two ropes on either side of the boat called genoa sheets. Unfurl the genoa by releasing the roller and pulling on one of the genoa sheets.

4 Check the wind direction. In order to move, the boat must be at an angle of about 45 degrees or more to the wind. Once you've decided which direction you're going, make sure the genoa is on the opposite side of the boat from which the wind is blowing.

5 Set a course at 45 degrees to the wind and adjust the genoa sheets until the sail stops flapping. The angle of the mainsail is controlled by a rope at the back of the boat called the mainsail sheet. Adjust this until the front edge of the sail stops flapping. Keep a steady course!

6 To change direction, ease out the sails as you head away from the wind. If you need to go the other way, let go of the genoa sheet and turn the boat until the wind is on the other side and the boat is again pointing at least 45 degrees to the wind. Make sure the genoa is on the other side of the mast, and adjust the sheets again.

TRAVEL & SPORTS

HOW TO DO THE FRONT CRAWL

It's great to be able to do the breaststroke, but you can only really swim once you can do the front crawl. It's not only faster and more efficient than any other swimming stroke, it also looks more impressive. Practice it in a quiet corner of the pool, when no one's watching. Start with just the arms and, once you've established a rhythm, the legs will follow. Pretty soon you'll be swimming in the lanes with the best of them.

INDISPENSABLE THINGS

- A straight body line
- Measured breathing
- Swimsuit
- Goggles

LEGS

Use the "flutter" kick, keeping your legs close to the surface of the water. Kick from the hips, bending your knee slightly going down and straightening for the up kick. Keep your ankles loose and your toes pointed. Use short, fast kicks.

A PRACTICAL HISTORY OF THE CRAWL

The superiority of the front crawl was proven beyond doubt when a group of Native Americans took part in a swimming competition in London in 1844. Although the stroke had been used for centuries in the Americas, it was unknown in Britain, where the breaststroke still prevailed. The Native American swimmers duly thrashed their European competitors. Because the front crawl entailed a considerable amount of splashing, however, the British considered it barbaric and stuck with their breaststroke until the 1870s.

ENTRY

Plunge your hand into the water directly in front of your shoulder, with the elbow slightly flexed and palm facing outward. Turn your palm down, as you stretch your arm forward.

DOWNSWEEP

Flex your arm at the elbow and sweep down until the hand is facing directly backward. As the arm sweeps up, extend the arm slightly (not completely) and move your hand backward, outward and upward. Think about your thumb touching your thigh as it exits the water. As your hand comes out of the water, move it forward, keeping your elbow high and your hand close to your body.

BODY

Swim with your body close to the surface of the water and keep your movements long and narrow. Imagine you are swimming through a tube and are not allowed to touch the sides. Do your best not to splash.

BREATHING

Turn your face down and forward. Your line of vision should be like the headlights on a car. When your arm is in recovery mode, turn your head into the triangle of your arm and the water, and take a breath. The "hollow" created by your bow wave will create a space for you to breathe. Raise your head as little as possible.

HOW TO DO THE BUTTERFLY STROKE

It might look like a lot of effort for not very much gain, but the butterfly stroke is undeniably cool. It also has the fastest peak speed of any swimming style—although, because of the long recovery time in between strokes, its average speed is slightly slower than the front crawl. Still, 2.177 meters per second (4.87mph/7.84kph) isn't anything to sneeze at. Unless you breathe in at the wrong moment and get a lungful of water. Try it next time you're in an empty swimming pool.

INDISPENSABLE THINGS

- Undulating body
- Swimsuit
- Goggles

A PRACTICAL HISTORY OF THE BUTTERFLY STROKE

The origins of the butterfly stroke are disputed. According to one version of the story, David Armbruster and Jack Seig, both from the University of Iowa, developed the butterfly breaststroke and the dolphin kick independently in the 1930s. They then combined their discoveries to create what we now know as the butterfly stroke. Another version of the story suggests that Jack Stephens, of Belfast, Northern Ireland, invented the elements of the stroke some 30 years before Armbruster and Seig. Either way, it was regarded as a variant of the breaststroke until 1952, when it was finally recognized as a style in its own right. It achieved Olympic recognition in 1956, when separate categories were created for the male and female 100-meter butterfly.

1 Extend the arms forward, thumbs down, shoulder-width apart. Your feet should be close together, like a fish's tail, legs straight. Kick your legs to get started.

2 Sweep your hands down and out, to create a "Y" shape, scooping the water with your palms. Keep your head down.

3 Bring your hands together under your belly to complete a keyhole shape. Bend your legs to prepare for the big kick.

4 Kick back strongly and point your feet down. As your body surges forward, streamline your arms by the side of your body, ready to fling them forward. Raise your head and breathe!

5 While your body still has forward momentum, throw your arms forward over the water in a wide arc. Kick your legs and repeat the process, undulating your body in time with your arms and legs.

TOP SWIMMING SPEEDS

- FRONT CRAWL 2.349m/s (5.254mph/8.4kph)
- BUTTERFLY 2.177m/s (4.87mph/7.84kph)
- BACK STROKE 2.0433m/s (4.57mph/7.35kph)
- BREASTSTROKE 1.839m/s (4.115mph/6.6kph)

TRAVEL & SPORTS

HOW TO MAKE A RAFT

It must be every child's dream to build a raft and paddle across the local pond/river/ocean. The trouble is, you'll probably upset the neighbors if you start chopping down trees to make your dream raft. Besides, have you ever tried lifting half a ton of unseasoned lumber onto a car roof rack? Here's an ingenious idea that saves the trees, uses up those plastic bottles that you keep forgetting to recycle and creates a raft that is genuinely unsinkable. Eat your heart out, Noah!

INDISPENSABLE RAFTS

In 2006, two MIT students built a raft using 129 empty bottles of Gatorade energy drink. It took them a year to collect the bottles, during which they drank 90 gallons (340 liters) of Gatorade. The finished raft used 64.5 gallons (244 liters) worth of bottles and carried their combined weight of 260lb (118kg) across Lake Charles, Massachusetts.

INDISPENSABLE THINGS

- Empty plastic bottles and lids
- Duct tape
- Broom handle
- A snack in case you get lost!

BOTTLE SIZE

You can use almost any size of bottle, but the smaller they are, the more you'll need and the more taping you'll have to do. Those gallon (5-liter) water bottles are ideal, or those sturdy 2-quart (2-liter) bottles that certain brands of carbonated drinks come in. If you're mixing different-size bottles, make sure the bigger bottles are at the center, with the smaller bottles attached to them in decreasing order of size. Save some sturdy bottles for the outermost layer, which will take the most knocks.

HOW MANY?

The number of bottles you need will depend on the number of people you're going to carry. If you allow about 1 quart (1 liter) of buoyancy per 1lb (450g) of weight, you should have ample buoyancy. Alternatively, a simple 10 x 10 grid of 1½-quart (1.5-liter) water bottles (100 bottles) will comfortably carry one adult.

MAKING THE RAFT

Tape the bottles together to create "cells" that you then join together to create bigger cells, until they are all taped together to make the raft. Start by taping two bottles together to make the first cell; then tape two pairs of bottles together to make a four-bottle cell; then tape two sets of four together to make an eight-bottle cell, and so forth. Make sure the bottles are upright, with lids firmly secured. Reject any bottles without lids. Use duct tape—don't settle for less.

MAKING THE PADDLE

A paddle can be made from a 3-quart (3-liter) plastic bottle cut in half down its length and taped to the end of a broom handle.

HOW TO DO AN OLLIE

Skateboard culture has been sweeping the world since the mid-1970s. The latest estimate puts the total number of users at 18.5 million, mostly under the age of 18. But why let the kids have all the fun? Practice on your offspring's skateboard while they are at school and—once you've worked out how to stay on it—try an ollie. It's the basic trick that every skateboarder has to master, and it will impress the kids to no end.

INDISPENSABLE THINGS

- Skateboard
- Sneakers or flat, rubber-soled shoes
- Padded clothing and gloves

A PRACTICAL HISTORY OF THE OLLIE

The ollie was invented in 1979 by Alan "Ollie" Gelfand, a Florida skateboarder, as a skate-park trick and later adapted for freestyling. The official record for the highest ollie is held by Danny Wainwright from England, who jumped 44in. (113cm)—although an unofficial video shows Peruvian skateboarder Jose Marabotto reaching an estimated 50in. (127cm).

1 This is your starting position. The front foot is placed about two-thirds of the way along the board, in between the middle of the board and the front truck, or wheels. The ball of the rear foot is resting on the tail.

2 Crouch down as low as you can. Basically, the lower you crouch, the higher (and, therefore, more impressive) your ollie will be. If you're worried about doing this on the move, practice first on grass—you'll have a softer landing anyway!

3 Strike the tail of the board on the ground as hard as you can, at the same time jumping up from your rear foot. Getting the timing of this move right is crucial, so you might want to practice it a little before moving on to the next step.

4 As you push off with your rear foot, roll your front foot and slide it up the board, raising your knee right up to your chest. The friction of the shoe against the griptape (the gritty layer on top of a skateboard) lifts the board higher and lets you guide it into position.

5 Raise your rear foot and, as you reach the top of your ollie, level the board under both feet. Once you start to get the timing right, it will all turn into one continuous move, with the board hovering under your feet as if it's being held by a magnet.

6 You can't defy gravity forever. As you come down, make sure your knees are bent. This will absorb the shock of landing and help you keep the board under control. Injuring yourself while trying to impress your kids is not cool.

HOW TO DIVE

Diving is easy, right? So why is it that, instead of the beautiful, elegant dive we imagine we're going to perform, we usually end up doing an ungainly belly flop? According to the experts, it's all due to that first push. Here are some step-by-step instructions that will ensure that the next time you dive, you'll cut the water like a knife—instead of bombing it like an elephant.

INDISPENSABLE THINGS

- Deep water
- Streamlined body

PRACTICAL TIP

Guys, if you really want to make an impressive dive, you'll have to sacrifice fashion. Those baggy swimming shorts really slow you down underwater. Buy a natty pair of Speedos or other tight-fitting swimming trunks. They're all the rage in Brazil.

1 Think. Check that you've got enough water before you dive. A general rule of thumb is that the water should be at least twice the height of the person diving. The higher you start from, the deeper the water should be. About 1,000 people a year in the US alone suffer from spinal cord injuries from diving into shallow water*—don't be one of them.

2 Stretch your arms in the air, palms facing downward, so that your biceps squeeze your ears. Bend your legs slightly—but don't bend your head.

* ThinkFirst National Injury Prevention Foundation & the North American Spine Society, quoted by the Mayfield Clinic of Cincinnati.

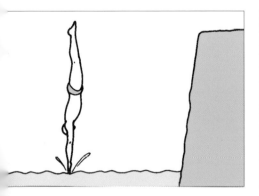

3 Lean forward. Just before you start falling, push off with your feet. Judging when to push is crucial because it will determine the angle of your trajectory: push too soon, and you can dive straight down and hurt your backside; push too late and you'll end up doing a belly flop.

4 A good push off at the right angle will raise your feet and legs and ensure that the top half of your body leads the dive. Follow an imaginary arc with your body, keeping your legs and hands together.

5 Make sure that your hands hit the water first to reduce the impact of the water on your head. It can be surprisingly painful if you misjudge it! Keep your body as straight and as streamlined as possible to avoid making a splash.

6 Once you're in the water, keep your body stretched out and arch your back backward to steer toward the surface. If you've gone too deep, don't panic; open your eyes and swim up toward the light.

HOW TO MAKE A KITE

Kites originated in China, where they were first flown some 2,800 years ago. Nowadays, stunt kites can easily cost more than $300 apiece, but you can have as much fun with a cheap kite made from bamboo skewers and plastic bags. You can get the kids to decorate it, and you won't worry so much when it (inevitably) gets tangled up in a tree.

INDISPENSABLE THINGS

- 2 bamboo skewers
- Electrical tape or thread
- 1 balloon stick
- Plastic garbage bag
- Felt-tip pen
- Straightedge
- Insulation tape
- Plastic shopping bags
- Fish netting line
- Scissors

JOINING THE SKEWERS

To join the bamboo skewers together, overlap them by about 3–4in. (8–10cm) and secure them with electrical tape or thread. The crosspiece skewers should be joined with a 2in. (5cm) length of balloon stick or similar to let you bend the joint slightly and create a "dihedral" (curved wing) effect. Very sophisticated!

MAKING THE SAIL

To turn a garbage bag into a sail, first cut it open and spread it out on the work surface. Lay the frame on top of it and mark out its extremities using a felt-tip pen. Join the points together with a straightedge and cut out the sail. Lay the frame over the plastic and secure the extremities with strips of insulation tape folded over each corner. Make sure the sail is stretched tightly over the frame.

MAKING THE TAIL

You can make a tail out of old shopping bags by cutting the bags in horizontal strips to create plastic rings. Loop the rings together until you have a tail four times the length of the kite.

MAKING THE FLYING LINE

Fish netting line makes ideal kite flying line. Make a harness by tying one length of string from top to bottom and another from side to side, leaving a little slack. Attach the flying line where the two cross. You'll need about 100ft. (30m).

HOW TO SKIP STONES

Stone skipping (or skimming) is a serious business, as the many competitors who traveled to Scotland for the 2008 World Stone Skimming Championships will testify. Finding the right stone is crucial, but after that it's all about technique. Here's how to beat the current Guinness World Record of 5I skips.

ANGLE
The optimum angle for skipping is 20 degrees. The faster the stone hits the water and the more spin it has, the farther it will go. Technique is more important than brute force; don't let your enthusiasm compromise the correct angle.

SMOOTH & CALM
The stone should be smooth and flat with well-rounded edges, and it should fit comfortably in the palm of your hand. What's more, it's best if the water is calm.

SKIPS
After extensive research, French scientist Lydéric Bocquet concluded that the maximum number of skips can be achieved by throwing a stone at an angle of 20 degrees, a speed of 39ft. (12m) per second and a spin of 14 revolutions per second.

TRAVEL & SPORTS

INDISPENSABLE THINGS
- Smooth, flat stone
- Calm water

THROWING THE STONE
Hold the stone between your index finger and your thumb, with your other fingers loosely curled under it. Stand sideways to the water and curl your hand in toward your body. Snap your wrist and arm out at the same time, releasing the stone when your arm is fully extended. It's a bit like throwing a Frisbee.

HOW TO JUGGLE THREE BALLS

If you can't wriggle your ears or make your eyes look in opposite directions, then juggling is a good substitute as a party trick. Anyone can do it. It's just a matter of persistence. Start with one ball, then add another, and another, and pretty soon you'll be juggling a whole crate of oranges. And if you can already wriggle your ears and make your eyes look in opposite directions, then juggling at the same time will impress your friends even more.

🖐 PRACTICAL TIP

If you don't have beanbags, you can try juggling tennis balls—although they are liable to bounce away when they're dropped. Some fruit works well, and if you practice on grass, it's less likely to get bruised when/if you drop it.

INDISPENSABLE THINGS

- Juggling balls
- Beanbags or fruit if you don't have juggling balls

A PRACTICAL HISTORY OF JUGGLING

The earliest evidence of juggling is on an ancient Egyptian tomb painting dating from c.1994–1781 B.C.E., which shows a line of dancers throwing balls. The pastime is still commonly practiced in many Pacific islands, especially Tonga, where most schoolgirls learn to juggle at least four tui-tui nuts at a time. The record for beanbag juggling, as recognized by the International Jugglers' Association's Numbers Competition, is 10 beanbags for 23 catches, performed by Bruce Sarafian in 2001.

1 Practice first with one ball. Beanbags are ideal for beginners because they don't roll away when dropped, but try also tennis balls, fruit and chainsaws (just kidding!). Start with the dominant hand, throw the ball in an arc to eye height and keep your elbows tucked in.

2 Try it with two balls now. Start with one ball in each hand, and throw the ball in your dominant hand (ball 1) in an arc. When it reaches eye height, toss the ball in the subordinate hand (ball 2) *under* ball 1. Catch the balls and stop. Repeat the exercise, starting with the opposite hand.

3 Now for the real thing: juggling three balls. Hold two balls (balls 1 and 3) in your dominant hand and one (ball 2) in the subordinate hand. Throw the front ball in your dominant hand (ball 1) in an arc.

4 When ball 1 reaches the top of its arc (such as your eye height), you need to throw ball 2 *under* ball 1, and then catch ball 1 with your subordinate hand.

5 When ball *2* reaches the top of its arc, throw the remaining ball in the dominant hand (ball 3) *under* ball 2. You can make things easier by rolling ball 3 down onto your fingers before throwing it. Catch ball 2 with your dominant hand.

6 When ball 3 is at the top of its arc, toss ball 1, which is now in your subordinate hand. Keep going! Don't be discouraged if you drop the balls. Even Marcel Marceau dropped his balls to start with.

HOW TO SHUFFLE A PACK OF CARDS

Can you do the Hindu shuffle? Or even the Corgi, Faro or Mongean shuffles? Nor can most people. There are dozens of ways of shuffling cards, all of which have the same objective: to rearrange the pack in a random order. But if there's one shuffle you should learn it's the riffle shuffle. Not only does it look good, it's surprisingly easy.

INDISPENSABLE THINGS

- Pack of cards
- Table (or lap)

1 Divide the pack into two roughly even piles. Hold one pile in each hand, facing downward, with the thumbs gripping the ends. Lever the ends up with your thumbs and line them up so that your thumbs are nearly touching.

2 Riffle the cards together by slowly sliding your thumbs up the edge of each pile, alternating between piles if possible (in practice, this will happen without you even trying). This can be done on a table or, with practice, on your knee.

3 Make sure the piles interlock enough to be secure. Now perform the cascade finish. Bend the cards together, pushing upward slightly with your fingers and using your thumbs to prevent them from spilling.

4 Square up the deck by tapping it gently on a hard surface. Shuffle again if necessary. You'll need to shuffle seven times to completely randomize the pack—although two or three times is usually sufficient for most purposes.

HOW TO SCORE IN TENNIS

"You have got to be kidding!" This famous exclamation by three-times Wimbledon champion John McEnroe sums up how many non-tennis people feel when someone tries to explain how to score the game. Yet, once you've accepted the concept of "love" being a valid score (or zero), it's all a matter of counting points.

SETS

A match is made up of several "sets" of games—up to five sets for men and three sets for women. The winner is the first to win more than half the sets, such as the first man to win three sets or the first woman to win two sets.

POINTS

Each game is made up of a number of points. The first player to win four points and be at least two points ahead of his/her opponent wins the game. The scoring sequence is as follows: 0 points = love; 1 point = 15; 2 points = 30; 3 points = 40. If both players reach 40, this is described as "deuce." The next player to win a point is said to have the "advantage." If this player wins the next point, he/she wins the game. If the other player wins the next point, the score returns to deuce, and they play on until one player has two clear points.

GAMES

Each set is made up of a number of games. The winner of each set is the first to win at least six games and be two games ahead of his or her opponent. If the score reaches 6–5, then another game is played. If the leading player wins this game, he/she wins the set by 7–5; if the trailing player wins this game, the score goes to 6–6 and a tiebreaker is played. The winner of the tiebreaker wins the set. In some countries, no tiebreaker is played in the final set of a match.

TRAVEL & SPORTS

HOW TO PLAY ROULETTE

Roulette has been around since the 17th century and is a lot more sophisticated than playing the one-arm bandits down the arcade. True, the pace is slower than craps or blackjack, which means you're likely to win less. On the other hand—and perhaps more realistically—it also means you'll have less time to lose all your money.

- Roulette wheel and layout
- Chips
- Roulette ball
- Dolly (winning number marker)

CHIPS

Special chips are used for roulette, with different colors for each player. At the end of the game, the chips are exchanged for regular casino chips, which can be exchanged for cash at the cage. Each table has a maximum and minimum bet.

INDISPENSABLE ROULETTE TABLE

Roulette is played at a long table with a wheel at one end, and a layout where the bets are placed. The wheel has 38 numbered slots (37 in the some countries), which correspond to numbers on the layout. The layout itself is made up of two parts: the "inside" area (usually red and black) and the "outside" area (usually green).

INSIDE BETS

Straight up: A bet on one number. Place your chip directly on the number. Pays 35:1.

Split: A bet on two numbers. Place your chip on thc linc between the two numbers. Pays 17:1.

Street: A bet on a row of numbers. Place your chip on the line at the end of a short horizontal row. Pays 11:1.

Corner: A bet on four numbers. Place your chip at the interjunction of the four numbers. Pays 8:1.

Double street: A bet on two rows of numbers (such as six in total). Place your chip on the line at the end of the short horizontal row, straddling two rows. Pays 5:1.

CROUPIER

A dealer (or croupier in Europe) spins the ball around the wheel. Once the ball has settled in a slot, the dealer places a marker (known as a "dolly") on top on the corresponding number on the layout and proceeds to collect the losing bets and pay out the winners.

ZERO

American roulette has an additional "00," which increases the odds in favor of the house. In some casinos, if the ball stops at "0" or "00" the "house" collects; in others, the "0" and "00" are treated as normal numbers, so check the house rules before you play.

OUTSIDE BETS

Red or black: A bet on the ball landing on either red or black. Pays 1:1.

Odd or even: A bet on the ball landing on either odd or even numbers. Pays 1:1.

1 to 18 and 19 to 36: Bets on the ball stopping at either set of numbers. Pays 1:1.

Dozens: Bets on the ball stopping at 1 to 12, 13 to 24, or 25 to 36. Pays 2:1.

Columns: Bets on the ball stopping at a number in one of the three long vertical columns. Pays 2:1.

HOW TO PLAY BLACKJACK

Blackjack has been around for at least 400 years and has become immensely popular in recent years thanks to the explosion in online gambling. So what is a blackjack, and do you need to get one to win the game? And why are you allowed to hit in the game, but you're not allowed to tap the table by mistake?

INDISPENSABLE THINGS

- Pack of cards
- 1–7 players
- Chips

THE CARDS

At start of play, each player receives two cards, face down if played with one pack, face up if played with two packs or more (the style at most casinos). The dealer also deals him- or herself two cards; one face up, the other face down. The 2–10 cards are valued at their face value, irrespective of suit or color. Face cards (jack, queen, king) are worth 10 points. Aces are worth 1 or 11 points, at the player's discretion.

BLACKJACK

Blackjack (also called 21) is played at a semicircular table, with a dealer and up to 7 players. Bets are placed before play begins, by putting chips in the designated spot in front of each player.

THE OBJECTIVE

The objective of the game is to beat the dealer by getting a higher score than him/her without going over 21. If either a player or the dealer goes over 21, they are "bust." Because one of the dealer's cards is hidden, you have to guess what his/her score is and play accordingly.

INDISPENSABLE OPTIONS

Once the first two cards are dealt, players have several options:

• BLACKJACK You receive an ace and a IO-point card, giving you 2I points—that is, a blackjack or a "natural"—and win. If the dealer also has a blackjack, it's a "push," and no one wins. If only the dealer has a blackjack, all the players lose.

• HITTING You want another card. Signal to the dealer by tapping the table with a card (or, if cards are face up, tapping the table).

• STANDING You are content with your hand and want to "stand." Signal to the dealer by sliding your cards under your bet (or, if cards are face up, by waving one hand horizontally).

• SURRENDER You give up your hand and lose half your bet.

• DOUBLING DOWN You double your bet by placing extra chips next to your original bet. You must now "hit," but you can do so only once.

• SPLIT HAND You have two identical cards, so you split them and play them as two hands. Place a second bet, equal to the first, next to the new hand.

• INSURANCE If the dealer's "up" card is an ace, you can make an additional bet, using half the chips you've already placed, that the "down" card is a ten. That way, if the dealer does get a blackjack, you have a consolation prize.

HOW TO CALCULATE ODDS

It's one thing to pretend you're James Bond in the casino, but if you don't understand odds, then you'll never outwit the bad guys. It's the same if you go to the races or gamble on your favorite football team. Thanks to our indispensable payouts table, you don't need to be a mathematician.

INDISPENSABLE ODDS

- **Killed in car crash: 1 in 5,000**
- **Struck by lightning: 1 in 700,000**
- **Killed in plane crash: 1 in 11 million**
- **Winning the lottery: 1 in 14 million**

ODDS AGAINST

Most odds are "odds against." That means the bookmaker is gambling on the probability of the event not happening. The number on the left is, therefore, bigger than the number on the right, for example, 5/2.

ODDS ON

"Odds on" means the bookie thinks the event is more likely to happen than not and is effectively challenging you to bet that it won't happen. The number on the right is bigger than the number on the left, such as 2/5.

INDISPENSABLE PAYOUTS

Payouts based on $10 (including original stake):

50/I	$510	5/I	$60	3/2	$25
35/I	$360	9/2	$55	7/5	$24
30/I	$310	4/I	$50	6/5	$22
20/I	$210	7/2	$45	I/I	$20
I7/I	$180	3/I	$40	4/5	$18
I5/I	$160	5/2	$35	3/5	$16
II/I	$120	2/I	$30	I/2	$15
I0/I	$110	9/5	$28	2/5	$14
8/I	$90	8/5	$26	I/5	$12
6/I	$70				

The basic formula to calculate the payoff is as follows:

$$\frac{(\text{stake x first number in the odds}) + (\text{stake x second number in the odds})}{\text{second number in the odds}}$$

EVEN ODDS

"Even odds" means that the bookie will pay out the same amount as the person's bet. The numbers are the same on both sides, such as 1/1.

HOW TO WIN AT MONOPOLY

No one really takes Monopoly seriously, do they? Wrong! As anyone who's spent rainy Sunday afternoons in with their family knows, it is a vicious game played (if that's the right word) to the death. Learn the odds and never again be the one storming out of the room in a temper.

INDISPENSABLE ODDS

- **Monopoly board game**

HOT PROPERTIES

Collect orange and red properties. Because of their position on the board, they receive the most visitors and provide the best return on your investment. Don't bother with blue, yellow and green—unless it prevents your opponents from completing a set. Buy stations, avoid utilities.

GET OUT OF JAIL

Pay to get out of jail during the first part of the game, when you need to collect properties. Stay in jail later when moving around is riskier.

POPULAR SQUARES

The most visited squares on the board are: Illinois Avenue, New York Avenue, B&O Railway and Reading Railroad. The least visited are: Mediterranean Avenue and Baltic Avenue.

ODDS

Remember the odds. You are most likely to throw 7 and least likely to throw 2 or 12. The order of probability, with the most likely outcome first, is: 7, 6 and 8 (equally probable), 5 and 9, 4 and 10, 3 and 11, and 2 and 12. On average, it takes around five turns to get back to "Go."

HOUSES

The optimum number of houses to have is three. Create a housing shortage by building three or four houses on each property, instead of building hotels.

BUY

Buy as much as you can early in the game to build up your earning power quickly. Aim to complete as many sets as possible.

TRAVEL & SPORTS

HOW TO ROLL A JOINT

According to Bill Clinton, it's not necessary to inhale to enjoy marijuana, but how is a joint rolled? Just in case you find yourself in the company of a former US president and he asks for a demo, this is how it's done.

INDISPENSABLE THINGS

- Cigarette papers
- Herb of choice
- Card

INDISPENSABLE WARNING

The publisher does not condone illegal activity of any kind. Consumption of cannabis is illegal in most countries, including the US. Penalties for possession vary from state to state. Studies have found that excessive use of cannabis, particularly by young people, can increase the chances of mental illness.

1 Take a lump of your herb of choice and break it up into small fragments. Remove any bits of twig as they are not potent and create lumps. Put the seeds aside.

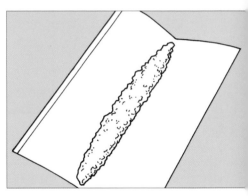

2 Sprinkle the herb down the center of the paper. If it's that stronger European herb, you'll need to thin it down with some tobacco—a 60:40 tobacco/herb ratio is recommended.

3 Roll a short length of thin cardboard into a cylinder to create a "roach" about ¾in. (2cm) long. The roach doesn't work as a filter, but it does prevent the end of the joint dissolving—saving every last bit of herb.

4 With the gum strip facing you, pick up the joint and roll it between your thumb and index finger. Once the contents feel firm, tuck the side nearest you under and roll the other side over it. Lick the gum strip and seal the joint.

IN THE WILD

There's no better way to put life back
in perspective than to spend a few days
living in the great outdoors. Leave behind
your camping gear and you'll learn
survival skills that will bring you even
closer to nature. And you never know
when you might need that.

HOW TO TIE A ROUND TURN & TWO HALF HITCHES

Pick up a book of knots and you'll find so many available
you might not know where to start. But, if you can learn
only one knot, learn this one. It's easy to tie, it can be
used in a multitude of situations and it's much stronger
than it might at first appear. Lash the loose, "working"
end to the "standing" part and it'll never come loose—
great for ocean liners, tow ropes and tree swings alike.

INDISPENSABLE RATINGS

- Strength rating: 4/5
- Security rating: 5/5
- Ease of tying: 4/5
- Ease of untying: 4/5

INDISPENSABLE USES

- Mooring a ship or dinghy
- Towing a broken-down car
- Climbing trees
- Hanging a clothes line
- Flying a kite
- Tight-rope walking

INDISPENSABLE KNOTS

No one knows how many knots exist in total,
but an astonishing 3,900 are listed in *The
Ashley Book of Knots*, the definitive tome
on the subject. In practice, most sailors
rely on about 10, which they use regularly.
Which 10 is a matter of debate (and personal
preference), but they are likely to include:
the figure-eight, the reef knot, the bowline,
the round turn and two half hitches, the
clove hitch, the rolling hitch and the sheet
bend. Top climbing knots include most of the
above plus the Prusik knot, the Klemheist
and the alpine butterfly.

Take a turn around the post, rail or whatever it is that will provide the anchorage for the rope. Note that the end of the rope actively involved in tying the knot is called the "working end," while the other extremity is the "standing end" and the part in between is the "standing part."

Pass the working end over and around the standing part, and tuck it under itself to form the first hitch. The number of turns and hitches you use depends on how great a load is being secured. Generally, more turns help spread the load, while more hitches prevent the knot from loosening.

Keep going in the same direction to create the second hitch. It's vital that the working end goes around the standing part in the same direction (clockwise or counterclockwise) for every hitch.

Once both hitches have been tied, tighten the knot by pulling the working end and the standing part in opposite directions. Any slack in the knot can be taken up either by pulling the standing part or feeding the slack through the hitches before final tightening.

HOW TO TIE A BOWLINE

There's something beautifully ingenious about a bowline. Of course, there are simpler ways to tie a loop, but the bowline is one of those clever knots that uses the strain on the rope to increase its strength—so the greater the load, the tighter the knot. And yet, no matter how tight it gets, it can always be undone. What's more, there's a simple trick for remembering how to tie it, which involves a rabbit, a tree and a hole.

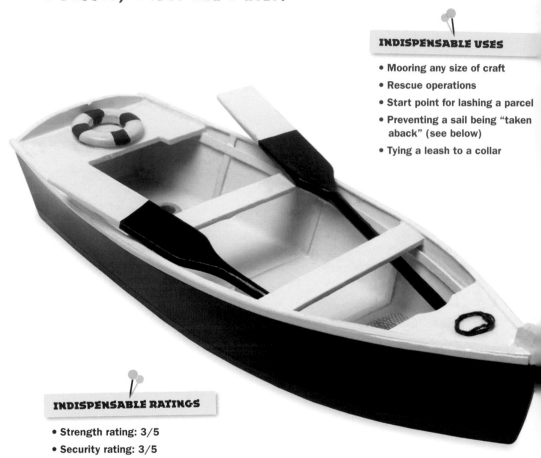

A PRACTICAL HISTORY OF THE BOWLINE

The bowline takes its name from its usage on the great square-riggers during the age of sail. A line was attached from the top of a square sail to the front, or "bow," of the boat to prevent the sail being blown from inside out—or, in nautical terms, being "taken aback." The earliest mention of the knot is in *A Seaman's Grammar* written by John Smith in 1627, which refers to a bowline being found in the rigging of the ancient Egyptian Pharaoh Cheops' "solar ship" during its excavation. The real age of the knot is therefore likely to be several thousand years.

1 Create a loop in the rope, making sure that the line nearest the "working end" (the active end of the rope) is on top of the loop. This is the rabbit hole, and the inactive, or "standing," part of the rope (at the top of the illustration) is the tree.

2 Pass the "working end" up through the loop. This is our rabbit popping up out of its hole to say hello.

3 Pass the "working end" around behind the "standing part." This is our rabbit running around the back of the tree.

4 Insert the "working end" back into the initial loop. This is our rabbit diving back down its hole—perhaps having seen an approaching fox.

5 To tighten the knot, pull the "working end" and the rope adjacent to it in the hole with one hand, while pulling on the standing part with the other hand. This is our rabbit snuggling down in its hole. To untie the knot, "break" it open by feeding the "standing" part through the top loop.

HOW NOT TO TIE A GRANNY KNOT

We've got nothing against grannies, but if you don't want your knot to come undone, then please don't use a granny knot. There's almost no difference between a granny and a proper square knot—except that one holds and one doesn't! Learn the difference and forever keep your shoelaces tied up and your mainsail reefed.

 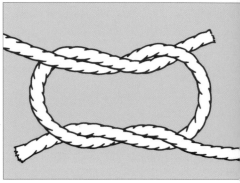

1 The simple rule to remember when you're tying this is: left over right followed by right over left (or vice versa, if you like—it will end up the same). Then pull the ends in opposite directions to tighten the knot. The key is that the working ends should come out snugly next to their adjacent "standing" parts, with a loop resting over both of them.

2 This is how NOT to do it. The granny knot is made by going left over right followed by left over right (or right over left followed by right over left). This results in the working ends coming out next to the opposite standing parts, which can lead to all kinds of trouble—from shoelaces coming undone to packages opening in the post and sails shaking loose. Heaven forbid!

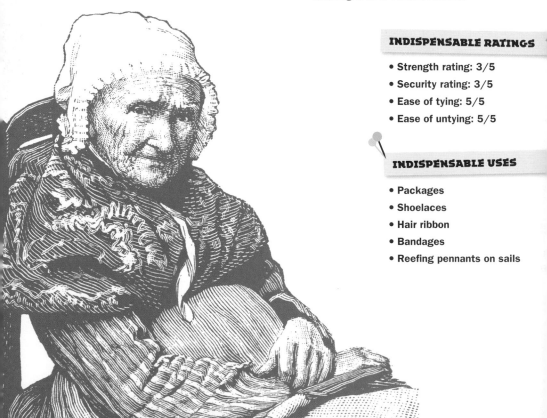

INDISPENSABLE RATINGS

- Strength rating: 3/5
- Security rating: 3/5
- Ease of tying: 5/5
- Ease of untying: 5/5

INDISPENSABLE USES

- Packages
- Shoelaces
- Hair ribbon
- Bandages
- Reefing pennants on sails

HOW TO TIE A ROPE HARNESS

Not everyone is happy to climb hand-over-hand down a rope—never mind up one. Lowering (or lifting) someone on a loop, such as a bowline, is one answer. An even better solution is a double-loop knot, such as the bowline in the right, where one loop can be used to support the person's backside and the other to support their chest.

INDISPENSABLE RATINGS

- Strength rating: 4/5
- Security rating: 5/5
- Ease of tying: 3/5
- Ease of untying: 3/5

INDISPENSABLE USES

- Rescue
- Climbing
- Child's swing
- Bosun's chair
- Hanging up bikes in the garage

1 First, make sure the rope is strong enough. Test it by hanging off a tree, where there's less chance of being seriously hurt if it breaks. Start the knot by doubling it—either just at one end or the whole thing. Then make a loop in the rope, allowing plenty of slack to make the "chair," and pass the doubled-up end of the rope up through the loop.

2 So far, much like an ordinary bowline, but this knot is even easier to tie than that. Simply open the doubled-up end and pass the large loop through it.

3 Once the doubled-up end has passed right around the loop, pull it down tight over the "standing" part to secure the knot. Before you finally tighten it, adjust the size of the two loops so that they pass around the thighs and chest.

HOW TO SPLICE ROPE

There are many ways to join two lengths of rope—nearly all of them much quicker and easier than splicing. But if you want a permanent joint that won't snag on things when the rope is in use and will be almost invisible, then a splice is the way to go. You'll also have the satisfaction of continuing a naval tradition that goes back to the 18th century and beyond. Please note this only applies to three-strand rope, and not to modern multistrand cordage.

INDISPENSABLE USES

- Sailing
- Climbing
- Tree swings
- Mooring lines
- Escape lines

INDISPENSABLE RATINGS

- Strength rating: 5/5
- Security rating: 5/5
- Ease of tying: 3/5
- Ease of untying: 3/5

A PRACTICAL HISTORY OF THE MAINBRACE

Braces are hefty ropes that were used to control the angle of the sails on a square-rigged sailing ship. The mainbrace is the heftiest of them all and, if damaged in battle, required considerable skill and effort to repair with a splice. A successful splice was often rewarded with an extra ration of rum and, in time, the expression "splice the mainbrace" became a euphemism for issuing a round of drinks. Bottoms up!

1 First, unlay the ends of both ropes by a few inches. Bring them together, so that the strands of one alternate with the strands of the other. If the ends continue to unravel, hold (bind) them with a short length of electric tape or twine.

2 When the two ropes are snugly entwined, secure the joint with a short length of electric tape or twine in order to prevent it from working loose while you are splicing. This tape can be removed once the splice is completed.

3 Pick any strand, pass it over the adjoining strand of the opposite rope and tuck it under the next strand. Work against the twist of the rope so that the strands are almost at right angles to one another.

4 Take the next untucked strand and pass it over and under the adjoining strand of the opposite rope, as before. Use a letter opener or similar (such as a marlin spike, if you've got one!) to tease the strands apart.

5 Take the remaining untucked strand and pass it over and under, as before. You should end up with three strands of one rope emerging between three strands of the opposite rope.

6 Take another tuck with each strand, before starting work on the untucked strands of the other rope. Keep going until each strand is tucked at least three times (four times for synthetic rope). Roll the splice underneath your foot, and trim the ends of the strands.

TRAVEL & SPORTS

HOW TO IGNITE A FLAME

Being able to light a fire when you're out in the wild can mean the difference between life and death. But what to do if your lighter has run out of lighter fluid and your matches have turned soggy? Rubbing steel wool against the terminals of a flashlight battery should produce a spark or two, and gunpowder from a bullet will quickly get a fire going. Or you can try more traditional methods.

INDISPENSABLE THINGS

- Length of wood
- Knife or rock for cutting
- Wooden spindle
- String
- Cane/wood for bow
- Wood, stone or bone for socket
- Tinder/bark (*see page 234*)
- Wooden shaft
- Flint
- Pocketknife (or other steel tool)
- Lens (from camera, binoculars, magnifying glass, spectacles)

1 A hand drill works best with dry, soft wood. Cut a V-shape notch in a board using a knife or rock. Stand a 2-ft. (60-cm) long spindle over the notch. Spin it between your hands, pressing down to increase the friction. Keep going until a red ember shows.

2 To speed up the process, string a bow and turn once around the spindle. Devise a socket in wood, stone or bone to hold the top of the spindle. Once you've got a rhythm, speed up and apply more pressure until an ember forms. Tap the ember into a piece of bark and transfer to the tinder. Blow into a flame.

THE FIRE PLOW is a neat alternative to the hand drill. This has the advantage of creating the tinder it then ignites. Cut a groove down a length of wood, and drag a wooden shaft up and down the groove, using the blunt tip to make wood shavings and create an ember. Blow to ignite the shavings.

FLINT AND METAL are hard to beat. Hold a piece of flint firmly in one hand, with a scrap of your favorite tinder placed on top of it. Strike it with a mild steel tool, such as a (closed) pocketknife, file or ax, until the tinder catches. It's possible to do this using stainless steel, but it's much harder to do so.

USE THE LENS of your binoculars, camera, magnifying glass or spectacles to light a fire—providing you have sun. Pile up your tinder and angle the lens so that the sun's rays are focused on one spot. Hold the glass steady until the tinder starts to smoulder. Blow into a flame.

HOW TO MAKE A CAMPFIRE

Lighting a fire outdoors without the benefit of fire lighters and a fireplace can be tricky—especially if it's raining. Here's a foolproof method that should give you a hearty fire on which to roast your freshly caught rabbit.

INDISPENSABLE THINGS

- Tinder
- Fuel

INDISPENSABLE MATERIALS

You'll need three types of material to light your fire—all should be as dry as possible. Avoid rotten or "green" wood.

- TINDER: This is the foundation of the fire and can be composed of twigs, wood shavings, leaves, bark, paper and pine needles.

- KINDLING: This is mostly small branches of softwood (such as pine) about I-2in. (3-5cm) in diameter, which should be broken up to fit inside the fire.

- FUEL: These are the large pieces of hardwood (such as oak) that keep the fire going. They should be about 3ft. (Im) long and as dry as possible.

CLEARING A SPACE

Clear a space at least 10ft. (3m) away from trees, tents and anything combustible, and make a ring of stones around it to provide a barrier. Have water on hand to put out the fire if it gets out of control.

LIGHTING THE FIRE

Place a handful of tinder in the middle of the fireplace, using the twigs to make a pyramid around it. Use the kindling to build a box around the tinder, overlapping the ends and making sure there are plenty of gaps to let the oxygen circulate. Place the fuel logs on either side of the box, and light the tinder (from the upwind side). The flames should spread from the tinder to the kindling to the fuel, creating a hot core of ashes as it goes

HOW TO BUILD A BIVOUAC SHELTER

You don't have to have a fancy tent to camp outdoors. Especially in summer, a simple bivouac will give you shade and protect you from rain, without blocking the view. All you need is a couple of tarpaulins, a length of rope, a saw, a knife—and a warm sleeping bag.

INDISPENSABLE THINGS

- **2 sheets of tarpaulin**
- **Rope**
- **Saw**
- **4–6 wooden stakes**
- **Knife**
- **Sleeping bag**

TREES

If you can, find a pair of trees about 9ft. (2.5m) apart, with clear, flat ground between them. Tie a line between them at chest height to make a ridge pole. If you can't find any suitable trees, cut two stakes, each with a Y at one end, and drive them into the ground. Use a branch stretched between them as a ridge pole.

CREATING THE SHELTER

Cut four stakes about 10in (25cm) long. Whittle one end into a point, so they can be driven into the ground more easily, and cut a notch at the other end to attach the tarpaulin string. Stretch the tarpaulin over the ridge pole, and drive a stake into the ground at each corner. Tie off the corners and lay a second tarpaulin on the ground. Now you've got a snug shelter.

LOCATION

Think about the location. If you camp too near the top of a hill, you'll be exposed to the elements; too far down a valley, you'll be cold and damp. Don't forget that heat rises.

TRAVEL & SPORTS

HOW TO MAKE A LATRINE

The call of nature is something no one can avoid, especially when camping. There are many ways of dealing with it, but probably the most hygienic is to build a latrine. At least that will save any unpleasant surprises. A latrine can be as fancy as you want, from a simple hole in the ground to a fully fledged shelter with washing area. If you're staying in one place for some time, remember that you'll need to move the latrine periodically when it becomes full.

INDISPENSABLE THINGS

- Burlap screen
- Spade
- Ash from the fire
- Wood shavings

CAT-HOLING

Some people believe that so-called "cat-holing" has less impact on the environment than building a latrine, because it spreads the feces over a wide area rather than concentrating it in one place. Making sure that you are at least 200ft. (60m) away from any water source, dig a hole about 6in. (15cm) square by 6in. (15cm) deep and squat over it. When you are done, stir in a little soil with a stick and fill the hole. However, this method is not recommended for large numbers of people camping in the same area.

CLEANING UP

Toilet tissue is generally acceptable, providing it is well buried after use. Alternatively, you can use nature's own toilet tissue—leaves, sticks (smooth ones!), stones or if you're camping in cold climes, snow. If you have toilet tissue, keep it in a sealed container or plastic bag to prevent it from getting soggy.

WET PIT

A properly equipped latrine should have a "wet pit" for urinating and a "squat pit" for defecating.

SCREEN

Screen off an area at least 200ft. (60m) away from your camp, your water source and any path or trail. A burlap screen is ideal, or get creative with some branches.

SQUAT PIT

The squat pit should be a rectangular trench about 3ft. (1m) long, 1ft. (30cm) wide and 2ft. (60cm) deep.

SOIL COVER

The dug-up soil is left next to the trench and used to cover the feces. When the pit has filled to within 4in. (10cm) from the top, it should be filled completely and camouflaged. A new trench can then be dug elsewhere.

LINING

The wet pit should be a shallow hole lined with stones or pebbles to help with drainage.

SURFACE DISPOSAL

Another method is surface disposal. This involves simply spreading the feces with a stick to speed up the process of decomposition. This should only be used in remote areas far away from human habitation and at least 200ft. (60m) away from your camp, water sources and trails.

ASH

Use ash from the campfire to cover the feces, and top it with a sprinkle of wood shavings to get rid of the smell.

HOW TO FIND WATER

The human body is made up of 60-75 percent water, depending on age and gender. We lose about 3 quarts (3.5 liters) of that a day through sweating and urination—more in the desert or if physically active—so finding water to replenish it is a priority in the wilderness. As for whether you should ever drink salt water, the jury's still out on that one, but you're probably safest avoiding it if you possibly can. They say it makes you go mad...

INDISPENSABLE THINGS

- Dew-covered foliage
- Plastic bags
- String
- Wood and pebbles, or large plastic container
- Sand
- Charcoal from fire (for purifying)

👉 PRACTICAL TIPS

- You need to drink between 2-3 quarts (2-3.5 liters) of water a day, depending on levels of heat and exertion.
- Don't eat ice or snow without melting it first. It will sap your energy.
- Don't eat without drinking. It will use up your bodily fluids.
- The maximum dew is just before sunrise.
- See where birds gather to drink, and follow animals' tracks to watering holes.

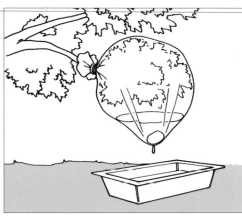

1 Look for obvious sources, such as rivers and streams. Check your map, and look at the landscape for clues. A crooked line of trees indicates there is probably a stream beneath. Get up early and collect the dew off (nonpoisonous) flowers and leaves. If it tastes funny, it's just that it doesn't contain the same minerals as stream water does.

2 Make a sun still (*see page 333*), or use the transpiration method. Put a clean rock in a plastic bag and, in the morning, tie it around the leafy branch of a tree (nonpoisonous). By evening, the perspiration of the tree will have collected in the lowest point of the bag, created by the rock. Prick a hole in the bag and collect the water.

3 If you're on a beach, dig a hole about 4ft. (1.2m) deep behind the first set of sand dunes—or about 100ft. (30m) from the sea. Put pebbles in the bottom of the hole and line the sides with wood—or insert a large plastic container with a hole in the bottom, if you have one. After a few hours, the cavity should fill with filtered water. If not, find a lower stretch of sand.

4 Filtering the water will remove sediment and improve the taste. Cut a hole in the bottom of a plastic bag, and fill it with alternate layers of rock and sand. Hang the bag from a tree, pour in the water and collect it in a container placed under the hole. Charcoal from the fire, if thoroughly washed, will help remove undesirable smells. Purify the water by boiling it for 10 minutes.

TRAVEL & SPORTS

HOW TO COOK WITHOUT UTENSILS

If you really want to commune with nature, leave the cooking utensils at home and cook straight over the fire. With a little imagination, most things can be skewered, baked or fried using organic utensils. Not only does it save you carrying cooking equipment around, but it also means no washing up!

INDISPENSABLE THINGS

- 2 Y-shaped stakes
- Sticks for skewering
- Large, flat stones
- Clay
- Fresh grass or leaves
- Half an onion
- Scooped-out orange peel

HOT COALS

Make sure the fire has burned down to hot coals without any large flames before you start cooking.

UTENSILS

Cut two stakes with Y shapes in one end and drive them into the ground on either side of the fire. Skewer anything you like: vegetables, chicken, wild boar—even eggs. Just prick a hole in either end of the egg, thread a thin skewer or string through it and hang over the fire for 20 minutes

ORGANIC EQUIPMENT

Place large, flat, nonporous stones in the middle of the fire and let them heat. Use them like a frying pan to cook meat, fish and eggs. Try covering vegetables in a thick layer of clay before placing them directly on the coals to cook. You can do the same with meat and fish, but first wrap them in (edible) fresh grass or leaves.

HOLE BAKING

Clear a space in the fire and dig a shallow hole in the ground. Place potatoes or washed corn (with leaves and silk) in the hole and bury. Relay the fire and let bake for 20 minutes for corn, 45 minutes for potatoes.

ORGANIC PAN

Cut an onion in half and scoop out all but the last two layers. Crack an egg into and place directly on the coals to cook. You can do the same with scooped-out orange either using an egg or bread/cake mixture

HOW TO DIG A PIT OVEN

It's a method that's been used for thousands of years and, if judged right, produces delicious results with minimal wastage and maximum nutrition. Pit ovens, also known as earth ovens, are holes in the ground into which you place hot coals and a large lump of meat or fish and leave to cook. Here's how it's done.

INDISPENSABLE THINGS

- Spade
- Hardwood for fire
- Flat, nonporous stones
- Edible leaves/grass to protect food
- Layer of soil
- Aluminum foil (optional)

DIG A HOLE

Dig a hole about three times the size of the item to be cooked.

LINING

Line the hole with flat, nonporous stones. Use the big ones to line the sides and spread the rest over the bottom.

LIGHT A FIRE

Light a fire inside the hole, using hardwood (such as oak or elm) if possible. Let the fire burn for 45 minutes or so, until it's reduced to coals.

WRAPPING

Wrap the food in edible leaves or aluminum. If you're using aluminum, you can lay the item straight on the coals. If not, clear the coals to the sides, put a layer of leaves on the hot stones and lay the wrapped item on the leaves.

LAYER OF LEAVES

Cover the food with another layer of leaves, sprinkle it with water to assist the steaming process and then place an animal hide, bark or carpeting over the food to protect it. Fill the hole with at least 4in. (10cm) of soil and let cook. About 1½ hours should suffice for a large fish, or 3–4 hours for a whole lamb.

TRAVEL & SPORTS

HOW TO CATCH A RABBIT

You've set up camp, built a latrine and found a supply of water. What you need now is a steady supply of fresh food. Rabbit meat is high in protein, as well as essential vitamins and minerals such as BI2 and iron. What's more, the little critters breed like, er, rabbits, so it's highly likely there will be a few hopping around nearby.

INDISPENSABLE THINGS

- 2 large empty cans
- Sharp knife
- Duct tape
- Length of string
- Gloves
- Length of wire
- Hinged wooden box
- Stick

PRACTICAL TIP

Bear in mind that the laws relating to trapping wild animals vary from state to state and country to country. Check before you trap.

SETTING A TRAP

Get two large empty cans and cut the bottom off one of them. Join them end-to-end with duct tape and place some enticing rabbit food in the bottom. Balance the trap on a stone so that, when the rabbit hops in for a nibble, it tips up and traps the bunny inside. Use a length of string to secure the trap to a high branch to stop it rolling over once the rabbit is inside.

LOCATION

Place your trap in an area regularly used by rabbits. Check for trails and droppings to find their favorite places. Keep your scent hidden by locating the trap elsewhere and wearing gloves while you are handling it. Mask your scent with wood smoke. Rabbits are crepuscular, which means they are most active around dawn and dusk.

MAKING A SNARE

Make a snare by bending a length of wire into a running loop (like a noose), and tie a length of string to the "standing" end of the loop. Find a place where the rabbit trail narrows, and secure the string to a nearby tree or bush. Place the snare about 3in. (8cm) off the ground and conceal it with twigs. When the rabbit pokes its head through the snare, the wire will tighten around its neck and trap it.

HUMANE TRAP

A more humane trap can be made from a simple box with a hinged lid. Place the box on its side and prop the lid open with a stick. Tie a piece of string to the stick, about 2in. (5cm) off the ground, and attach a carrot or other favorite rabbit food to the other end. Put the carrot in the box and wait for the rabbit to hop along for a nibble.

KILLING THE RABBIT

Kill the rabbit humanely. One of the most humane methods is a sharp blow to the head with a heavy object. Your aim should be to kill it quickly and to cause as little suffering as possible.

TRAVEL & SPORTS

HOW TO SKIN A RABBIT

Catching a rabbit is just the beginning of the process.
Next, you've got to skin and gut it. It's not a job for the
fainthearted, but if you're going to survive in the
wilderness, it's got to be done. And at the end of it you'll
have the satisfaction of knowing that you were involved
in the food-gathering process from start to finish, as
nature intended, rather than handing over all the messy
jobs to someone else.

INDISPENSABLE THINGS

- Cutting board
- Sharp knife
- Ax
- Strong stomach

☞ PRACTICAL TIPS

- About ¼ cup of animal blood contains
as much nutritional value as 10 eggs.
- Bone marrow is also rich in nutrients.
Crush the bones, boil them and strain the liquid
for a rich, nourishing stock.
- Intestines and sinews are surprisingly strong
and can be twisted and used as rope. Wash them
thoroughly first. Expect flies.
- The human body can't survive on meat
alone. Balance your diet by foraging for
nonpoisonous berries and vegetables.

1 Lay the rabbit on a cutting board and pinch the loose skin in the lower part of the belly. Cut a neat incision, being careful not to puncture the stomach lining. Be careful to avoid piercing the animal's organs in the process, because this may contaminate the meat with urine or feces.

2 Extend the cut all the way around the rabbit's torso, either by tearing or cutting the skin with a knife. The fur will pull away from the trunk easily.

3 Turning the skin inside out, pull the rear end over the hind legs and the front end over the head, until both ends tear off completely. It feels similar to pulling a rubber glove off your hand.

4 Use an ax or a knife to sever the head, paws and tail. Save the blood to add to a soup or stew—it contains iron and other essential nutrients.

5 Cut the stomach lining open, being careful not to pierce any organs. Remove the guts. If you see any blotches or growths on the organs, discard the rabbit because it may be diseased and, therefore, unfit to eat.

6 If the organs look healthy, keep the heart, liver and kidneys to eat, but discard the rest. Wash the carcass and soak overnight in salted water, prior to roasting over a campfire.

HOW TO CATCH A FISH

Fish is a fantastic source of nutrition and probably the single most valuable food if you are stuck in the wilderness, far away from your favorite sushi bar. Tasty and easy to cook, it contains essential protein, iron, vitamin D and Omega 3 fatty acids. However, first you've got to catch the slippery critters. There are many ways of catching fish. Try out several different approaches and find out which works best in your particular environment.

INDISPENSABLE THINGS

- Wooden stakes
- Stones
- Paper clips, safety pins, pins, needles, nails, wire or metal strips for hooks
- Sliver of wood, bone or metal
- Sharp knife
- Shoelaces, dental floss, wire, thread or twisted bark for line
- Tree branch
- Worms, insects, berries or meat for bait, or a strip of red cloth
- Shirt or pants for a net

FISH TRAPS

Fish traps are very effective. Drive stakes into the bottom of shallow water to create a three-sided rectangle, with the open side facing the current. Upstream, make a V-shape wall to funnel the fish into the trap. In tidal areas, use stones to create tidal pools to trap fish when the tide goes out.

A PRACTICAL HISTORY OF FLY-FISHING

There are references to anglers in ancient Greece and Rome tying red feathers and wool to their hooks. But the first detailed descriptions of artificial flies being used for fishing comes in *The Treatyse of Fysshynge Wyth an Angle*, published in 1496 at St. Albans, England. This popular work describes twelve artificial flies made from silk, wool and feathers in many colors. The most famous work on fly-fishing is *The Compleat Angler*, by Izaak Walton and Charles Cotton, which was first published in 1653 and is still in print today—some 400 editions later.

MAKING A FISHING LINE

Hooks can be bent, twisted and cut from objects you may already have with you: paper clips, safety pins, pins, needles, nails, wire or a strip of metal cut from a can. Or find them in nature: thorns, bone, wood, shells and bird claws can all be fashioned into hooks.

GORGE

Even easier to make than a hook is a gorge. Sharpen both ends of a short sliver of hard material (for example, wood, bone or metal) and cut a notch in the middle. Tie a line to the notch and bury the gorge in the bait. When the fish swallows the bait, the gorge will stick in its throat.

NATURAL BAIT

Find bait in the immediate environment, such as worms, insects, raw meat or berries. A simple lure, such as a strip of red cloth tied above the hook, can be equally effective. Fish just before dawn or just after dusk, when the fish are most active.

LINES

Line can be made from shoelaces, dental floss, wire, thread from clothes and equipment, twisted bark or the sinews of dead animals. Use a branch as a rod, or make a simple hand line. Make up several lines and leave them out overnight.

NET

Make an improvised net by stretching a shirt between the limbs of a Y-shape branch—making sure you tie the sleeves up first to prevent the fish from escaping. Or use the leg of a pair of pants, with the loose end tied tightly as a net.

TRAVEL & SPORTS

HOW TO GUT A FISH

Contrary to what most children think, nature doesn't supply fish in neatly breadcrumbed sticks ready to cook under the broiler. That's Captain Birds Eye's job. But it's really not that difficult to scale and gut a fish yourself, and then you've got a bundle of goodness all ready to grill over the fire. If you're feeling squeamish, go find some wild berries to eat instead.

INDISPENSABLE THINGS

- Sharp knife
- Spoon or fork
- Nimble fingers

PRACTICAL TIP

There are several ways to kill a fish. The fastest and probably most humane is to hold it by the bottom of the tail and swing it sharply against a solid object. Alternatively, you can strike its head with a heavy object. The cruelest way is to let it "suffocate" on air.

1 Decide if your fish needs descaling by scraping from tail to head with a knife; if the scales lift up, descale the fish, otherwise just wash it. To descale, hold it firmly by the tail and scrape up both sides with a knife held at right angles to the body. Now do the smaller scales around the fins, tail and collar.

2 To gut the fish, hold it firmly by the tail and push a sharp knife into its anus. Draw the knife toward the head, cutting its belly open right up to the bottom of the gills. Don't cut too deeply because this will pierce the digestive system and contaminate the meat with feces.

3 If it's a small fish, simply reach inside with your hand or fingers and scoop out the organs. If it's a bigger fish, you'll need to cut the organs off directly behind its head and at the anus before pulling them out. Remove the black vein from the backbone by scraping it off with a spoon or fork.

4 Clean the abdominal cavity thoroughly in cold water. Don't use river water unless you are absolutely sure it's clean.

5 The fish is now ready to cook, but there are other steps if you want to make it more palatable. You can cut fillets off the bone by inserting a sharp knife into the flesh directly behind the gills until you feel the vertebra. Slide the knife along the bone, pulling the flesh away with your other hand.

6 Some people don't like being looked at while they are eating—particularly not by the creature they are eating. Using a sharp knife, cut off the fish's head directly behind the gills, pushing hard to cut through the vertebra. The head is full of goodness— save it to make a nutritious fish soup.

TRAVEL & SPORTS

HOW TO READ A MAP

GoogleEarth may give us the illusion of seeing Earth in three dimensions, but even the most modern map technology still relies on grid references and contours to show the way. So, how do you represent three-dimensional mountains and valleys on flat paper or a screen? How do you find where you are on a map? And how do you know whether your map is large or small scale?

INDISPENSABLE THINGS

- Map
- Sense of direction

PRACTICAL TIP

Most maps are drawn with north at the top. That means that west is to the left, east to the right and south is pointing downward. To make life easier, turn the map until it matches the real lay of the land.

CONTOUR LINES

The height of the land is represented by contour lines. Each line represents a standard height above sea level. Imagine the tide is coming in and, at regular intervals, a line is drawn around the sea's edge; that's what contour lines are like. The closer the contour lines are, the steeper the gradient. The farther apart the lines are, the flatter the gradient.

ROADS & RIVERS

Roads are shown in a variety of colors, depending on their size. Buildings are usually shown as gray or black, woods as green and mountains as brown or white, depending on height, but this varies from map to map. Rivers and the sea are always shown in blue. A key will explain what the symbols on the map mean.

SCALE

A "large-scale" map shows features close-up (big!), but doesn't have space to show much (such as 1:25,000). A "small-scale" map shows features from afar (small), but can fit more on the page (such as 1:24,000,000).

WORKING OUT THE SCALE

Maps come in different scales, depending on their intended purpose. The scale is indicated at the bottom or side of the map in the form of a ratio, such as 1:100,000. This means that 1 unit on the map is the equivalent of 100,000 units in real life. A 1:25,000 map has enough detail for walking, a 1:190,000 map is good for driving, while a 1:24,000,000 map shows the whole world.

LATITUDE & LONGITUDE

The numbers on the sides of the map represent latitude, or the distance in degrees north or south of the equator. The numbers at the top and bottom represent longitude, or the distance in degrees east or west of the Greenwich Meridian Line. Each degree is divided into 60 minutes. Each minute represents one nautical mile (or 1.15 land miles/ 1.85km), so one degree equals 60 nautical miles (or 69 land miles/111km).

HOW TO USE A COMPASS

Did you know that Earth is a giant magnet? Well, there is a magnetic field running north to south, which is why the needle of a compass always points north. The Chinese invented the first compass at least 2,000 years ago, and the same concept has been used by voyagers ever since, from Christopher Columbus to every Boy Scout and Girl Scout in the land. Clever, hey? But what happens when you don't want to travel north? Well, let's see...

INDISPENSABLE THINGS

- Compass
- Steady hand

👆 PRACTICAL TIP

To use a compass, stand in a clear space and check that the compass is level. Make sure there are no large metal objects nearby, which may create a magnetic attraction and affect the reading. Once the needle has settled down, turn the compass until the colored end of the needle lines up with north on the dial.

NEEDLE & DIAL

Most compasses are made of a needle balanced on a pivot. The end of the needle that points to north is usually painted either red or fluorescent green. A dial around the compass shows north and the other cardinal points (south, east and west).

GET YOUR BEARINGS

To find the direction, or bearing, of an object, turn the compass until the "direction of travel" arrow is pointing at it. Turn the dial until the colored end of the needle lines up with north. Read off the bearing next to the arrow.

FIND A DIRECTION

To find a direction apart from north, turn the dial until the desired direction (for example, southeast) lines up with the "direction of travel" arrow. Now turn the whole compass until the colored end of the needle lines up again with north. The arrow will now be pointing to the desired direction (say, southeast).

CARDINAL POINTS

The four cardinal points of the compass are north, south, east and west. In between these are the intercardinal points, such as northwest and southeast. These can be divided again, to give north-northwest and east-southeast, although for orienteering the intercardinal points are usually accurate enough.

CHECK

Use your common sense. If you are walking toward the sun in the northern hemisphere, you are heading south (north if you are in the southern hemisphere). If you are supposed to be traveling the other way, check your compass again. It's a common mistake to line up the wrong end of the needle.

DEGREES

The compass dial can also be divided into 360 degrees, with 000° standing for north, 090° for east, 180° for south and 270° for west. Courses can be set to the nearest degree, allowing for more accurate navigation, suitable for a ship or an airplane.

HOW TO MEASURE THE DISTANCE WALKED

Knowing how far you've traveled is key to knowing where you are now. It also enables you to work out how far you've still got to go and, crucially, whether you'll reach your destination before the bar closes. A GPS (Global Positioning System) will give you an exact location and a pedometer will measure precisely how far you've walked, but there are simpler ways to work out these things, using just your eyes, arms and legs—plus a little mental arithmetic.

👉 **PRACTICAL TIPS**

To work out how far away an object is—for example, a barn on the other side of a valley, approximately 100ft. (30m) wide—extend one arm and stick your index finger in the air. Close one eye and line up your finger with one end of the object. Without moving your finger, open just the other eye and observe how far your finger appears to have moved. Estimate the distance between the two apparent positions (for example, three times the length of the barn). Times that distance by 10; that is how far away the object is ... very approximately.

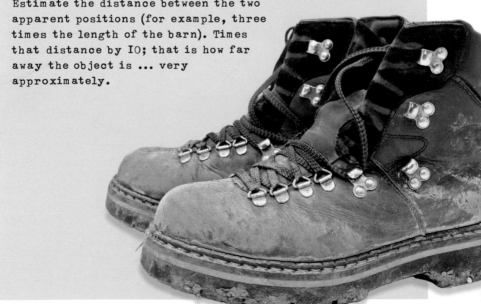

PACE YOURSELF

Measure your pace. A double pace is easier to count than a single pace. Walk two paces, starting with your dominant foot (such as left foot/right foot/left foot) and measure how far you've walked. Better still, count how many double paces it takes to walk a set distance. Divide the distance by the number of double paces and you've got an average measure of your pace, for example, 100ft. (30m)/20 double paces = 5ft. (1.5m) per double pace.

PREVAILING CONDITIONS

Your pace will vary according to the terrain and the prevailing conditions. It will be shorter walking uphill than downhill. It will be shorter walking into a head wind than with a tail wind. Gravel and sand will also shorten your pace, as will snow and ice. Fatigue will affect your pace. Measure your pace in different conditions and over different types of terrain and adjust your calculations accordingly.

TALLY

Use the "tally and pace" system, where 100 paces = 1 tally. Keep track of the number of tallies by tying a knot in a piece of string or by putting pebbles in your pocket. Get several people to count and work out the average result. An average pace is 2½ft. (0.8m), or 5ft. (1.5m) for a double pace. It therefore takes 528 double paces to walk half a mile (800m).

USE TIME

With experience, you can use time to measure the distance you have traveled. Use a stopwatch to time how long it takes you to walk a mile (1.6km). To work out your hourly rate, divide 60 by the number of minutes it takes you to walk a mile, such as 60/20 minutes = 3mph (4.8kph). The average person walks at 2–3mph (3.2–4.8kph), depending on the terrain, any load carried and level of fitness.

HOW TO ESTIMATE REMAINING DAYLIGHT HOURS

It's late afternoon and the sun will be setting soon. But how soon? Should you set up camp now, or keep going to the next valley? Should you eat the last piece of chocolate, or save it for later? With access to an almanac or the Internet you can find out the time of sunset to the nearest second, but here's an ingenious method, using just your fingers, that will give you an approximation.

INDISPENSABLE THINGS

- Sunlight
- Steady hands

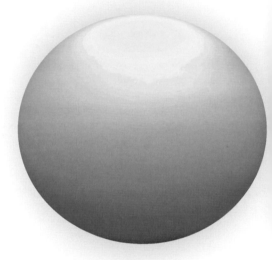

1 Extend both arms in front of you at eye height. Turn your hands inward so that both palms are facing toward you and place one on top of the other, so that your eight fingers are stacked up in front of you (ignore the thumbs). Line up the bottom of your lower hand to bring it level with the horizon below the sun.

2 Starting from the top, lift your fingers until the sun is peeping over the top of the uppermost finger. Count how many finger there are left between the sun and the horizon and times that number by 15. That's how many minutes it will be before the sun sets, for example, 6 fingers x 15 = 90 minutes. Size of fingers varies, of course, so experiment to work out what each of your fingers is worth—they might only be 10 minutes or they might be a whacking 20 minutes thick.

HOW TO FIND YOUR BEARINGS USING A WATCH

Did you know you can find north and south using an ordinary analog watch? OK, it's not as accurate as a compass and you do need some assistance from the sun, but it will give you an approximate bearing that will get you out of trouble in an emergency. Or try it just for fun.

INDISPENSABLE THINGS

- Watch
- Sunlight

INDISPENSABLE BEARINGS

- In the northern hemisphere, the sun is in the south
- In the southern hemisphere, the sun is in the north
- Facing the sun (in the north), east is to your left
- In the southern hemisphere, east is to your right

IN THE NORTHERN HEMISPHERE, place the watch horizontally and line up the hour hand with the sun. The line that lies halfway between the hour hand and midday points to south. Use standard time; if the watch is set to daylight saving time, the south–north line lies between the hour hand and 1:00 p.m. If in doubt, bear in mind that the sun rises in the east, sets in the west and is due south at noon.

IN THE SOUTHERN HEMISPHERE, place the watch horizontally and line up the 12 o'clock mark with the sun. The line that lies halfway between 12 o'clock and the hour hand points to north. If the watch is set to daylight saving time, line 1:00 p.m. with the sun; the north–south line will lie between it and the hour hand. If in doubt, bear in mind that the sun rises in the east, sets in the west and is due north at noon.

HOW TO FIND NORTH USING A STICK

Who needs a compass when you can find north using just a stick? Unfortunately, the stick method is less portable than a compass and considerably less accurate. What's more, it's not much use on overcast days or at night or if you're in a hurry. Apart from that, it works great. Just don't try to use it at sea.

INDISPENSABLE THINGS

- Stick
- Open ground
- Twig or stone
- Sunlight

INDISPENSABLE SUNDIAL

You can turn your stick compass into a basic sundial by driving the stick vertically into the ground at the intersection of the east—west and north—south lines. The west side of the east—west line represents 6:00 a.m., while the east side represents 6:00 p.m. The north—south line represents midday. The path of the shadow through the arc will vary, depending on location and time of year, but, with a little attention, can make an acceptable substitute for a clock.

1 Find some open ground that is reasonably level and free of undergrowth. Drive a stick about 3ft. (1m) long into the ground—it doesn't matter how straight or upright the stick is, providing it casts a distinct shadow on the ground.

2 Mark the tip of the shadow with a twig or stone, or a mark in the ground. This is the west mark, irrespective of whether you are in the northern or southern hemisphere.

3 Wait for 10–15 minutes, until the shadow has moved a short distance. Mark the new position of the shadow tip as before. This is the east mark.

4 Draw a straight line between the two marks, extending the line slightly past the second mark. This gives you an approximate east–west line.

5 Stand on the line with the west mark to your left. You will now be facing north, irrespective of whether you are in the northern or southern hemisphere. Draw a line perpendicular to the first line to give you a north–south line.

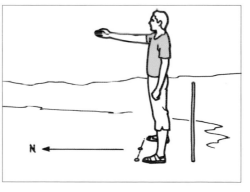

6 For a more accurate reading, mark the first shadow 15–20 minutes before noon and, using the mark as your radius, draw an arc around the bottom of the stick. Wait for 15–20 minutes after noon, and the tip of the shadow will touch the other side of the arc. Mark that point and join the two marks to create an east–west line as before.

TRAVEL & SPORTS

HOW TO FIND THE NORTH STAR

No need to stop walking just because the sun's gone down. Traveling by night can be a magical experience and, even without a compass, you can navigate with reasonable accuracy using the stars. There are 5,000 stars visible to the naked eye but, in the northern hemisphere at least, you only need one to find your way: the North Star.

INDISPENSABLE THINGS

- Night sky
- Sharp eyes

THE NORTH STAR

The constellations in the sky vary from season to season because of the journey of Earth around the sun. They change their position from hour to hour because of the rotation of Earth on its axis. The one star that remains virtually constant every night, all night, is the North Star. That's because it's located above Earth's axis, just 1 degree off true north.

URSA MAJOR

The North Star is the last star in the "handle" of Ursa Minor, also known as the Little Dipper. Two constellations rotate counterclockwise around the North Star: Ursa Major and Cassiopeia. Ursa Major (also known as the Big Dipper) is a group of seven stars shaped like a saucepan. To locate the North Star, follow the line of the two stars which form the outer edge of the "saucepan." These are called the "pointers," and they point toward the North Star.

CASSIOPEIA

If the Big Dipper isn't visible, locate Cassiopeia, which is a group of five stars in the shape of an "M" or "W," depending on the time of night. The middle star of Cassiopeia points straight to the North Star.

HOW TO FIND THE SOUTHERN CROSS

The North Star isn't visible in the southern hemisphere, and there's no other star conveniently parked under the South Pole to use in its place. Instead, the voyagers of the south have devised an ingenious alternative for night-time navigation without a compass. And this time it's got nothing to do with dippers.

FINDING THE CROSS

The Southern Cross is a constellation of five stars, visible only in the southern hemisphere. The four brightest stars form a cross, tilting to one side. The two stars farthest apart in the group are the pointer stars.

INDISPENSABLE THINGS

- Night sky
- Even sharper eyes

FINDING SOUTH

To find south in the southern hemisphere, draw an imaginary line from the pointer stars in the Southern Cross. Extend the line so that it is 4.5 times the distance between the two stars. Where the line ends is the point above the South Pole. To avoid having to repeat this process, find a landmark on the horizon below this imaginary point and use that to navigate by.

🖝 PRACTICAL TIPS

Don't confuse the Southern Cross with the Diamond Cross and False Cross, both of which are located in the southern sky. The Southern Cross is distinguished by its two pointer stars, which stand out from the rest. It's also more kite-shaped than the others, which are more diamond-shaped.

TRAVEL & SPORTS

HOW TO CLIMB A TREE

Climbing a tree gives you a different perspective on life. It frees you from your usual attachment to the ground and makes you look at familiar things with new eyes. It also makes you feel like the king/queen of the world—it should be on everyone's list of things to do to stay young.

INDISPENSABLE THINGS

- Tree with evenly spread branches
- Good balance

CHOOSING YOUR TREE

Choose your tree carefully. Find one that has evenly spread branches, not so close that you might get stuck and not so far apart that you won't be able to move from branch to branch easily.

TESTING THE BRANCHES

As a rule of thumb, if a healthy branch is as thick as your bicep, it should be strong enough to take your weight. Test the branches before you put your full weight on them.

TREES TO AVOID

Some trees, such as sycamore, are prone to splitting suddenly. Avoid them and choose something more trusty, such as an oak. Never climb a dead tree. It might look all right at first sight, but is probably rotten on the inside.

CLIMBING TIPS

Keep your weight as close to the main trunk as possible, where the branches are strongest. Use your legs more than your arms; it's less tiring. Keep a firm grip with your hands at all times in case your feet slip.

HOW TO CLIMB A CLIFF

There are times when climbing up (or down) a cliff is the only sensible option. There are other times when it's simply the most fun and/or daring option. Either way, there are some precautions you can take that will prevent it from becoming the most dangerous option.

INDISPENSABLE THINGS

- Even balance
- Small steps

POSITION
Unlike the guy in this illustration, you should face the cliff, with the inside of your feet facing in toward the rock. Keep your hands low, preferably between waist and shoulders. Avoid overstretching and becoming spread-eagled. Use several short steps, rather than one long one.

BALANCE
Don't hug the cliff. Keep your body away from the rock face, with your center of gravity over your feet. Use your foot to power you and your arms for balance. Move only one limb at a time, and keep three points in contact with the rocks—that is, two hands and one foot, or one hand and two feet. Don't use elbows, knees or buttocks.

TEST & REST
Test the rock before putting your weight on it. A crack in the rock face can be used as a hold by placing a hand flat in the crevice and clenching it into a fist to jam it in. Rest regularly, keeping your hands low to maintain circulation.

TRAVEL & SPORTS

☞ PRACTICAL TIPS
Plan your route carefully. You can minimize the risks by avoiding obvious hazards. The direct route is rarely the safest. Gullies often provide the easiest route, but beware of rockfalls. Don't climb when it's wet.

ACCIDENT &
EMERGENCY

GOING TO THE RESCUE

You may not feel like Superman or
Superwoman, or look anything like them,
but there may come a time when you have to
act like them——or, better still, act like a
trained paramedic. You can't become one of
these in an instant, but here are some very
practical guidelines that could help
you help someone in distress.

HOW TO SAVE SOMEONE'S LIFE

As implausible as it may seem, at some point during your lifetime you may find yourself in an emergency situation during which your actions could determine whether someone lives or dies. Certainly an unappealing thought for most of us, but every day, around the world, members of the general public are faced with this scenario. Fortunately, if you follow the advice here you'll dramatically improve somebody's chances of living by learning your ABCs.

INDISPENSABLE THINGS

- Cell phone
- Calm manner
- Safe approach

A PRACTICAL HISTORY OF ABC

The mnemonic or *aide-memoire* ABC was devised in the early 1960s by three doctors, Peter Safar, James Jude and Guy Knickerbocker. Together, along with others, the three developed the ABC protocol along with the closely associated CPR technique (*see pages 268–69*). They presented the procedures during a far-ranging lecture tour and also through the training video "A Pulse of Life." Since its inception, ABC has undoubtedly helped to save many thousands of lives.

ABC Accepted by the vast majority of first-aid organizations, ABC stands for Airway, Breathing and Circulation. After you've alerted the emergency services, ABC are the first three essential checks that should be undertaken before proceeding with any subsequent first-aid treatment. The checks should be made in that order because without a clear airway, breathing cannot take place, and unless the casualty is breathing, the blood cannot circulate around the body.

AIRWAY The airway is the passage running from the nose and mouth to the lungs, down which air travels nourishing the blood with vital oxygen. The most common blockages found at the scene of an emergency are caused by food, vomit or the casualty's own tongue. It is vital to remove any blockage (to prevent it from falling farther into the airway) before effecting a "head tilt—chin lift" position so that the person can breathe. Lift the casualty's chin with two fingers while at the same time placing your other hand on the casualty's head and tilting it well back.

BREATHING With the airway clear, the casualty should be able to breathe. To check this, place your head close to the casualty's mouth and nose—you should be able to feel the person's breath on your cheek and determine how regular the breathing is. If the casualty is not breathing, you'll need to begin CPR (*see pages 268–69*).

CIRCULATION With a clear airway and the casualty breathing, the heart should be able to pump blood around the body, enabling the exchange of the gases oxygen and carbon dioxide. If the heart is pumping you should be able to feel a pulse. To check for a pulse, place two fingers on the side of the neck in the space between the large neck muscle and the windpipe. If you cannot detect a pulse, begin CPR (*see pages 268–69*).

HOW TO PERFORM CPR

CPR stands for "cardiopulmonary resuscitation," so we are going to stick with CPR—or you can also think of "ComPRessions." Learning how to perform CPR is something that everybody should do. While the steps shown here provide a good introduction to CPR, they're no substitute for going on a first-aid course and learning the procedure from a qualified first-aid instructor. However, these instructions should help you keep someone alive if they've stopped breathing and the heart's no longer beating until paramedics arrive at the scene and take control—and all the glory (they deserve it).

INDISPENSABLE THINGS

- Cell phone
- Clear head

PRACTICAL TIP

Before you begin performing CPR, call the emergency services. That way they can get an ambulance on its way and give you reassuring instructions over the phone while you're attending to the casualty.

INDISPENSABLE WARNING

If the casualty is an infant, don't do this because it's too heavy. Hold the back of the neck and press with just two fingers on the midline of the sternum, a finger's breadth below the nipple line.

1 First ensure the airway is clear before tilting the casualty's head back. With the casualty lying flat on his or her back, tilt the head back by gently pushing on the chin while at the same time using your other hand to push the person's forehead back. This is the same procedure used for checking the airway in ABC (*see pages 266–67*). Listen for signs of breathing.

2 If the casualty is breathing, check for circulation (*see pages 266–67*)—DO NOT PERFORM CPR. If, however, the casualty is not breathing, close the nose by pinching with your fingers, open the mouth and cover with your own mouth. Take a normal breath and slowly breathe into the casualty's mouth for about a second. The chest should rise as you breathe for him or her. Repeat a second time. This is referred to as rescue breathing.

3 Begin chest compressions as soon as you have performed two rescue breaths. Place one hand on the person's chest between the nipples. Place your second hand on top of the first and interlace your fingers. Move your body directly over the patient's, lock your elbows and, using your weight, push down with the heel of the bottom hand. Compress the chest by 1½–2in. (4–5cm). Push hard and fast while counting up to 30.

4 After 30 chest compressions, provide two more rescue breaths and repeat the chest compressions. Perform this cycle five times and then check for a pulse (*see pages 266–67*). If there's no pulse, repeat the cycle until paramedics arrive. If you do detect a pulse, check the casualty's airway and circulation and keep monitoring the pulse to ensure it doesn't fade.

PRACTICAL TIP

Remember you're trying to pump blood around the body from outside the chest wall, so don't be too hesitant. Push hard and fast while counting up to 30.

ACCIDENT & EMERGENCY

HOW TO STOP A NOSEBLEED

Although often visually spectacular and capable of setting off minor panic in young children, most nosebleeds are perfectly harmless—the person with the nosebleed being likely to sustain less damage than any fabric caught within the vicinity of the incident. Caused by ruptured blood vessels, usually due to a strike on the nose, or from picking, sneezing or blowing the nose, most nosebleeds should come under control within 20—30 minutes.

INDISPENSABLE THINGS

- Chair
- Handkerchief/box of tissues
- Bowl (optional)
- Clean cloth and warm water
- Sympathetic ear

🖐 PRACTICAL TIPS

- Encourage the person to relax and lie down for 30—60 minutes to avoid the bleeding restarting.
- If the nosebleed persists after 30 minutes, consult a physician or take the patient to the hospital, particularly if bleeding has followed a blow to the head and the blood appears thin and watery.
- If a child has repeated nosebleeds, it may be that he or she is picking his or her nose. Keep fingernails trimmed and advise the child against doing it.

KEEP THE HEAD UPRIGHT

Ensure the person doesn't tip his or her head back in an attempt to stop the flow of blood. By tipping the head back, blood may flow down the throat and induce vomiting.

KEEP CALM

Keep the person calm and reassure the person that there's nothing to worry about. Ask him or her to sit down on the chair and to lean slightly forward. This will enable the blood to flow from the nostrils and into a bowl. Offer a handkerchief to mop up any blood on the person's hands or face.

PINCH THE NOSE

Ask the person to pinch the soft part of the nose (just below the hard cartilage) for about 10 minutes. As well as slowing the blood flow and so encouraging the blood to clot, this will force him or her to breathe through the mouth, which will have a calming effect. After 10 minutes the person can release his or her fingers. If the bleeding continues, pinch the nose for another 10 minutes. Usually the bleeding will stop after this time, after which you can gently clean around the nose with a clean cloth and some warm water.

🖛 PRACTICAL TIP

Ask the person not to sniff, blow their nose or attempt to clean the nostrils for about 4 hours, if possible. Otherwise the bleeding may start again

ACCIDENT & EMERGENCY

HOW TO PERFORM THE HEIMLICH MANEUVER

The Heimlich Maneuver is a medical procedure used to stop someone from choking. The Maneuver comprises a series of abdominal thrusts that are intended to expel the choking object out of the casualty's mouth. First described by Henry Heimlich in 1974, the Heimlich Maneuver is estimated to have saved around 100,000 lives in the US alone including those of Ronald Reagan, Elizabeth Taylor and Goldie Hawn, to name just three.

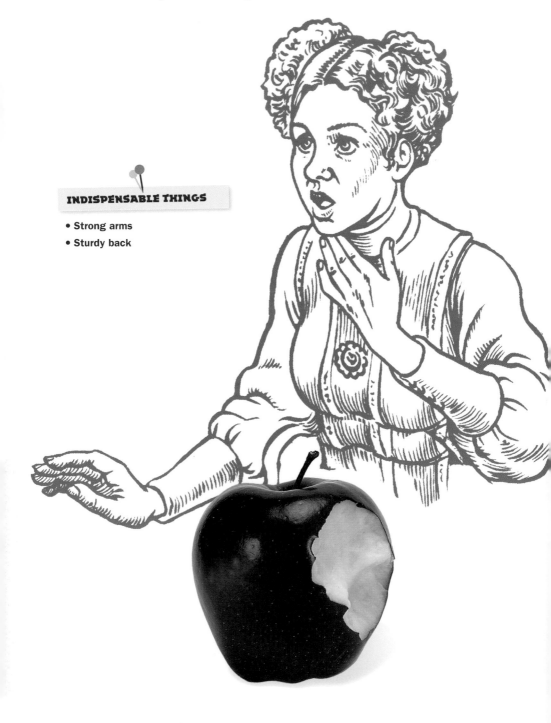

INDISPENSABLE THINGS

- Strong arms
- Sturdy back

IMPORTANT

Before attempting the Heimlich
Maneuver, first ask the casualty to
lean forward and cough. This may
force the object out. If not, try
slapping the casualty on the back
five times, between the shoulder
blades, with the heel of your hand.
You don't have to use all five blows
if one is all it takes. If this fails, it's
time for the Heimlich.

POSITION

Ideally, you need
to get the person
to stand to perform
the Heimlich
Maneuver. Stand
behind the person,
lean him or her
forward slightly, and
put your arms around
the waist. It may help
your balance to place
one of your legs
between those of the
casualty. However, if
the casualty is seated
and is too frail or
elderly to stand, you
can position yourself
behind the chair and
perform the same
procedure.

PULL

With one fist clenched,
place it, with the thumb
against the stomach,
between the casualty's
navel and the bottom
of the diaphragm (or
sternum). Place the other
hand over the first and pull
sharply inward and upward.
This action compresses
the lungs and will hopefully
force the object out of the
casualty's mouth. If the
object is not expelled,
repeat the Maneuver. DO
NOT repeat the Maneuver
more than five times.

☞ INDISPENSABLE WARNING

While the arm action of the maneuver needs to be short and sharp,
it mustn't be too strong. There have been a number of cases of
overzealous administrators damaging the casualty's sternum, liver
or stomach. Even when performed with an appropriate amount of
pressure, the abdomen is likely to suffer some bruising as a result.

HOW TO MAKE A SLING

One of the more unpleasant side effects of gravity is that it can make little boys and girls fall out of trees and big boys and girls fall off ladders. In fact, gravity is responsible for all kinds of accidents that can often result in broken arms, dislocated collarbones and sprained wrists. Ouch! If you have family members who like trying to cheat gravity, you may find making a sling a useful skill. A sling will keep the injured arm still, preventing further injury, and elevated, which stops swelling.

INDISPENSABLE THINGS

- Piece of cloth about 40in. (1m) square or a pillowcase cut open
- Soft material for padding
- Large safety pin or tape
- Second bandage or piece of cloth or a belt

1 Take the cloth or pillowcase and fold or cut it in half to make a triangle. Ask the casualty to support the injured arm across his or her chest so that it is as comfortable as possible. Ideally the hand should be slightly higher than the elbow. Gently place the cloth under the injured arm so that half is above the elbow and half below.

2 Bring the top end of the sling around the neck and lift the bottom end up to form a cradle for the injured arm. Talk soothingly while performing this operation because it will help you assume the role of nurse.

3 Tie the top and bottom ends of the bandage together at the neck. Use the knot to adjust the height of the sling, ensuring that the arm remains in the most comfortable position. Place a pad underneath the knot because it can be uncomfortable for the patient. Make sure that you leave the hand of the injured arm exposed and accessible so that you can check for circulation and sensation. Next bring the third end around the elbow and attach it to the front of the sling using a safety pin. Be aware, particularly in the elderly, of any neck problems that could be exacerbated.

4 Finally, to prevent the sling from moving backward and forward as the casualty walks or moves about, take a second bandage and fold it into a long strip. Place it under the uninjured arm, around the casualty's back and around the front of the sling. Tie the ends together or attach them using a safety pin. If you don't have a second bandage, a loosely buckled belt will suffice.

☞ INDISPENSABLE WARNINGS

Remove all rings and any tight jewelry from the patient's injured side, particularly if the arm or wrist is damaged, because swelling can occur.

HOW TO MAKE A SPLINT

If your little one comes dashing to you gingerly holding an arm that appears swollen and/or bruised, and has difficulty moving his or her fingers, the arm may well be fractured—and if the broken end of a bone is poking through the skin, then you have a strong indication that things aren't as they should be. If you can't get medical attention quickly, you'll need to make a splint so that the sharp ends of broken bones don't inflict further damage to veins, arteries or nerves.

INDISPENSABLE THINGS

- Soft material for padding
- Rigid but lightweight lengths of material
- Lengths of flexible material for ties

ARM WOUND If you are dealing with an injury to the arm, clean any visible wound as thoroughly as possible before attaching the splint to prevent infection. Do not attempt to straighten the injured arm, simply surround it with soft padding, attach the rigid lengths along the length of the arm and secure them with the ties. Get the casualty to hospital as quickly as possible.

LEG WOUND If you are dealing with a leg wound, ask the casualty to sit or lie to take any weight off the injured leg. Clean any wound and stem the flow of any bleeding. Wrap the leg in blankets or other padding. Apply the rigid lengths to the back of the leg and the bottom of the foot. Add additional rigid lengths to the sides of the leg if necessary, and use the ties to keep the splint together. Get the casualty to hospital as quickly as possible.

HOW TO MEASURE A PULSE

The pulse is an indication of the body's heart rate. There are a number of reasons why you might want to measure and record a person's, or even your own, pulse, whether to assess how well a casualty is responding to treatment, to monitor the effectiveness of your aerobic exercise routine or just to check how fast your heart's beating—although you're unlikely to be checking that yourself.

INDISPENSABLE THINGS

- Sensitive fingers
- Watch

WRIST

The wrist is the most effective location for measuring the pulse. Place your first and second fingers on the casualty's wrist, just below the base of the hand between the tendons and the bone (in line with the thumb is about right). Apply gentle pressure until you can feel the pulse.

COUNT

Count the number of beats you feel in your fingers for 15 seconds. Multiply this by four and you have the casualty's pulse, which is traditionally measured as beats per minute (bpm).

HOW TO RESPOND TO AN EPILEPTIC SEIZURE

Epilepsy was first described some 3,000 years ago, an although physicians know a great deal about the conditio: today, the specific causes are often hard to pinpoint. Th good news is that epileptic seizures are usually successfull; managed with a variety of drugs—around 80 percent o epileptics lead perfectly normal lives. However, the ris of seizure cannot be ignored—here's how to respond.

INDISPENSABLE WARNING

Call the emergency services if you think that this is the person's first seizure; if the seizure lasts longer than 5 minutes; if a second seizure begins before the person has regained consciousness; or, if the patient's pregnant.

INDISPENSABLE THINGS

- **Anything soft to place under the person's head**
- **Ability to remain calm**

1 In the case of a severe seizure, do not attempt to hold or control the person or administer any medication. Do not check to see if the person has swallowed his or her tongue—this cannot happen during a seizure. Move all objects, such as furniture, well away to prevent injury. Place something soft under the casualty's head to prevent accidental injury and loosen any restrictive clothing, such as a tie or collar.

2 As the seizure begins to pass, gently rol the sufferer into the recovery position as shown above—this will help to keep the airways clear. Do not be alarmed if the person's lips become blue; they should return to normal color after the seizure. When the person regains consciousness, be calm and reassuring—he or she will soon make a full recovery.

INDISPENSABLE FACTS

Seizures vary in severity. In some cases the person may simply appear dazed, in which case all you need to do is stay with him or her and be reassuring when the seizure has passed. If the person suffers from epilepsy they are likely to be wearing a special medic-alert necklet or bracelet.

HOW TO TREAT A SNAKEBITE

ost poisonous snakes are shy creatures that rarely come
nto contact with humans. So while the risk of being bitten
y a venomous snake is small, that's little consolation
or the 2.7 million people who are bitten on average around
he world each year, of whom some I25,000 don't survive.
enomous snakes live on all continents, so all of us need
o be aware of the risk.

INDISPENSABLE THINGS

- Bandage or length of cloth
- Soap and water

KEEP CALM

If you or someone with you is bitten by
a snake and you're in a region where
venomous snakes are found, stay
calm, but assume it's poisonous.

ROCEDURE

ow follow these generally
greed-upon procedures:
f possible, wash the bite with
oap and water.
Keep the bitten area immobile
nd below the level of the heart
reduce blood flow.
Call the emergency services and
et the victim to a hospital as
uickly as possible. Try to provide
description of the snake.
DO NOT give the victim anything
eat or drink, especially alcohol
-this will cause the circulation
accelerate and spread the
oison more quickly.

EASSURANCE

is vital that the
ctim should be
lmed as much
possible. It is
nportant to keep the
eathing slowed to
ep the entire body
ot just the affected
mb) immobile in order
reduce the speed
th which the poison
rculates in the
oodstream.

INDISPENSABLE WARNING

A venomous bite is more likely to be fatal
in the young and the old. Do not hesitate
to call an ambulance to get the victim
to a hospital.

ACCIDENT & EMERGENCY

HOW TO TREAT A BEE STING

It is almost comical that something the size of a bee ca
ruin many a relaxed picnic and can cause displays o
panic in humans, creatures who are comparatively huge
And for the great majority of us it is comical, aside fro
the risk of a minor sting; it's far less amusing, however
if you know you will develop anaphylaxis, or a sever
allergic reaction.

INDISPENSABLE THINGS

- Knife or piece of thin cardboard
- Clean dressing
- Soap and water
- Ice/cold compress

STAY STILL

The first thing to do if anyone around you is stung is to ask him or her to stay still and identify exactly where the sting is. If it's a bee sting, there may well still be a venom sac and stinger visible. Brush this off with the back of a knife or a piece of thin cardboard. Don't attempt to pull it out using your fingertips or tweezers because you might inadvertently squeeze the venom sac, releasing more venom into the victim.

DRESS THE WOUND

Wash the sting with soap and water and apply a dressing to the wound. Placing some ice against the dressing may reduce any pain and swelling.

☞ INDISPENSABLE WARNING

Watch the casualty carefully for any signs of an anaphylactic reaction, such as breathing difficulties or a swollen face or neck. If such symptoms arise, call the emergency services immediately and explain what has happened.

HOW TO TREAT A DOG BITE

No doubt most of us at some point have enjoyed the cartoon of a dog chasing a mailman. What mischievous little creatures our canine friends, are, eh? Actually, in real life it isn't something to snigger about. A whopping 4.7 million people are bitten each year in the US—the majority of them children.

INDISPENSABLE THINGS

- Soap and water
- Gauze swabs
- Clean plaster or dressing

INDISPENSABLE WARNING

There is the risk that dogs, particularly a wild dog, is carrying rabies. If you are bitten by a dog, always seek medical advice—it may be necessary to have anti-rabies injections.

CHECK FOR TETANUS

Always ask the person if he or she has had a tetanus injection in the last 10 years. Even if the wound is small, without immunization it's best to seek medical advice.

KEEP IT CLEAN

Not only are dog bites painful, but they also carry a real risk of infection. First wash your own hands (or put on disposable latex gloves if they're available) and then clean the wounded area thoroughly with soap and warm water.

DRESS THE WOUND

Dry the area with clean gauze swabs and apply a dressing. If the bite is deep, take the person to the hospital or call the emergency services.

ACCIDENT & EMERGENCY

HOW TO TREAT A BURN

Although we occasionally laugh at comedy bee stings an[d] long-legged mailmen in flight from an excitable pup[py,] cartoonists rarely get much humor mileage from bur[n] victims—and that's because they aren't funny. As mos[t] of us know, even the smallest burn, such as those sustaine[d] through careless cooking, can be incredibly painful, an[d] the thought of anything more severe really doesn't bea[r] thinking about. Unfortunately, burns are relativel[y] common, so it's best to know how to deal with them.

INDISPENSABLE THINGS

- Access to water
- Sterile dressing and bandage or plastic wrap

CATEGORIES OF BURNS

- First degree—only the topmost layer of skin affected. Skin turns red and, when pressed, white. Blisters don't form and risk of infection is slight.
- Second degree—more layers of the skin are affected, including the wetter tissue layers and those layers containing the nerves. Blisters will form and the area will swell up. Risk of infection.
- Third degree—skin potentially charred or missing altogether. Extremely high, overall health risk to victim.

INDISPENSABLE WARNINGS

- Do not apply creams or ointments—they will have to be scrubbed off, which can be extremely painful for the patient. And they may introduce infections to the wound.
- NEVER burst blisters. They help to keep the burn moist and clean.

1 The risk of infection with a burn, particularly one in which the skin is broken or actually burned away or has caused bleeding, is very high. Before you attempt any first aid, quickly but thoroughly wash your hands. Alternatively, use disposable latex gloves if they're available.

2 After you've made the casualty as comfortable as possible, pour cool (not cold) water over the injured area for at least 15 minutes (depending on the severity of the burn). Preferably immerse the injured part in a bowl or bath to keep it under water. It's essential to lower the skin temperature to minimize damage and to keep loss of body fluids to a minimum.

3 Once you've lowered the temperature of the burn, remove any items of jewelry or clothing located near the burn. Depending on the severity of the burn, the area is likely to swell up and items such as these may well restrict blood flow and cause additional pain. Do not, however, attempt to remove any clothing or any other item caught in the burn area because this will aggravate the injury.

4 Cover the burned area with a sterile dressing and wrap a loose bandage around it to keep it in place. If you don't have a dressing, cover the area with anything that won't introduce fluff or other particles into the wound, such as plastic wrap. If more than redness persists after this time, take the patient to the ER for the proper burn dressing to be applied. Ideally, travel by car to minimize exposure to the air and any germs.

ACCIDENT & EMERGENCY

HOW TO TREAT A GUNSHOT WOUND

In view of the high-profile reporting that gun crime attracts, you'd be forgiven for thinking that the Wild West was constantly being replayed in many of our cities. In fact, gun crime accounts for around 9 percent of violent crime in the US. But we can't be complacent—every day firearms are used to perpetrate a variety of crimes, and on each occasion someone could end up being shot.

INDISPENSABLE THINGS

- Blanket
- Cell phone
- Clean dressings/towels

☞ INDISPENSABLE WARNINGS

• Do not touch any protruding internal organs. Cover them with plastic wrap or a clean plastic bag to prevent them from drying out and to reduce the risk of infection. If you have a sterile dressing, use that.
• Do not raise the victim's legs above the wound in an attempt to treat for shock, because this will only exacerbate the bleeding. For a chest injury, secure any dressing on only three sides—you must leave one side open for air to escape from the pleural cavity.

1 Before going to the aid of someone who has been shot, be certain that you are safe to do so. You can't help the victim if you become one yourself. If the casualty is still conscious, try to make him or her as comfortable as possible, put a blanket around the victim and get him or her to stay as still as possible—unnecessary movement will only aggravate the injury. Call the emergency services.

2 If the victim is unconscious but breathing, place him or her in the recovery position (as illustrated above). Call the emergency services. First check the airway for blood (see ABC, pages 266–67), especially if the injury is to the chest. Make regular checks to ensure that the victim is still breathing. If breathing stops, you may need to begin CPR (see step 4 below).

3 With the casualty as comfortable as possible, try to identify the source of any bleeding—you may need to remove clothing to be sure of the exact locations. This is important because next you need to use pressure to stop the bleeding. Ideally, press on the wound with clean dressings. If these aren't available, use towels or anything that will help to soak up the blood.

4 If the victim becomes unconscious and stops breathing, check to ensure the airways are clear and proceed with CPR (for full instructions, see pages 268–69). If the victim has been shot in the chest, be extra careful when performing the chest compressions.

HOW TO TREAT A STAB WOUND

Recent years have seen a sharp rise in knife attacks. Much of this is due to inter-gang rivalry among teenage boys, made worse by the fact that an increasing number of youngsters feel the need to carry a knife as a form of protection. Add to this that, unlike guns, knives are readily available.

INDISPENSABLE THINGS

- Clean dressings/towels
- Bandage or strips of tape
- Cell phone
- Blanket

1 As in any violent crime scenario, do not go to the victim's aid until you know it is safe to do so. First check the airway for blood (see ABC, *pages 266–67*), especially if the injury is to the chest. Carefully remove any clothing to help you pinpoint its exact location. Use any clean absorbent material, ideally a clean dressing, and press it to the wound to slow the rate of bleeding.

2 Now cover the dressing with a bandage or strips of tape to hold it in place. For a chest injury, secure on only three sides (see box below). Reassure the victim and make him or her as comfortable as possible. Get him or her to sit up and to try to keep the wounded area above the level of the heart to help reduce additional blood loss. Phone the emergency services.

3 Continue to monitor airway, breathing and circulation. Use a blanket or coat to keep the victim warm. Loss of blood and suffering from shock can lower the body temperature. Ensure that the casualty is comfortable and is lying as still as possible. Keep reassuring the casualty and let him or her know that medical help is on its way.

☞ INDISPENSABLE WARNINGS

• To avoid the risk of infection, use disposable latex gloves if they're available. Ensure your hands are as clean as possible before undertaking first aid.
• If the victim has suffered a stab wound to the chest, use kitchen foil, plastic wrap or a clean plastic bag over the dressing—it's vital to leave one side open for air to escape, and prevent it from entering the pleural cavity, which would cause the lungs to collapse (when the victim inhales, the patch adheres to the skin).
• If the knife has remained in the victim, do not attempt to remove it if this is likely to cause additional bleeding. Dress the wound around the knife as best you can.
• If the victim becomes unconscious but is still breathing, place him or her in the recovery position (*see page 285*) and monitor his or her breathing.
• If the victim is not breathing, begin CPR (*see pages 268–69*).

ACCIDENT & EMERGENCY

HOW TO DELIVER A BABY

It's the scenario that strikes fear into every expectant father (and mother, no doubt). The car won't start and you've called for an ambulance, but there's a fallen tree on the road and the paramedics can't get through—and now mom-to-be's water has broken! So what next? Well, the first and most important thing is to stay calm. Remember, women have been giving birth in all types of environments for hundreds of thousands of years and the vast majority of them coped without sterile maternity wards and banks of monitoring equipment. Don't worry, it'll be fine...

INDISPENSABLE THINGS

- Pillows
- Plastic sheeting (or newspapers)
- Clean towels
- Disposable latex gloves (if available)
- Blankets
- Plenty of warm water
- Sanitary napkins

☞ **INDISPENSABLE WARNINGS**

- Do not cut the umbilical cord.
- Do not throw away the placenta; medical staff will need to check this is complete.
- Do not smack the baby.

1 Offer plenty of support and reassurance. Start timing the contractions and let he mother assume whichever position she eels most comfortable in, and provide her with pillows. Try to get the mother to take deep, slow breaths during and after the ontractions. This will help her to remain alm and ease the pain. In the meantime, quickly prepare a clean delivery area. Place the plastic sheeting (or newspapers) on a ed and cover with towels. When the time etween contractions is less than two minutes, the baby is ready.

2 Ask the mother to lie down on the area you've prepared. Thoroughly wash your hands and arms or put on latex gloves if available. When the baby's head is visible, tell the mother to push when she feels a contraction starting. Ask her to take a deep breath, hold it and push. Get her to relax and breathe deeply between contractions. As the baby's head emerges, gently support it with your hands—DO NOT pull.

3 As the head continues to emerge, it will naturally turn to one side. Gently move to one side and wipe away any membrane that may be covering the baby's face so that he or she can breathe easily. Ensure the umbilical cord is not going to wrap itself round the baby's neck as he or she emerges. If the cord is wrapped around the baby's neck, ensure that it is loose before carefully pulling it over the baby's head.

4 While the mother continues to push, guide the head downward to let the top shoulder emerge first. The rest of the body will follow with the next contraction. Guide and support the baby using a towel so that he or she doesn't slip in your hands. When the baby is fully born, hold him or her so the feet are higher than the head, cover fully in blankets with just the face exposed and lay the baby on the mother's stomach. Encourage her to feed the baby, because this will help to bring about contractions that will expel the placenta. Clean the mother with warm water and provide sanitary napkins to absorb any final bleeding.

ACCIDENT & EMERGENCY

HOW TO TREAT FOR ELECTRIC SHOCK

The improved design of electrical appliances and more sophisticated electrical circuitry have resulted in fewer cases of electrocution over the years, particularly around the home. Yet it's important to remain mindful when handling any form of electrical appliance—particularly those that use a powerful motor and are used outdoors, such as lawn mowers and hedge cutters. Always check the condition of any appliance and its cord for signs of exposed wires and use a circuit breaker when recommended.

INDISPENSABLE THINGS

- Broom handle
- Towel

☞ INDISPENSABLE WARNING

Don't attempt do-it-yourself repairs on any electrical appliance by removing protective covers— certainly not while it's plugged in.

1 If someone has an electric shock and is still in contact with the appliance, the priority is to turn off the appliance. You can do this either by unplugging the appliance at its local outlet or by turning off the main circuit breaker switch at the main service panel.

2 If either of the above steps is not possible, knock the appliance away from the person's hands using a wooden broom handle. Never attempt this with a metal pole, or the current may pass through you. Nor should you attempt to drag the person away, because again, the current may pass through you.

3 If the appliance cannot be easily moved, it may be necessary to drag the person away. Use a towel wrapped around the casualty's leg to pull him or her away. Alternatively, if a towel or similar piece of material is not available, pull on any loose article of clothing that is not in direct contact with the casualty.

4 Once the casualty has been removed from the appliance and is conscious, cover him or her in a blanket and, depending on the severity of the shock, call the emergency services. If the casualty has sustained burns, try to take the heat out of the burns by running cool water over them and await the emergency services.

If, once freed, the casualty is breathing but unconscious, place him or her in the recovery position (*see page 285*) and periodically check that he or she is still breathing while waiting for the emergency services. If the victim is not breathing, begin CPR (*see pages 268–69*) and continue until paramedics have arrived on the scene.

ACCIDENT & EMERGENCY

HOW TO RESCUE SOMEONE FROM DROWNING

Statistics indicate that the risk of drowning in most developed countries is somewhere in the region of I in I00,000, or 0.00I percent. Also, when you factor in that a good proportion of those who do perish in inland waterways, swimming pools, rivers, lakes and seas are, unfortunately, young men who have had too much to drink, then the risk to a responsible, sober adult like yourself is pretty small. However, although you might not be the one in the water, one day you may find yourself having to fish someone out.

INDISPENSABLE THINGS

- Buoyancy aid
- Long, sturdy stick
- Length of rope
- PRE (Public Rescue Equipment), if available

☞ INDISPENSABLE WARNING

If you see someone in trouble in the water, suppress any thought of simply diving in and "pulling" him or her out. It just doesn't happen like that. Someone drowning will acquire immense strength and in his or her panic will do anything to get out of the water, and that includes climbing all over you and pushing you underwater.

1 After you've called the emergency services, look around for some form of buoyancy aid or flotation device. If you're at a swimming pool, beach or resort, or on a boat, there should be one on hand. Ideally, the device should have a rope tied to it. Throw it to the person in the water. When he or she has a firm hold, pull him or her gently to the edge.

2 In areas of water less well known for swimming, there may not be a buoyancy aid on hand, in which case you will have to improvise. Again, don't be tempted to jump in yourself. Many lakes and riverbanks are near stands of large trees. Find a long, sturdy branch to hold out to the person in the water. Alternatively, a piece of rope will do the job.

3 If there is nothing on hand to throw out or offer, lie on the side on your stomach. Ideally, there will be someone there to hold onto your legs. Now reach out to the person in the water and try to get him or her to grasp your wrist.

4 Of course learning to swim is one of the best ways to prevent drowning. Most professional swimming instructors begin by getting people to feel comfortable with the idea of just floating. Go to a part of the pool where you can touch the bottom. Pull your feet up and push forward, and try lying on your back in the water with your face above the surface. Take deep but measured breaths and the air in your lungs, together with gentle leg and arm movements, will keep you afloat.

ACCIDENT & EMERGENCY

HOW TO PERFORM AN ICE RESCUE

Perhaps it's the fault of the *Omen II* (you remember th[e] man trapped under the ice looking pleadingly up at hi[s] would-be rescuers) that icy lakes create such universa[l] dread—or perhaps it's because they're just plai[n] dangerous. Yet every year, thousands of people seem t[o] think it's fine to go tearing off onto the ice with littl[e] more concern for health and safety than getting the larges[t] guy to jump up and down on the ice a few times.

INDISPENSABLE THINGS

- Rope
- Long, sturdy stick
- Cell phone
- Blanket

LAST RESORT ONLY

If there is nothing with which to reach the victim or throw to him or her, and no way to call the emergency services, as a very last resort crawl out on your stomach. If he or she is a fair way from the bank, form a chain. Lying on your stomach will spread your weight.

USE A STICK OR ROPE

Don't attempt to approach the victim on the ice; if it hasn't supported the casualty's weight there's no reason why it will support yours. Try reaching them with a long stick or pole, or throw them a rope. Naturally, the victim will be struggling against the cold, so get him or her to tie a rope around his or her body so you can pull him or her in. If his or her hands are too cold to do this, the victim should wrap coils of rope around his or her arm, which should hold for long enough to pull the victim out.

DEALING WITH EMERGENCIES

When you sit down to think about it, you're
risking your life every time you go out the
front door. So don't sit down and think
about it. Sure, some people endure bad
things all the time, but they're a drop in
the ocean compared with the billions of us
who go about our emergency-free existence
blissfully unaware. But just suppose...

HOW TO PUT OUT A FIRE

According to statistics, fire crews in the US respond to domestic fires every 17 seconds—a very sobering figure. And while most domestic fires start in the kitchen, it is the careless disposal of smoking materials—in other words, people falling asleep in bed or in a chair while smoking—that causes the greatest fatalities.

INDISPENSABLE THINGS

- ABC-rated fire extinguisher
- Fire blanket
- Baking soda
- Cell phone

PRACTICAL TIP

ABC-rated fire extinguishers are so called because they can be used on all three types of fire: A = wood, paper, etc.; B = fat, oil, etc.; C = electrical. Individual types of extinguisher (such as A, B or C) are available, but should be used only on the relevant type of fire.

DISCOVERING A FIRE

On discovering a fire in the home, assess its severity and, if in any doubt as to whether or not you can get it under control, evacuate the building. Remember, fire develops quickly —don't lose valuable time trying to gather up important possessions. Just leave via the safest route and contact the emergency services.

If you're absolutely certain that you can tackle the small blaze, assess the type of fire it is and act accordingly. There are three types of fire, as shown here:

TYPE A For any fire that involves paper, wood, cardboard, clothing and other material, it is safe to douse the fire with water. If the object on fire is sufficiently small and you are able to hold it safely in some way, take it to the bathtub or sink. This will contain the fire and prevent it from spreading.

TYPE B This type of fire involves cooking oil or fat—two of the most common causes of domestic fires. If attended to quickly, they may be controlled. Either put the lid back on the pan or throw a damp cloth or a fire blanket over the pan and turn off the heat. Starved of oxygen, the fire will quickly fade. Never move the pan or throw water over this type of fire—the burning fat will splatter everywhere, spreading the fire.

TYPE C The third type of fire is electrical, usually caused by overloaded outlets, poorly wired electrical appliances or frayed electrical cables. First of all, go to the main service panel and turn off the electricity supply. The best way to tackle electrical fires is by covering them in baking soda. Again, do not throw water on an electrical fire, or you may get a powerful electric shock.

HOW TO OPERATE A LIFE RAFT

There you are enjoying a gin and tonic astern before dinner, when a loud crunching and grinding sound followed by shouts and exclamations indicates that you're about to have your own mini *Titanic* episode. Fortunately, unlike the *Titanic*, the ship you're on is fully equipped and has sufficient life rafts for everyone. Unfortunately, the small crew are behaving in a most un-*Titanic* fashion and have already abandoned ship with one of the life rafts, leaving you and your companions to fend for yourselves.

 PRACTICAL TIP

Give everyone a task, such as opening and assessing the emergency kit, looking out for other passengers in the water, attending to first aid and operating any signaling equipment that might be available. Ensuring that everyone has a job to do will help them work together as a team.

INDISPENSABLE THINGS

- Life raft
- Survival kit
- Cell phone

A PRACTICAL HISTORY OF HYDROSTATIC RELEASE

The best life rafts have a hydrostatic release device. This device will instigate the automatic inflation of the raft if it hasn't been manually inflated. As the ship sinks, pressure builds in the hydrostatic release until a cutting blade is activated, which cuts the raft free. The activation line itself, however, remains attached to the release and, as the boat continues to sink, the line is stretched tight by the floating raft container on the surface. Eventually the activation line will pull on the gas canister and the raft will inflate. The activation line will then break free from its weak link.

1 If the ship is relatively small, you may have to launch the raft yourself. Ask someone to help you. They don't have to have superhero strength, but two is definitely better than one. Free the raft from its cradle while still in its container and lift it to the ship's rails. Don't undo the retaining/ activation length of rope, which will be attached to a device (hydrostatic release) on the cradle. Ensuring there is nothing sharp in the water to puncture the raft, throw the raft container over the side. Pull the activation line until it is taut, then give it a sharp tug. The raft will automatically inflate. Using the retaining/activation line, pull the raft closer to the ship.

2 Choose the strongest-looking person to get in the raft first. Hand him or her the retaining line to stop the raft from floating away. Ask individuals to then climb into the raft. They should all help to ensure the raft doesn't float away and help the next individual in. Once everyone is in the raft, cut the retaining line at the hydrostatic release end using the knife in the raft, so that you have a length of line attached to the raft. Ask your fellow survivors to spread themselves around the life raft so that it is evenly balanced and not to stand up.

HOW TO OPERATE A LIFE JACKET

Frequent fliers, you might think you're exempt from this section, but you're not—so listen up. And while we're at it, this section applies just as much to the boating fraternity as it does to our fliers—so you need to pay attention, too. In fact, whenever you go out in a boat, no matter how small it is, or how near to the shore you intend to remain, always wear a life jacket—modern designs aren't overly bulky and allow for free movement.

INDISPENSABLE THINGS

• Life jacket

1 As soon as you are informed by the captain or the steward to put on your life jacket, reach under the seat and retrieve the package containing the folded jacket.

2 Remove the life jacket from the package and unfold it so that the front is facing away from you.

3 Place the life jacket over your head and pull it down so that it sits firmly on your shoulders.

4 Pass the drawstrings around behind you and back to the front. Some models of life jacket are then secured by tying a double knot in the drawstring.

5 Other models, particularly Type III marine life jackets, are fastened by pushing together two plastic clips. The fit of the jacket can then be adjusted by pulling on the adjustment straps attached to the clips. There are other types of marine life jacket, however, so always refer to the specific instructions that come with your jacket to ensure it fits and will work efficiently.

⚑ PRACTICAL TIPS

• If you're traveling with a young child, it's important that you put your life jacket on first before helping the child. It may seem counter-intuitive, but if you're flailing around in the water trying to put on your life jacket, you won't be in a position to offer assistance to your young companion.

• Always make sure any life jacket or vest you buy is a good fit.

ACCIDENT & EMERGENCY

HOW TO COPE IN A FLOOD

Reports of flooding are on the increase. Some blame climat
change, others the fact that in most developed an
developing countries we are building an increasing numbe
of homes, factories and offices in high-risk flood area
and not successfully managing rivers and their floo
plains. It's likely that increased flooding is due to
combination of several factors—but that's scan
consolation as the flood water is rising in your kitchen

INDISPENSABLE THINGS

- Emergency first-aid kit
- Food
- Drinking water
- Radio (batteries)
- Flashlight (batteries)
- Clothes
- Any prescribed medication
- Cell phone

PRACTICAL TIP

In the majority of flood incidents,
there is usually a fair amount of
warning given before the floodwaters
arrive. If you live in a high-risk area
and are concerned about flooding,
listen to the local radio station and
watch local news bulletins for flood
warnings. This should give you ample
time to undertake the following before
you evacuate the area. It's always best
to secure your home, putting as many
essential items upstairs as possible,
and leave if you can.

1 Turn off the main electricity supply to your house and unplug all electrical appliances. This will help protect your property as well as making it safer when you return after the floodwaters have receded. However, never touch any electrical appliances if you're standing in flood water.

2 Along with the electricity supply, also turn off any gas supply you have to the house. Again, this will protect your home and make it easier to recommission the supply after the flood.

3 If you don't have time to secure your home and leave the area, gather together the things listed on page 302, along with important documents, such as birth certificates and insurance policies, and any easily portable valuables, and move to a higher floor away from the floodwaters. Keep listening to the radio for information.

4 As an extra precaution in extreme flood conditions, wash out bathtubs and sinks with antibacterial cleaning products or bleach, rinse well and then fill with cold water. That way you'll have something to drink if the emergency services can't get to you for a couple of days.

☞ INDISPENSABLE WARNING

Don't evacuate if it means having to drive through flooded roads; you may get swept away in your car. Don't walk through fast-flowing flood water; even 6in. (18cm) of water can knock you down. Don't go near any fallen power cables.

ACCIDENT & EMERGENCY

HOW TO REACT IN A CAR ACCIDENT

In the US, around 41,000 people each year lose their lives on roadways. According to the Federal Highway Administration, 115 people every day, or one person every 13 minutes. Fortunately, the majority of the 6.4 million accidents that occur on US roads result in minor or no injury. However, you still need to know what to do if you are involved in an accident.

INDISPENSABLE THINGS

- Emergency first-aid kit
- Disposable/inexpensive camera
- Breakdown kit
- Pen and paper
- Cell phone

🐾 PRACTICAL TIPS

If you are in an accident involving another car, motorcycle, cyclist or pedestrian, you must stop. You should then exchange the following information:

- Name, address and phone numbers
- Name, address and phone numbers of any witnesses
- Licence plate numbers
- Details of insurance companies
- Year, model and make of car

Take photos of any damage sustained to all vehicles. Try to avoid discussing who was responsible for the accident with anyone other than the police. As soon as you can, contact your insurance company, and they will begin to process the accident claim by contacting the other parties' insurance companies.

1 Today, most cars come with some accident/breakdown equipment, such as warning triangles and a basic first-aid box. However, we strongly recommend that you assemble your own kit, comprising an adequately stocked first-aid kit, warning triangles, flares, a high-visibility vest, a camera, pen and paper, and always ensure you have your cell phone with you.

2 If you're involved in an accident but are still in control of the vehicle, pull safely into the side of the road at the first available opportunity. Turn off the ignition and turn on your hazard warning lights.

3 Assess any passengers in the car for signs of injury. If anyone appears injured, phone the emergency services immediately. Do not move the casualty. Assess them using ABC (*see pages 266–67*) and if necessary begin CPR (*see pages 268–69*). Reassure the casualty while waiting for assistance and if necessary reduce any bleeding by pressing lint pad or a clean towel against the wound.

4 Having attended to any passengers in your car, approach any other vehicle involved in the accident and ask the driver and passengers if they are injured. If necessary, call the emergency services.

ACCIDENT & EMERGENCY

HOW TO REACT IN A BOMB BLAST

Thanks to the work of national security services and their cooperation with the services of other countries, domestic terrorist attacks, although a real and constant threat, are mercifully few. Of course, this is no guarantee that terrorists won't successfully detonate a bomb in a busy city center sometime in the future. Additionally, for those working or living in countries with significant terrorist activity, explosions can be an almost daily occurrence. We should try not to let the threat affect our lives and continue with normal routine as best we can.

INDISPENSABLE THINGS

- Cool head
- Nerves of steel

1 Of course, much easier said than done, but immediately following an explosion try to remain as calm as possible. If you can, find something solid to hide under, such as a sturdy table, to protect you from collapsing ceilings or walls; there may well be additional explosions. Assess whether you personally have sustained any injuries—surprisingly, it may not always be obvious.

2 If you are sure it is safe to do so, go to the aid of others. If someone is seriously injured but conscious, do not attempt to move the person unless not doing so will result in further injury. If someone appears seriously injured and is unconscious, assess him or her using ABC (*see pages 266–67*) and if necessary begin CPR (*see pages 268–69*). For any minor injuries, implement any first aid you can.

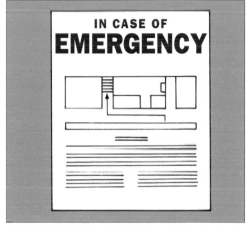

3 Under no circumstances should you use a lighter or matches immediately following a blast. Gas supply pipes may well have broken in the explosion, and you don't want to cause another one.

4 Most public buildings will have emergency information signs posted. Read these carefully because they may offer valuable information on how to evacuate the building as safely as possible. Given the potential risk of subsequent explosions, you should consider carefully whether or not to evacuate immediately. Again, if not doing so will endanger your life, evacuate; but if you're not in any immediate danger, it may be safer to wait under the shelter until emergency services reach you, or you are given the OK to evacuate by staff members.

HOW TO SURVIVE A HURRICANE

Hurricanes have hit the headlines a lot in recent years, notably Katrina in August 2005, which was responsible for flooding around 80 percent of New Orleans, resulting in the loss of some 1,500 lives. Fortunately, not all hurricanes are as devastating as Katrina, but every year, during the Atlantic hurricane season (June—November), vast areas of the Caribbean and much of the coast around the Gulf of Mexico live under the threat of potentially deadly tropical storms.

INDISPENSABLE THINGS

- Emergency first-aid kit
- Food
- Drinking water
- Radio (batteries)
- Flashlight (batteries)
- Clothes
- Any prescribed medication
- Cell phone

INDISPENSABLE ADVICE

Thanks primarily to the meteorologists of the US National Hurricane Center, it's impossible for a hurricane to form and gather impetus without being spotted. So, in the vast majority of cases, people are given adequate warning to board up and lock up their homes and evacuate the area before the hurricane strikes.

Hurricanes can, however, change course drastically in a very short period of time, and in these cases people can get caught. In other cases, if a hurricane is of a low category, many people will choose to sit out the storm. Here are a few steps to take to make life a little more bearable.

1 It's likely that you'll have some time before the hurricane is actually upon you. Use this time to cut down any weak-looking branches in the yard, and put inside any garden ornaments or objects, such as garbage cans, that are likely to get caught up by the wind and potentially smash into your own or your neighbors' property.

2 Board up your windows with specially made hurricane shutters or at least homemade shutters made out of strong plywood nailed to the frames. If you live in a hurricane area, you should have these made in advance. Some people tape their windows to stop the glass from shattering, but recent evidence suggests that this will offer little protection. Shutters are most effective.

3 Assemble items on the list given on page 308. It may be a day or two before you can get to any stores, so ensure you have plenty to eat and drink. A battery-operated radio will keep you informed about the status of the storm.

4 Put all your important documents, such as medical records, insurance policy details and bank account details, together in one safe place and carry them with you.

5 It's a wise precaution to unplug all your electrical appliances, because lightning strikes may cause a power surge in your home that will damage such items.

HOW TO SIGNAL SOS

Although now superseded by other systems, for much of the 20th century "SOS" was the generally accepted international maritime distress signal. A popular misconception is that the letters were an abbreviation for "Save Our Ship" or "Save Our Souls," but such phrases were used to help people remember the letters themselves. The reason SOS was used is because in Morse Code S is "..." (or dot/dot/dot) and O is "— — —" (or dash/dash/dash), and easy to signal when icy water was pouring into a ship, and also easy for anyone listening to decipher and realize a ship was in trouble.

INDISPENSABLE THINGS

- Whistle
- Foghorn
- Flashlight
- Anything that makes a noise

ON LAND OR AT SEA

The widespread recognition of both the signal and the letters can help greatly if you find yourself in trouble, not necessarily while on the sea, but also on land. For example, if you find yourself stranded in your car with no access to a telephone in a remote location, periodically sound the horn with three short, three long and another three short blasts. Anyone listening will instantly recognize that as a distress signal rather than an errant car alarm. Alternatively, if you have a flashlight, periodically flash the SOS signal to attract someone's attention.

IN POOR VISIBILITY

Similarly when hiking, if you or a member of your party is injured and cannot walk to safety and visibility is poor or it's getting dark, signaling SOS on a whistle, with three short, three long and three short blasts will alert any potential rescuers and help them to locate you. No whistle? Use anything that will make a distinctive and penetrating sound, such as metal on metal or a hollow wooden object. Keep repeating the SOS signal, and anyone who hears it is likely to recognize it as a cry for help.

HOW TO SIGNAL SOS WITH SMOKE

You might instantly think of Native Americans, and why not? They knew a thing or two about signaling over great distances. Seeing smoke signals rising into the sky must have been an eerie sight for those adventurous folk heading West. So if you find yourself stranded and lost in the wilderness, take a metaphorical leaf out of the collective Native American book and signal for help using smoke.

INDISPENSABLE THINGS

- Matches or lighter
- Dry kindling
- Blanket or coat

MAKING A SMOKY FIRE

The first thing you need to do is to make a fire (*see page 234*). Start your fire with good, dry kindling to generate a lot of heat. Once your fire is burning steadily, add handfuls of damp grass or leaves—anything wet that will make the fire smoke.

SIGNALING

When the fire's really smoking, use a blanket or a coat to carefully cover the fire periodically to prevent the smoke rising. Try signaling three "puffs" at a time—this is the universal number for help and will alert people to the fact that it's not just a natural scrub or forest fire.

ACCIDENT & EMERGENCY

HOW TO SIGNAL SOS WITH LETTERS

So what at first seemed like a really great idea, to get away as far as possible from all human contact, has backfired drastically—either you're in the middle of nowhere with a broken 4x4 or truly stranded on a desert island with a boat that won't start. There's nothing with which to start a fire, but at least you know that after two or three days people will start wondering where you are.

INDISPENSABLE THINGS

- Large rocks or stones
- Flat area of cleared land
- Book to read

USING ROCKS

It's likely that your rescuers will first start to look for you from the air; but without any decent firewood, how can you attract their attention? Easy, make a sign. Using large stones or rocks (or anything else that comes to hand), spell out the letters "SOS" and you'll quickly grab the attention of any eagle-eyed pilot. Make the letters large!

BE VISIBLE

Remember to choose rocks or other objects that are easy to distinguish in terms of color or texture from the ground, otherwise your cry for help won't be sufficiently visible from above.

HOW TO SIGNAL SOS WITH MATERIAL

"No good," you cry. There's nothing to make a fire with and there aren't enough rocks to spell out S, let alone SOS. Don't panic: there is another way of attracting an aerial search party. This one utilizes the shape of the internationally recognized distress flag used by ships all over the world. All you need are blankets, rugs or any largish piece of material—a newspaper will do.

INDISPENSABLE THINGS

- Blankets or rugs
- Newspaper
- Rocks or stones

CLEAR SPACE
Clear an area of land of all other debris (rocks, bushes, and so forth) so that you have an uncluttered canvas to work on. Now form a circle and a square as best you can with the materials you have on hand. Try to make sure that they're relatively similar to one another in size, and weigh down the edges with stones or rocks. Help will be on hand in no time.

CIRCLE & SQUARE
Officially, the distress flag is a black square and a black circle on a bright orange background. But as this is an emergency, we won't argue if you struggle to find the correct colors.

ACCIDENT & EMERGENCY

HOW TO SURVIVE A BLIZZARD IN YOUR CAR

OK, so when you set off, there was just a flurry of snow and you couldn't possibly miss your great-aunt's special Christmas Eve celebration. Besides, it was only supposed to be a 30-minute drive because you were taking the back roads to avoid the traffic, and now where did all this snow come from? And where's everybody else gone? Suddenly the festive spirit has deserted you and you feel very alone. Here's what to do, and what not to do, if you're caught in a blizzard while driving.

INDISPENSABLE THINGS

- Cell phone
- Flashlight
- Water
- Something to eat
- Blankets
- Gloves
- Extra clothes
- Roadside emergency kit
- Signal devices

1 As tempting as it might be to "just keep going," it's not worth it. In poor visibility, you run the risk of either crashing into an object by the side of the road or having a head-on collision with another vehicle. Pull over to the side of the road and stop. If you have a cell phone, call 911 to alert the emergency services to your situation and provide them with as much information as you can about your whereabouts.

2 Having stopped, unless you can see a building very close to you, don't be tempted to walk for help. You'll get lost in a blizzard, particularly at night, and may end up with hypothermia or freezing to death. There are likely to be emergency services in operation and they're much more likely to find a car than an individual, especially if you keep the emergency lights on; these will also act as a warning to other vehicles.

3 To keep yourself warm, run the car with the heater on for about 10 minutes at hourly intervals. It's tempting to run it for longer, but you could run out of gas before you're rescued, or inadvertently introduce carbon monoxide into the car. As a safety precaution, open a window very slightly.

4 Depending on how heavily the snow is falling, every so often go to the rear of the car to check that the exhaust is still free of snow. If the exhaust becomes blocked, you may find that carbon monoxide will find its way into the car when you're running the engine to stay warm.

> **PRACTICAL TIP**
>
> As well as staying in the car (apart from getting out to check the exhaust), it's also recommended that you keep your seat belt on in case you're hit by another car.

5 In very cold conditions, it's essential to maintain good circulation. To do this, either clap your hands or stamp your feet. You don't need to move much at all to keep the blood flowing freely around your body.

HOW TO BUILD A SHELTER

Somehow you've miscalculated the time needed to complete the trek. The sun's going down and you've still got another three hours hiking before you make it back to the car. You estimate that it will be dark in an hour, so there's no alternative but to spend the night in the woods, and it looks like rain. The first thing is not to think about *The Blair Witch Project* (if you haven't seen it that shouldn't be hard—just be thankful you haven't) and the next is to go about making a shelter—here are a couple of ideas.

INDISPENSABLE THINGS

- Dead wood, branches and leaves
- Length of rope
- Tarpaulin

👉 PRACTICAL TIP

No matter how convinced you are that your hike in the woods won't involve an overnight stay, always carry a tarp in your backpack. It's portable, lightweight and you never know when you might need to rig up a makeshift shelter.

DEBRIS HUT SHELTER

1 The debris hut shelter is very simple to make, but you need access to a good supply of dead wood, branches and leaves. The basic structure utilizes a long central pole supported at one end by two shorter branches crossing over one another near the top. Alternatively, you can simply rest one end of the pole in the crook of a tree. (If there's a strong wind, consider where the opening will be.) Now find or cut suitable lengths of shorter branches to rest against the central pole to form the structure shown.

2 Once you have completed the basic structure, next cover it with any suitable material that you can find lying around, such as large fern leaves, leafy branches, pine boughs, grass, earth sod—literally, anything that won't fall between the branches or won't get blown away too easily. You'll need to lay on and overlap a lot of material to ensure the shelter is watertight. Use a coat to block the entrance to the shelter to help you keep warmer if necessary.

TARP SHELTER

1 The tarp shelter is one of the easiest and quickest of emergency shelters to put up. Begin by tying the length of rope between two trees. Again, ideally consider where you want the two openings to be. Also, you can make the shelter lower at one end if that will help protect you from the wind.

2 Next simply throw the tarp over the rope and secure the corners. You can use sharpened sticks as pegs to do this, although it's probably best not to puncture the tarpaulin because it may tear or let in water. It's better to use heavy rocks to weigh down the corners.

HOW TO SURVIVE AN AVALANCHE

With the largest examples moving some 9.8 million tons (10 million tonnes) of snow at speeds of up to 190mph (300kph), avalanches are a serious force of nature. Of course, the best way to survive an avalanche is to avoid them altogether by steering clear of steep slopes with thick powder snow. If you are about to be engulfed by an avalanche, the following procedures may help you to survive.

INDISPENSABLE FACT

The authorities responsible for the safety of the numerous people who go skiing each year take their responsibility very seriously. In 1999, the mayor of Chamonix, France, was convicted of second-degree murder for not evacuating an area that was subsequently hit by an avalanche, killing 12 people.

INDISPENSABLE THINGS

- Ski clothing and equipment fitted with RECCO reflectors

STAY ON YOUR FEET

Try to stay on your feet for as long as possible. If you're caught in the snow, try to remove your skis and any other heavy equipment, because it will drag you deeper into the snow.

HOLD ON

Hold on to any nearby branches for as long as possible.

KEEP TO THE SIDE

If you have time, try to ski or walk to the side of the avalanche slope. The center of the avalanche carries the highest risk because it's where the snow is at its greatest volume and speed.

"SWIM"

Once subsumed by moving snow, try to make swimming motions with your arms and legs to keep as close to the surface as possible before the snow settles around you.

CUP YOUR HANDS

As the avalanche is about to stop, but before it has done so, cup one hand in front of your nose and mouth to create a pocket of air. The majority of people die of suffocation when caught in an avalanche, so creating a region of air may buy you valuable time. With the other hand, reach up so that it is visible to rescuers.

SURVIVING IN EXTREMES

Just think how dull life would be without a little risk. It's good for us to put ourselves in a bit of danger every now and again—particularly you adrenaline junkies. So what if every now and again you have to fight off sharks or survive a riot—we've got all the answers here.

HOW TO DEFEND YOURSELF

Hopefully, you'll never be in a situation in which you have to defend yourself against an attack. Of course, there are things that you can do to avoid the scenario altogether, such as being aware of your surroundings, not going into high-risk areas alone and using public transport or taking a taxi in areas you're unsure about. But however careful you are, there is still a possibility that one day you may have to confront an attacker.

INDISPENSABLE THINGS

- Small can of hair spray
- Pepper spray (where legal)
- Car keys or pen
- Personal attack alarm

PRACTICAL TIP

If you think you're going to be attacked, ascertain as quickly as possible whether you're being attacked for your money or whether it's an intentional physical attack. If the attacker just wants your money, hand it over. If it's clear, however, that the attack is going to lead to an assault, you'll need to physically deter your attacker.

1 In countries where pepper spray is legal, by all means use this if you're absolutely certain you're about to be assaulted. In some countries, such as the UK, pepper spray is classified as a firearm, and you'll be breaking the law if you use it, even to defend yourself. One alternative is to carry a small can of hair spray and spray that in the attacker's face—it should give you enough time to run away.

2 If the attacker has grabbed you by the arms or around the neck, lift your knee as hard as you can into his groin. If well aimed, you will inflict severe pain on the assailant, giving you time to escape.

3 An alternative to kneeing the attacker in the groin is to stamp as hard as you can, ideally with the heel of your shoe, on the attacker's ankle or foot. Again, this will cause quick, sharp pain.

4 Use anything sharp you have on hand to poke into the attacker's eyes, such as your car keys, a pen or even your fingers.

5 Remember that your prime objective is to get away—once you've inflicted any form of pain that has forced your attacker to release you, run away as fast as you can. Use a personal attack alarm to attract the attention of passersby; this should also help to deter your attacker.

HOW TO SURVIVE A BEAR ATTACK

With an ever-increasing number of us enjoying outdoor pursuits, whether at home or on vacation, it's logical that the number of encounters with bears is also on the rise. Bears have very wide-ranging territories and will eat just about anything. The number one rule, therefore, if you want to avoid running into a bear, is not to leave food lying around your campsite—that really would be one picnic you'd best avoid.

INDISPENSABLE THINGS

- Bear pepper spray (where legal)
- Whistle
- Air horn

PRACTICAL TIP

The best way to defend against a bear attack is to avoid an encounter altogether. Find out from local sources if there are bears in the area. If there are, and particularly if it's the breeding season, find an alternative place to camp. If you must stay in the area, make your presence known by talking loudly, singing or clapping your hands periodically. Unless feeling threatened or very hungry, bears will avoid contact with humans.

1 If you do happen to come face to face with a bear, slowly back away so that the bear doesn't feel threatened. You might try talking calmly and gently moving your arms so that the bear knows you're human—this may deter it, and you'll both be happy to go your separate ways.

2 If you accidentally stumble upon a bear and her cubs, she will certainly perceive you as a threat and may react by standing up on her hind legs. Remain as calm as possible; don't shout and wave your arms because this may further upset her. Simply back away, talking quietly. Hopefully, that will diffuse the situation and the bear will back down.

3 If the bear looks as if she is about to charge and there are trees nearby, one option is to climb a tree, although black bears are proficient climbers. Again, hopefully by climbing a tree you'll have indicated you're not a threat, and the bear won't bother to pursue you.

4 If you're going to be attacked, it's important to know which species of bear you're dealing with. If it's a black bear, your best chance of survival is to fight back as fiercely as possible with any weapon you have on hand, making as much noise as possible. If you're confronted with a grizzly bear, the only option is to play dead. Curl up into a ball and try to protect your neck and stomach. A backpack will provide some protection.

HOW TO SURVIVE A SHARK ATTACK

OK, so we know the odds of being attacked by a shark are pretty small. In fact, I in II.5 million according to the International Shark Attack File. But as a gruesome end, being attacked by a shark has to rank in the top IO. So what, practically, can you do if this disturbing nightmare should turn into stomach-churning reality one day as you're enjoying the warm waters of the coastal states?

INDISPENSABLE THINGS

- Anything solid or sharp with which to hit the shark
- Diving or swimming buddy

1 If you see a shark coming straight toward you, don't try to swim for safety right away, unless you're certain you can get out of the water before the shark reaches you. Stay calm and vertically still in the water (vertical because it makes it harder for a shark to bite you, because its nose will get in the way). The shark will hopefully realize you're not it's usual prey and leave.

2 If the shark approaches in a zigzag fashion, that indicates it's likely to attack. Get back-to-back with your swimming partner (you're not swimming alone, are you? so that one of you can always see what the shark is doing. If you are on your own in the water, stay as calm as possible and try to keep watching the shark. If there's a reef nearby, put your back toward it.

3 If a shark begins to circle you, that doesn't necessarily mean that it's about to attack. Recent evidence seems to suggest that it may just be curious about you—most sharks won't have encountered humans before. Stay calm and watchful—it may simply swim away.

4 If you are actually attacked by a shark, fight back as aggressively as you can. Don't play dead, because the shark will only attack more. The best option is to hit the shark in the gills or the eye with any appropriate object. Punching a shark on the nose may also deter it. If you have a spear gun or a knife, use it. Again, aim for the gills and eyes. Whatever happens, keep fighting back, remembering to breathe when you get a chance to surface.

HOW TO SURVIVE A DOG ATTACK

Although not as exotically terrifying as being attacked by a shark or bear, attacks by dogs are naturally far more numerous and can often result in horrific injuries and even death. In 2008, 23 people in the US died as a result of being attacked by dogs. Most people who require serious medical treatment following a dog attack are children, many of whom are bitten in the face. If not trained or well cared for, man's "best friend" can become a savage animal reverting to basic attack instincts.

INDISPENSABLE THINGS

- Pepper spray (where legal)
- Thick coat or jacket
- Rocks/sticks

POLICE DOGS The easiest dogs to "defend" against are well-trained police dogs—as long as you give yourself up. If you find yourself caught in a disturbance where police dogs have been deployed, face the dog (but do not engage in eye contact), stand still and keep your arms by your side. Police dogs are trained to recognize these submissive gestures and will simply stand guard until their handler calls them off.

SINGLE UNTRAINED DOG If a single, untrained dog begins to bark and snarl at you, shout and make yourself appear large and powerful. At the same time throw rocks or anything else appropriate. The majority of untrained dogs will run away if confronted by something that appears more powerful than them. If possible, try to put an obstacle or barrier between you and the dog, such as a garbage can lid, a gate or a large plant pot.

GUARD DOGS Poorly trained guard dogs are usually the hardest to defend against. They may not recognize submissive gestures and will simply be trained to attack. Try offering your arm (preferably the one you don't normally use) wrapped in a coat. Just over half of all dogs will bite on this. With your arm in its jaws, fall as heavily as you can into the dog in order to disable it.

A GROUP OF DOGS If you're being attacked by more than one dog, try to back up against something solid to stop them from encircling you, and fight them off with anything you can lay your hands on until help arrives. If they get behind you, you're in big trouble.

PEPPER SPRAY In countries where it is legal, carry a can of pepper spray with you if you live in an area where dogs roam freely. This will temporarily disable any dog.

HOW TO ESCAPE FROM A SINKING CAR

While for the inhabitants of some countries the risk of running off the road into a river or canal may seem remote, in others it's a real danger. In Holland, for example, people take the risk so seriously that they pay around $150 to be dropped in a large tank while in a car to practice escaping. In the US, instances of drivers leaving the road and ending up in the water reach around 10,000 each year and subsequent fatalities average 300. Here's how to give yourself the best chance of survival.

INDISPENSABLE THINGS

- Autoglass-breaking hammer

1 In most cases, when cars enter the water the impact, fortunately, is slight. Of course, this depends on the speed at which the car was traveling before leaving the road and whether there was any significant drop to the water. Usually, cars aren't traveling at excessive speed and the water, whether river, canal or levee, is only slightly lower than the road. One victim compared it to entering the water in a log-plume amusement ride.

2 Having entered the water, the priority is to open the window and release the seat belt. (Trying to open the door will be futile due to the water pressure on the outside and will only waste valuable time.) If you have electric windows, opening the window before releasing the seat belt makes more sense because the water will at some point interfere with the car's electrical systems (some cars have wind-up windows in the back). Tell all passengers to do the same.

3 With the window open you should be able to climb out relatively easily and swim to dry land. Only go back to the car if someone is in difficulty and needs help escaping through the window. Under no circumstances reenter the car for any possessions. If for whatever reason you cannot open the windows, try breaking a side window with anything with a pointed end. Car windows are extremely tough, so you may need an autoglass-breaking hammer, which you may want to keep in the glove compartment at all times. Don't try the windshield because it's very unlikely you'll be able to break this.

4 As a last resort, if there's no way of escaping through the windows, you'll have to wait until the car is submerged and filled with water, at which point the pressure inside and outside the car will be equalized, enabling you to slowly push the door open. Take a deep breath at the very last minute before the car is entirely filled with water. Ensure the door is unlocked and push it open. You will need to push quite hard, although the pressure is equal inside and out, as you push the car door you'll also be pushing against a heavy body of water—but it will open.

ACCIDENT & EMERGENCY

HOW TO ESCAPE FROM A HOUSE FIRE

No matter how carefully we guard against a fire in the home, there is always the possibility that we become victim to one—whether through an accident in the kitchen, a poorly maintained electrical appliance or from smoking. And while domestic fires can break out at any time, perhaps the most alarming and distressing, and potentially the most life-threatening, are those that start in the middle of the night when the occupants are asleep. According to one set of statistics, around 25 percent of casualties of house fires were asleep when the fire broke out.

PRACTICAL TIP

It's essential that your house has a sufficient number of well-maintained smoke alarms (change the batteries regularly). These, above everything else, are likely to save your life. In addition, make sure everyone in the house knows which route to take in the event of a fire (and an alternative route, should the principal escape route be inaccessible) and a convenient place to meet outside.

INDISPENSABLE THINGS

- Well-maintained smoke alarms
- Flashlight
- Cell phone

1 Keep a flashlight by your bed in case the fire has disabled the lights. It can be very disorienting and quite scary to wake up to the smell of smoke and a smoke alarm screeching. Try to stay calm. You may have inhaled smoke in your sleep already, so it's essential that you stay as low to the ground as you can when you get out of bed to avoid as much smoke as possible.

2 When moving around the house to alert all the other occupants to the fire, continue to stay close to the floor, where the air is cleaner and cooler. Find something appropriate, such as a cloth, to cover your mouth to help reduce smoke inhalation.

3 Always test to see how hot a door is by feeling with the back of your hand before opening it. A fire may be blazing on the other side and opening the door will introduce additional oxygen, causing the fire to spread more rapidly, if not causing a minor explosion. If anyone's clothes catch fire, drag the person to the ground before he or she can start running (which will only fan and spread the flames) and roll the person, ideally in a rug or large towel, to smother the flames.

4 When a room has been safely evacuated, always close the door behind you. This will slow the rate at which the fire spreads around the house. Head for the emergency meeting place and phone the fire department.

ACCIDENT & EMERGENCY

HOW TO SURVIVE IN THE DESERT

You were told by your guide that the 4x4s they use were the most reliable on the market, and so yours has been. But if only your guide had been as reliable, perhaps the vehicle would not have become stuck in sand while you were still three hours away from civilization without any means of contacting anyone. There's no other choice but to set off on foot, and you're not exactly swimming in water.

INDISPENSABLE THINGS

- Long-sleeved shirt
- Pants
- Broad-brimmed sun hat
- Clear plastic bag
- Cup
- Length of tube
- Sheet of plastic wrap
- Water bottle

1 Surviving in the desert is all about the relationship between air temperature, physical activity and water consumption. It's essential to lose as little water as possible from your body, so if you have to walk in the desert, wear a long-sleeved shirt and pants. You may feel hotter, but the material will retain your sweat for longer than your exposed skin, from which any moisture is likely to evaporate almost instantly. Wear a broad-brimmed hat to protect your head from the sun.

2 If you can, find a sheltered place in which to rest during the heat of the day. Only walk at night, when it will be a great deal cooler than during daylight hours. Again, doing any physical activity in the cooler air temperature will reduce the rate of necessary water consumption. Visibility in the desert at night is usually sufficient to walk by, due to the lack of moisture in the air.

3 If you're running out of water in the desert, tie a clear plastic bag over the end of a plant or small branch of a tree, ensuring that the bag is sealed as tight as possible. During photosynthesis, the plant will transpire, releasing water vapor that will collect in the bag. Keep the bag attached to the plant until after sunset in order to collect as much moisture as possible.

4 If there aren't any plants growing in the vicinity, try building a sun still. Dig a hole in the ground until you reach the moist subsoil. Place a cup in the bottom of the hole and run a plastic tube from the cup to the edge of the hole. Cover the hole with a taut sheet of plastic wrap held in place by stones or sand. Ensure there is a good seal all the way around. Place a small stone in the center of the sheet so that it dips over the cup. The moisture in the subsoil will evaporate under the heat of the sun and collect on the inside of the sheet. From here it will flow down to the center and drip into the cup. You can then suck the water through the tube.

ACCIDENT & EMERGENCY

HOW TO PERFORM A FIREMAN'S CARRY

Although it was the standard for many years, the fireman's carry is no longer the recognized method by which to carry someone out of a burning building. This is due to the fact that toxic fumes could potentially asphyxiate someone being carried at shoulder height. The preferred method is now to drag someone along the ground (away from potentially harmful fumes)—but the lift can still come in handy in numerous other situations.

INDISPENSABLE THINGS

• Relatively strong back

1 Lift the casualty into a standing position with both arms wrapped around his or her waist so that you are facing one another. This position will also prevent the casualty from falling backward.

2 While still supporting the casualty with one arm around the waist, with your other hand lift one of the casualty's arms by the wrist so that the arm is fully extended.

3 With the casualty's arm extended, quickly duck under the raised arm and hold it by the wrist, while going down on one knee to start supporting the weight on your shoulders. Pass the other hand through the casualty's legs and hold him or her by the back of the knee.

4 Pass your arm farther through his or her legs so that you can take hold of the casualty's wrist, which should now be released by the hand that was originally used to raise the arm. This frees up your arm and helps you keep your balance as you're about to stand up.

5 Ensuring that the casualty's weight is evenly balanced across both of your shoulders, now stand up—you may need to lean forward a little to help you do this. Once you're standing, you should be able to carry the casualty easily over a fairly long distance before having to set him or her down. To do this, crouch down and gently roll the person off your shoulder onto his or her back.

> **PRACTICAL TIP**
>
> When performing the fireman's carry, it's important that the carrier uses his or her legs to lift the casualty, instead of the back. That way the carrier will avoid any injury to his or her back.

ACCIDENT & EMERGENCY

HOW TO PREVENT HYPOTHERMIA

Essentially, hypothermia is a cooling of the body's core temperature as it drops below 95°F (35°C). There are three recognized phases of hypothermia, each increasingly more severe than the last, starting with numb hands and goose bumps, going through blue lips and mild confusion, and culminating in a point when walking is almost impossible and the pulse and respiration are dramatically lowered. Death will happen when the main organs can no longer function normally, which will usually occur when the body temperature dips below a teeth-shattering 86°F (30°C).

INDISPENSABLE THINGS

- Blankets
- Dry clothes
- Someone with whom to share body heat
- Shelter
- Hot, sweet tea

1 Of course, as with so many things, avoiding hypothermia altogether is the best cure. Always dress appropriately for cold weather, even if you intend to be outside for only a few minutes. Plenty of layers, a warm hat, gloves and warm boots are essential if you intend to spend time outdoors in cold weather.

2 Anyone participating in outdoor sports in a cold environment should be aware of hypothermia, particularly if there's a chance of becoming wet in the process. Wet clothes, particularly cotton, will increase the rate at which hypothermia advances, because they lose about 90 percent of their insulating properties. Don't stay out in the cold in wet clothes—change into dry ones at the earliest opportunity.

3 Shivering is a sign of the onset of hypothermia—do not ignore it. If you can't get back to camp or your car, try to find a natural shelter from the wind and rain, somewhere where you can perhaps start a fire and dry out wet clothes. Along with wet conditions, wind will also speed up hypothermia, because it drives cold air through and under your clothes, therefore taking valuable heat away from the core of your body.

4 If you're in a really exposed location with no natural shelter to escape to, you must at least erect a makeshift camp using anything you have on hand in order to combat the worst of the conditions. On pages 316–17 we showed you how to make some primitive types of shelter using the most basic materials. If there are two of you, share body heat once you're in the shelter by clinging to one another. And a thermos of hot, sweet tea will literally be a life saver—just sip it slowly.

HOW TO STOP A PANIC ATTACK

Usually caused by major anxiety, hyperventilation brought on by a panic attack will cause the person to feel out of control with a sense of impending terror, accompanied by the physical symptoms of numb hands and feet, red face, tingling fingers, chest pains and light-headedness. The cause of all these symptoms is the intake of too much oxygen due to unnaturally fast deep breathing.

INDISPENSABLE THINGS

- Calming manner
- Removal of all onlookers

REASSURANCE IS VITAL

It is important to approach someone having a panic attack with a calm and confident demeanor (even if you don't feel that way). Separate the casualty from any bystanders or passersby—it is easier to calm a patient down one to one. If possible, sit him or her down on a chair in a quiet room. Reassure the patient and encourage him or her to slow their breathing down. Do not expect him or her to answer any questions immediately. Be calm and reassuring. The symptoms (tingling fingers, feeling faint, chest tightness, dizziness) should start to abate after around 5 to 7 minutes.

IF SYMPTOMS PERSIST

If, however, symptoms persist or indeed should the victim lose consciousness, call the emergency services and monitor the casualty's breathing and pulse.

INDISPENSABLE WARNING

If the patient's appearance is pale and clammy instead of flushed, then call an ambulance immediately. They may be suffering from something more than a panic attack.

HOW TO SURVIVE A RIOT

What initially sounded like a carnival procession coming up the road is, on closer inspection, a baying mob smashing windows, setting fire to cars and generally causing a commotion. It's a full-fledged riot, and you're about to get caught in all the action. Assuming that you're unwilling to join in with all the looting, tear gas, water cannons and other festivities, here's how to extricate yourself.

INDISPENSABLE THINGS

• Cell phone

CALL SOMEONE
At the first sign of trouble, surreptitiously phone someone to let them know where you are and what's happening. Try to avoid getting caught in the middle of the riot by looking for side roads down which you can quietly walk—don't run. Running will attract attention to yourself and may cause people to chase you.

LOOK FOR REFUGE
Look for refuge in a hotel, large apartment building or ideally an embassy—make it absolutely plain to anyone on the door that you're not part of the disturbance and are looking for safety.

IF YOU'RE IN A CAR
If you're in a car, drive slowly away from the disturbance if you can, looking for back roads rather than the main streets. Reverse away from the trouble rather than taking time attempting to turn the car around.

ACCIDENT & EMERGENCY

HOW TO SURVIVE A BIOLOGICAL OR CHEMICAL ATTACK

It's an unsavory fact of modern life, but we're living in turbulent times when international terrorism appears to be a constant threat in most regions of the world. Terrorists exist whose aims are to cause widespread fear among the public and to seed self-doubt in established governments. To achieve this they will attempt any form of atrocity, including the use of biological and chemical weapons, to inflict as many casualties and generate as much fear as they can. We should all be prepared.

INDISPENSABLE THINGS

- Duct tape
- Damp towels
- Radio (batteries)
- Cell phone
- Emergency kit
- Canned food
- Bottled water

🖎 PRACTICAL TIP

Terrorist activity, by its very nature, does not come with a warning. So you're unlikely to be able to choose where to be when an attack takes place. If you're outside when an attack occurs, enter the nearest safe, accessible building and aim to get up as many storeys as possible—gas used in such attacks is usually denser than air and will, therefore, stay low to the ground.

1 If you're at home and near the vicinity of the attack, quickly gather together the items listed on page 340 and move to the highest, least accessible room—that is, the one with fewest windows and doors. Lock the door to prevent others who may have been contaminated from entering the room.

2 Turn off any air-conditioning units and ventilation systems and use the duct tape to tape any gaps in doors and windows. Use damp towels to block any large gaps under doors. This will help to stop gas or a biological agent, such as anthrax, from entering the room.

3 In the case of a biological attack, follow standard hygiene practice. Thoroughly wash yourself, especially your hands, and don't come into close contact with anyone who may have been contaminated.

4 Wash all surfaces and clothes that have been in contact with someone you suspect of being contaminated, and under no circumstances rub your eyes.

5 Stay indoors and listen to the radio for any information that will help you determine the severity of the attack and whether or not you need to evacuate the area. Use your cell phone to stay in contact with other members of the family who may have been elsewhere at the time of the attack.

ACCIDENT & EMERGENCY

HOW TO SURVIVE AN EARTHQUAKE

Earthquakes can happen pretty much anywhere in the world, but there are recognized regions where the incidents and risk of earthquakes, due to the local instability of the earth's crust, are much greater. Our knowledge of these regions has, in most cases, led to the implementation of "quake-proof" construction techniques. However, every now and again the failure to use such construction techniques can result in horrific loss of life, as witnessed on May 12, 2008, when an estimated 69,000 people lost their lives in Sichuan Province, China, many of them children trapped in poorly constructed schools.

 PRACTICAL TIP

If you live in a region recognized as a high-risk earthquake zone, have a plan. Decide which room is likely to be the safest in which to take shelter— remember you're looking for something sturdy under which to hide, and avoid rooms with plenty of heavy objects such as shelves and cabinets that could easily fall over during the quake.

INDISPENSABLE THINGS

• Sturdy table or desk

1 As soon as you feel the room begin to shake, seek shelter under a sturdy table or desk. Even a large chair, if you can fit under it, will afford you some protection against falling masonry or other large objects. Make yourself as small as possible and tuck your head in, covering your head and neck with your arms.

2 If there is nothing suitable under which you can take shelter, go to the nearest interior wall and take cover there in the same position. When ceilings fall in, they are more likely to collapse in the center of the room than at the edge. Only shelter under an internal doorway if you know it is strongly constructed.

3 If the earthquake strikes while you're in bed, it's often best to stay in bed, curl up into a ball and cover your head with a pillow or two. Evidence suggests that people who get out of bed to seek shelter are more likely to get injured. If, however, you can quickly roll out of bed and under a table, this is the best option.

4 If you're outdoors when an earthquake starts, try to make for open ground away from tall buildings and other constructions. This way you will avoid being hit by falling masonry and other debris.

ACCIDENT & EMERGENCY

HOW TO AVOID A LIGHTNING STRIKE

The risk of being struck by lightning is far greater in some regions of the world than in others, but it's something that we should all take seriously. In the US, between 80 and 90 people die each year after being struck by lightning. However, bear in mind that the number of people who have burns and other serious injuries is far greater in the country than in towns and cities.

INDISPENSABLE THINGS

- Cool head
- Car

PRACTICAL TIP

If you find yourself outside in a thunderstorm with lightning present, the first thing is to assess the risk of a lightning strike. Count the seconds between hearing thunder and seeing lightning—if it's less than 30 seconds, there's a risk of a lightning strike.

1 Avoid high ground and don't take shelter under a tree. Lightning will strike tall, isolated objects, such as trees, and the current can easily pass from the tree through you to the ground. In addition, trees have been known to literally explode when struck by lightning.

2 If you're out camping and a storm is approaching, don't take shelter in your tent, particularly if it's in an exposed location. The tent is likely to have metallic components that will attract lightning.

3 If you're caught out in the open, make yourself as small a "target" as possible. Crouch down low to the ground (but do not lie flat) and minimize the amount of contact you have with the earth.

4 If you can get to your car, do so. Put all the windows up and don't touch any metallic element inside the car. If the car is struck by lightning, the metallic body of the car will take the charge and conduct it safely to the ground.

5 If you're inside during the storm, stay well away from all electrical appliances, wall outlets and switches, and don't use the telephone. If the house is hit, the current may well surge through these objects.

> ☞ **PRACTICAL TIP**
>
> If someone with you is struck by lightning, he or she may well be rendered unconscious. If so, check that they are breathing and that he or she has a pulse. If not begin CPR (*see pages 268–69*). If breathing but unconscious, place the person in the recovery position (*see page 285*). Don't worry about touching someone who has been struck by lightning because he or she will not be carrying a charge.

ACCIDENT & EMERGENCY

INDEX

INDEX

INDEX

ACKNOWLEDGMENTS

The publishers would like to thank Christine Evans, Marie-Eve Foisy, Martin Lusk, Vivienne Macey, Colin Richardson, Dr. Christopher Van Tilburg, Tony Wafer and Professor Greg Whyte for their invaluable advice.

ABOUT THE AUTHORS

HOME & GARDEN: Sara Rose has written many books on nutrition, health and fitness, and is the best-selling author of *Vitamins and Minerals*. A busy mother of two and proud possessor of a vegetable plot, her indispensable advice will help you maintain your home, impress others with your culinary skills and make the most of your yard in a practical, time-saving way.

HEALTH & BEAUTY: Kim Davies is a writer, adventurer and practical mother who has changed diapers on moonlit roadside shoulders, crossed India on a shoestring, and applied emergency first aid to jellyfish stings. She practices yoga and knows how to tie a bow tie. Her published titles include *Go Green*, *Save Money* and *The Baby and Toddler Meal Planner*.

TRAVEL & SPORTS: Nic Compton was brought up on boats in the Mediterranean, and one of his earliest practical memories is of his father teaching him to tie a bowline knot at the age of six. He has worked as a carpenter and shipwright, and rebuilt bicycles before turning his attention to more academic matters. He has written six books, including *Sailing Solo* and *The Great Classic Yacht Revival*.

ACCIDENT & EMERGENCY: David Martin is an adventurer and explorer whose favorite pastimes include sailing, motorcycle touring, trekking and camping. To pursue safely his love of the outdoors, David has undergone a number of first-aid and other sport-related safety courses, as well as developed a good understanding of field craft and how to react in adverse conditions.

PICTURE CREDITS

The publisher would like to thank the following individuals and organizations for their kind permission to reproduce the images in this book. Every effort has been made to acknowledge the pictures, however, we apologize if there are any unintentional omissions.

CORBIS: 84/Brand X.

GETTY IMAGES: 7/Rubberball; 8, 226/Stockdisc; 136/Stockbyte; 160/Dorling Kindersley; 298/Riko Pictures.

DAVID MELLOR DESIGN (www.davidmellordesign.co.uk): front cover image (green dessert spoon).

PHOTOLIBRARY: 70/Denkou Images.